THE
SHROUD
AND THE
CONTROVERSY

THE
SHROUD
AND THE
CONTROVERSY

KENNETH E. STEVENSON &
GARY R. HABERMAS

THOMAS NELSON PUBLISHERS
Nashville

Special thanks to Vernon Miller, who granted permission for us to use the photographs appearing in this book as well as the photograph appearing on the jacket cover.

Published in Nashville, Tennessee, by Thomas Nelson, Inc. and distributed in Canada by Lawson Falle, Ltd., Cambridge, Ontario.

Printed in the United States of America.

Library of Congress Cataloging-in-Publication Data

Stevenson, Kenneth.
    The Shroud and the controversy : science, skepticism, and the search for authenticity / by Kenneth E. Stevenson and Gary R. Habermas.
      p. 256 cm.
    Includes bibliographical references.
    ISBN 0-8407-7174-6
    1. Holy Shroud. I. Habermas, Gary R. II. Title.
BT587.S4S72   1989
232.96 '6—dc20
                                            89–13248
                                             CIP

DEDICATION

To my precious children, Jejchelle, Kenneth, Sean, and Angela, and the loving, supportive members of Everlasting Covenant Christian Ekklesia.

Ken Stevenson

To Dad and Mom Wrobel, with love and appreciation for your Christian commitment.

Gary Habermas

CONTENTS

1

THE CLOTH AND THE CONTROVERSY

Where We Are Today

Contemporary interest in the Shroud of Turin is truly an amazing and multifaceted phenomenon. During the last decade and in the last several months, in particular, the controversy over the nature of this cloth has "heated up" dramatically due to the results of carbon dating.

Response to the dating can perhaps be said to have taken at least a couple of broad directions. Some persons have concluded that the matter of the Shroud's authenticity is now forever cleared up and that the Shroud cannot be the burial garment of Jesus. Others have decided to challenge the results of the testing on several counts, postulating that the Shroud is every bit as likely to be authentic as they had previously concluded. And, of course, there are important possibilities in between these two extremes. In one important sense, the debate might hinge on two crucial issues: the age of the cloth and the cause of the image on it.

Measuring 14 ft. 3 in. long by 3 ft. 7 in. wide and known to exist since at least 1354 A.D., the Shroud might at first appear to be an odd object for the serious studies and debates which have characterized its most recent history. Caught in a fire in 1532 and almost destroyed by dripping molten silver, the Shroud survived with a twin series of burn marks down its entire length. Almost every destructive burn is mirrored by a similar one across from it, reminiscent of paper doll cutouts.

11

But most compellingly, this cloth reveals the frontal and dorsal images of a man, the whole body of an apparent crucifixion victim. The double image, arranged head to head with the feet at opposite ends of the cloth, appears to have been created after being wrapped lengthwise around the dead body. The person apparently suffered wounds popularly associated with crucifixion—a pierced scalp; serious beatings in the face and down the length of the body, both front and back; pierced wrists and feet; and a larger wound in the side of the chest.

These more traditional points had long been noted when the entire discussion entered a new phase in the last half of 1988. In August, rumors began to fly regarding the long-awaited results of the carbon-14 dating on the Shroud of Turin. Some reported that the tests showed this ancient cloth to be a first-century artifact. Others, however, reported that carbon-14 testing indicated a medieval date, somewhere between the eleventh and fourteenth centuries. The earlier date, of course, seemed to confirm the belief of many that the Shroud was the authentic burial cloth of Jesus. On the other hand, the medieval date threatened to undermine this belief and confirm what the Shroud's most ardent critics had claimed all along: "The Shroud is a forgery, a clever one, but a forgery nonetheless."

The confusion intensified with the rumors. Both sides claimed victory—the Shroud's supporters over its skeptics and the skeptics over the supporters. Although more reports favored inauthenticity, the conflict seemed stalemated. But then in late September, it was reported that the scientific advisor to the archbishop of Turin, Professor Luigi Gonella, had ascertained that the late-date rumors were, in fact, true. The Shroud had been dated to the fourteenth century.[1] Later, Cardinal Anastasio Ballestrero concluded that the Shroud could not have been that of Jesus.[2]

The news media had a heyday: science had wielded the deathblow. The Shroud was a fake to be put on the mantel of forgeries along with such greats as Piltdown man—or so the public was led to believe.

Is the Shroud a clever forgery? Has carbon-14 completely settled the issue? We think that while the date *does* present a very serious objection, a great deal of other new material has not received much attention in the press. And as we will show in this book, a number of eminent scientists, archaeologists, physicians, and scholars from other disciplines join us in our caution. There is much more to this cloth than many people care to admit. Though we are *not* willing to say that the Shroud is, beyond any shadow of a doubt, Jesus' burial cloth, we believe that the evidence for its authenticity is still supported by strong arguments.

What is it that makes this cloth so intriguing? What provokes the great interest in this ancient piece of linen?

THE APPROACH OF THIS BOOK

Since many people believe that this cloth once wrapped the crucified and dead body of Jesus, interest in it has been understandably high. In our 1981 evaluation of the evidence, *Verdict on the Shroud,*[3] we explained why we believe not only that the Shroud was most likely Jesus' but that it might also tell us some very important things about the most influential life ever lived.

Has carbon-14 changed all of this? In the present confusion, public opinion seems split about as much as is possible. Is the subject settled for sure, or are there reasons to reassert the possibility that the Shroud is, genuinely the burial garment of Jesus? The results of the dating do present a serious challenge to any pro-Shroud enthusiasts, including to us, the authors of this book. But it would be quite premature to assert that there are no significant scientific challenges to the specific dating technique that was used. Perhaps it might be said that much caution is due in light of the current confusion.

Interestingly, we have some differences of our own, perhaps a small-scale reflection of the public attitude. While I [Habermas] have become more skeptical in light of the recent data, Stevenson remains as convinced of the Shroud's authenticity as when our initial conclusions were published in 1981.

So we now begin again by encouraging an open-minded look at the data. We must avoid both idolatry on one side and a closed-minded unbelief on the other. We need to be cautious, carefully following the data wherever they lead. While we wish to arrive at carefully reasoned conclusions, we also need to be sensitive to alternative theses. Open-mindedness requires a critical but fair investigation of all worthwhile views.

How do we intend to promote this open-mindedness? We propose a careful reevaluation of some of the major conclusions in our study of the Shroud. We will pay special attention to issues with direct bearing on the question of authenticity. For example, how authoritative are the results of the carbon dating? Can they be challenged in any valid way? Concerning the cause of the image, have any worthwhile hypotheses surfaced since 1981? Or do any older theses of image development become more important in light of the doubts cast by the carbon-14 dating results? Our method, and one of the most important features of this book, will set the data before you so that you can arrive at your own conclusion.

To be sure, one's own presuppositions play a crucial role in how one views and analyzes the Shroud and the evidence and theories surrounding it. We, the authors, are likewise influenced by our own thoughts on this subject. Religious persons sometimes tend to accept the authenticity of the Shroud regardless of the objections, and critics and atheists usually reject its authenticity no matter what the evidence in its favor. But these radically opposed views are examples of bias, not of an honest wrestling with the data to arrive at an objective conclusion.

We ask you to reconsider your own biases and view the

data as carefully as possible. We want to help by laying out the major options. Of course, after our own studies on the Shroud, we have reached our own conclusions, which we will share with you. But these are not necessarily the last word. We want no one to blindly accept our conclusions but rather to arrive at a personal conclusion through careful examination of the evidence. We will begin by asking whether any of our former conclusions ought to be rethought.

SOME SECOND THOUGHTS ON THE SHROUD OF TURIN

The Shroud of Turin is certainly a complex and multifaceted subject. As in any scientific enterprise, new data can provoke a reconsideration of certain issues. After relevant data are gathered and organized, a hypothesis is formulated and tested. Scientific investigation then confirms or discredits the temporary thesis.

After careful consideration,[4] we have rethought several topics in light of new data or courteous, scholarly critiques. Certain other issues are still open for discussion.

A few reviewers of *Verdict* mentioned our over exuberance on the subject, indicating that we were too enthusiastic in our endorsement of the Shroud. One noted, "The problem is *not* that their conclusions are groundless speculation, *but* that it is just premature to render a final decision."[5] This writer's point appears to be that, while the facts indicate that the Shroud is intriguing, we should not jump to conclusions concerning its authenticity. While our facts were not necessarily wrong, we should have waited for more data.

This is a fair comment. In spite of cautions we carefully voiced in *Verdict,*[6] we do *not* wish to cause undue excitement, which might encourage some to look at the cloth as an object of worship or faith. As researchers, perhaps we should have expressed less enthusiasm and used less emotionally laden language. I [Habermas] have already admitted this in print.[7]

15

Another issue we have reevaluated is the use of statistical probabilities to argue that the Shroud is very likely that of Jesus.[8] In our earlier volume we asked how likely it was that another victim was crucified in the same manner that Jesus was, including all of the abnormal features that marked His death, as the New Testament accounts relate. We judged that this would be a highly improbable occurrence. Some reviewers have correctly noted that this procedure is fairly subjective. In the absence of enough detailed historical reports on which to predicate such analysis, our effort did not carry as much weight as we might have hoped. We should have been content to examine the evidence that the man buried in the Shroud might have been Jesus, leaving the *strength* of the conclusion to our readers.

Another problem with the use of statistical probabilities is the implication that our final figure is the *actual* likelihood that the Shroud is Jesus' even though we reported alternate hypothetical possibilities.[9] We should not have implied that an actual figure can be ascertained.

With regard to the nature of the death and burial of the man in the Shroud, other issues arise. Can we know the specific cause of death? Was the man's body washed before burial? Challenges have been offered to the more traditional answers and we explain and evaluate them in detail in Chapter 7.

Other questions about the burial concern the nature of the face band (and other cloths) or whether there is sufficient data about the actual condition of the bloodstains to decide whether the cloth was removed from the body. On the crucial issue of the cause of the image, should we be more open to the alternative theses? Chapters 2 and 8 deal with this important concern.

Other questions could be raised,[10] but these are some of the more crucial topics for reevaluation. At the same time, other conclusions need not have changed even though a great deal of new data has emerged in the past eight years. So we wish to be cautious in our conclusions, realizing that we need to be open-minded about some new considerations. One of our chief purposes in this book is to explore the new data and determine if any reconsiderations of our previously published conclusions are appropriate.

THE PRESENT STATE OF THE QUESTION

Since the publication of *Verdict* in 1981, numerous books and articles have appeared on the subject from a wide variety of sources and viewpoints, both scientific and otherwise. While even a brief review of these writings could itself be the subject of a book, we would like to make some general observations. Besides the subject of carbon dating, what have recent researchers been most concerned with studying?

Among the more popular topics for discussion have been such medical issues as the nature of the blood stains, burial procedures, the washing of the body, and, perhaps most important, the nature of the Shroud image. On the last topic, a primary concern is the continued testing of alternative theses to discover a possible image mechanism.

It is fair to say that most scholarly publications on the subject have favored the authenticity of the Shroud, at least as an actual archaeological artifact. Alternative hypotheses have been proposed, carefully tested by various scholars, and generally rejected. Popular treatments, in general, have been even more outspoken in their support of the Shroud.

In spite of these trends, a number of articles have opposed one or more major aspects of Shroud research. Frequently these sources have been critical of virtually every aspect of the study. Most of these critiques appear to come from more radical publications that generally question all supernatural claims. Largely supportive of the work of Walter McCrone and Joe Nickell, they regularly resort to very strong (even *ad hominem*) attacks against those who disagree with them.

Sadly, such open attacks are common in the radically

17

anti-Shroud material. In an excellent forum on the Shroud in *Current Anthropology,* Steven Schafersman referred to a pro-Shroud presentation in the same journal with the words, "such a blatant example of human credulity rarely finds its way into the professional scholarly literature." Later, Schafersman called the Shroud "a forged relic with no other purpose than to awe and deceive an ignorant and credulous stream of pilgrims willing to pay to view it."[11] In the same forum, John Cole made a comparison: "High-tech shroudology, like 'scientific creationism,' ultimately fails."[12] Atheist Gordon Stein referred to *Verdict* as "dangerous," a book appealing to "gullible people." To this he added, "neither [Habermas or Stevenson] is competent by training or background to either do or evaluate scientific research," a charge ignoring the fact that Stevenson, who wrote the scientific material, has a degree in engineering. Stein also said, "Habermas is blissfully unaware of the progress of philosophy during the past 1000 years," ignoring that Habermas holds a doctorate in this general field.[13]

The point here is definitely *not* that pro-Shroud researchers should go uncriticized, for we may have been mistaken at any of several points. But such caustic verbiage has no place in scholarly discussions. William Meacham, in the forum mentioned above, pointedly stated: "Beyond misunderstanding lies invective, and the comments of Cole, Nickell, Schafersman, and Mueller are phrased in an emotive tone not conducive to reasoned discussion. They bristle with intemperate rhetoric."[14] Again, the only point is that, while dispute can and should be part of scholarly dialogue, the views of others should be challenged courteously and rationally. And these critics should be answered in factual terms.

By whatever means, like many scholarly questions, the study of the Shroud has benefited from interdisciplinary interaction. The topic is now so broad that such participation is necessary. Through such measures, old theories have been largely abandoned and the current discussions appear to revolve around certain more finely-tuned issues. Even before *Verdict* was published, views ranging from various types of fraud on the one hand to the "flash of light" thesis on the other had already been laid to rest (although the latter is not to be confused with other scorch theses).

And what about the public as a whole? As we mentioned earlier, most popular works on the Shroud have favored the authenticity of the artifact. Though these publications have sometimes been too uncritical in their evaluations, it would appear that many have been convinced that the Shroud is the actual burial garment of Jesus. But even within this viewpoint, many opinions exist. Some have wondered if the Shroud is a sign from God to persons living in the last days—a witness to skeptics. Whether this is or is not the case, science cannot decide.

At a variety of levels, it is easy to get caught up in the fascination of the data, and, once again, we must remain as objective as possible. We have already mentioned some of the topics that perhaps need to be rethought. If we add to these the current questions concerning carbon dating, some new options emerge.

SOME IMPORTANT CAUTIONS

In a Shroud of Turin study like ours, several critical points must be emphasized. First, we only speak for ourselves. We do not presume to be stating a position for anyone else. Stevenson edited the 1977 proceedings that presented the most extensive theorizing prior to STURP's (Shroud of Turin Research Project's) 1978 trip to Turin,[15] and he was the editor for STURP. He also served as the official spokesman for the group during the scientific testing in Turin in October 1978. But it should be carefully noted that we do *not* speak for that group. I [Habermas] assisted Stevenson in his work for STURP, though I was not a team member, and used my research on the subject of Jesus' death and resurrection[16] to explore the possibility that the Shroud is the authentic burial garment of Jesus. But we are not speaking for STURP in this book.

19

Second, we, along with many others, believe that there are problems with the 1988 carbon-14 dating of the Shroud. While we acknowledge that the dating presents a serious challenge to authenticity, it is faced with major objections, many of which will be outlined in this book. In particular, the testing method calls its reliability into question.

Also, William Meacham, an archaeologist, has raised several problems regarding carbon dating itself, from both published research and personal experience. Citing several non-Shroud studies, Meacham has observed peculiarities relevant to Shroud research, such as the wide dating variations in certain same-sample testings and inconsistencies with known historical ages. He has also pointed out similar problems in research of which he was a part, testing which was conducted at reputable laboratories around the world, just as the Shroud carbon-14 testing was done in 1988.

Furthermore, there is the problem of many known contaminants on the Shroud as well as the effects of a fire and dousing in water, plus many unknowns like contacts with many who have held or copied it. The image formation process also minimally changed the cellulose in the fibers.[17] The problems here are profound. If the cloth was not sufficiently cleaned before testing, these contaminants could significantly alter dating conclusions.

Then again, as critics note, a first-century date would not necessarily prove that the Shroud is that of Jesus, either. If we are correct in our assessment, the question of dating is still not solved, and considerable caution is called for.

Third, *whatever* the final conclusions of any study of the Shroud, another type of caution needs to be exercised. And this may be the most important warning of all. There are too many examples of religious misuses of the Shroud, such as claims and advertisements of healing, prayers to the Shroud, and even worship of it. We firmly believe that the Shroud should not be esteemed as an object of faith. Christianity is faith in a person, not in a cloth or in any other artifact, whether it is Jesus' or not. Practices of worshiping or venerating the Shroud blatantly disobey Exodus 20:4–6:

> You shall not make for yourself carved image—any likeness of anything that is in heaven above, or that is in the earth beneath, or that is in the water under the earth; you shall not bow down to them nor serve them. For I, the LORD your God, am a jealous God, visiting the iniquity of the fathers upon the children to the third and fourth generations of those who hate Me, but showing mercy to thousands, to those who love Me and keep My commandments.

God has forbidden the use of images of any sort, particularly in worship. Blessings and punishments are promised to those who obey or disobey this command.

Giving a similar warning, we addressed this vitally serious matter in *Verdict;*[18] we did not wish to be guilty of breaking such a command. Yet one reviewer still levels this criticism: "The proponents of the Shroud are attempting to replace the Word of God with an image; as such they are, I would suggest, at variance with the intentions of Divine Providence."[19]

Therefore we wish to stress once again that we are investigating the Shroud as a possibly authentic archaeological artifact. *Even if the Shroud is the actual burial garment of Jesus* (and especially if it is not), *it is only a cloth.* It dishonors God to venerate or worship the Shroud or to celebrate it as a means of healing or to treat it as an object of prayer or faith. We strongly disavow all such nonbiblical practices. We have no desire to encourage any of them. Taking our work otherwise misconstrues its purpose.

CONCLUSION

So we turn now to our reinvestigation of the Shroud of Turin. Our chief emphasis will be to present research results that have developed since 1981, paying particular attention to carbon-14 and the other tests for age, as well as presenting recent data on the nature of the image. It is our desire to outline some of the recent findings and draw some conclusions from them, while leaving the final verdict to the reader.

That our conclusions are stated in terms of probability indicates that proof is not available here. As in all scientific arguments, results can change with different data. Nothing in the Bible, church history, science, or medicine demands that the Shroud be genuine. And Christianity itself would *not* suffer one iota even if the Shroud's authenticity were totally disproven. Neither Jesus nor Paul made any comments about this cloth, so their views are not in question here. Granting this, however, the Shroud still possibly provides evidence for the validity of Christianity. But even if it did not, studying it appears to involve few negatives: If the Shroud is *not* the burial garment of Jesus, comparatively little is lost. Beyond the accuracy of the researcher's own views on this subject, the unfortunate possibility of worshiping the Shroud or misusing it in other ways is about the only other drawback. At any rate, one should not reject the Shroud as a fake before a thorough investigation is conducted. We have written this book to help meet this need.

2

SCIENCE, SKEPTICISM,
AND THE SHROUD

The air in the New London auditorium was tense as
STURP laboriously presented their findings in October
1981. Tension created by the controversy surrounding the
early release of *Verdict on the Shroud* and the one naggingly
unanswered question that STURP could not or would not
address—Is the Shroud the actual burial garment of Jesus
Christ?—filled the room. Finally, in exasperation, one re-
porter confronted the group of scientists:

> We understand and appreciate your need to remain scientifically
> objective as well as remain within the limits of science. Now, we
> just want to know as one human being to another, what you think—
> an educated guess—a feeling. Isn't there one of you that will admit
> from the stage officially what all of you whom I've personally cor-
> nered will admit even if only grudgingly when a microphone isn't
> in your face?

Before anyone could respond, he pointed to one of the
founders and directors of STURP and said, "You told me you
believe it's Jesus'. Why can't you say that here and now?"
While other reporters echoed his sentiments and applause
enveloped the room, another STURP director attempted to
brush off the issue and restore order. That episode, more
than any other, clearly identifies the key issue for this chapter on science, skepticism, and the Shroud.

The one question that everyone wanted answered—Is the Shroud the burial garment of Jesus?—can never be answered by science, for it is by definition outside the realm of science alone. Science, advanced as it may be, has no tools at its disposal to identify positively any relic of Jesus. Even the identification of the mummies of known Egyptian rulers requires the interfacing of multiple interdisciplinary fields to achieve widespread acceptance. Moreover, everyone has expected all along that modern science would somehow be able to at least address the issue of identity between the Shroud image and Jesus (which we cover in Chapter 6). Certainly many Shroud enthusiasts felt as though scientific fields such as pathology, archaeology, microbiology, anthropology, and pollen analysis would provide enough corroboration with history to enable at least an educated guess. Finally, the public has expected STURP to render personal opinions on the identity issue if for no other reason than that they are the only human beings in our generation to have had enough exposure to the Shroud and the attendant data to give a reasonably educated statement concerning the identity of the man of the Shroud.

Despite the fact that science alone can't address this major issue, science can and does address many areas that contribute dramatically to our ability to answer the question of identity. Unfortunately, in the Shroud story, personalities, politics, and other nonscientific issues have severely muddied the waters of objectivity on authenticity and identity issues.

In this chapter, we will delineate the newest findings of scientific research on the Shroud, specifically as they relate to the critical Shroud question. We will also discuss general scientific research blunders in the past and how STURP tried to avoid those errors. Furthermore, we will address our own errors in *Verdict* and try to provide a scientifically accurate picture of where we are today.

STURP AND THE SHROUD

One major failing of STURP was in not producing a true final report intended for popular consumption and at the same time providing the public with timely updates of their progress. Such a report and periodic updates were necessary to satisfy the demands of a public whose curiosity was at a fever pitch by October 1981. In fact, STURP was largely responsible for the high public interest by virtue of the caliber of its members, their dedication to the research of the Shroud, and the media coverage of STURP's investigation. In addition, the appetite of the public was further whetted by articles in print on STURP and its work, from the very superficial coverage in *Time-Life* to the excellent, in-depth report in *National Geographic*. Unfortunately, STURP consciously limited its final publications to arcane journals like *Applied Optics, Archaeology, Analytica Chemica Acta* (ACA), and the *Proceedings of IEEE*. While these are excellent avenues for establishing scientific credibility and peer review, they're hardly normal public fare. The average person would require a translator even to begin to wade through the technical jargon in some of these articles. Consequently, the only true final report of STURP's findings has remained widely unknown to the vast majority of the public because of its publication in just such a journal (namely, *ACA*).

When *Verdict* appeared in print, some of STURP's team members declared that we had grossly misunderstood the scientific method and findings and therefore misrepresented the state of the Shroud question. Assuming that I [Stevenson], an engineer who worked with STURP from its inception, could have been far enough off to warrant that comment, what hope did the average reader have of understanding what the quarrel was all about? In my humble estimation, most of the concern over *Verdict* was a matter of semantics, as we shall see later in this chapter.

SKEPTICS AND THE SHROUD

On the other hand, articles by Shroud opponents have appeared in numerous popular journals, such as *Discover, Geo, Popular Photography, Christian Century,* and *Biblical Archaeology Review,* and have led to widespread confusion at best and downright misinformation at worst. Some of these articles contain some pseudo-scientific statements, poorly researched (if researched at all) conclusions, and much *ad hominem* argument.

Most articles purporting to disprove the authenticity of the Shroud are partly based on Dr. Walter McCrone's work, which is touted far and wide in the popular press. Even many Christian writers have cited his work favorably, including Josh McDowell, Father Wild, and Ralph Blodgett. However, STURP's work clearly disproves McCrone's theories. Let's examine McCrone's work and then that of some of those who followed him until their findings and conclusions were irrevocably intertwined with his errors.

McCrone reported that in his opinion the Shroud image is a human artist's creation painted with a gelatin-based paint pigmented by iron oxide and mercuric sulfide[1] (iron earth and vermilion). However, McCrone contradicted even himself, for in *Chemical and Engineering News* he apparently agreed with STURP that the Shroud's yellow fibrils (image threads) are dehydrated cellulose.[2] The article reported, "McCrone, who was once a member of STURP himself, generally agrees with the group's explanation of the yellow color on the cloth."[3] Yet, in a rebuttal of William Meacham, a world-renowned archaeologist, McCrone stated, "All of the image on the shroud fibers consists of common and well-known pigments and a stain on the fibers due to aging [sic] of the paint medium."[4] Furthermore, according to Natalie Angier, he claimed the yellow in the Shroud's fibrils is caused by the threads being dried up because they had been coated with *collagen tempera* (an egg-based medium for applying a pigment or dye).[5] During one STURP meeting, he even suggested hematite or jeweler's rouge as the cause of the yellowing until someone gently reminded him that it wasn't even available until the twentieth century, long after the image was known to exist. Without batting an eye, McCrone declared that certainly it was because an earlier image was being enhanced in anticipation of the 1898 photography.[6]

Equally bizarre are the numbers of McCrone supporters who glibly repeat his internal contradictions, without even being aware of how far they stray from the documented facts. For example, Marvin M. Mueller, of the Los Angeles Alamo Laboratory, made a glaring error in stating, "[samples] showed significant amounts of pigment . . . identified . . . as micron-size hydrous and anhydrous iron-oxide. . . .These particles . . . coat the individual fibrils."[7] Less than three paragraphs earlier, he concluded that the paint "medium" had "virtually disappeared leaving behind only cellulose fibrils."[8] Is there pigment on the Shroud or not? Apparently, Mueller isn't sure. Yet STURP and peers insist there is absolutely none.

Perhaps McCrone's most incredible claim is that STURP believes that the image is blood. As reported in Meacham, McCrone contended that STURP's members "prefer to believe the image is blood."[9]

Also McCrone implied in *Discover* that STURP declares the Shroud to be a miracle.[10] Once again, McCrone misrepresents the facts. The single major statement to which STURP publicly agreed concerning the image is this: ". . . it is concluded that the image is the result of some cellulose oxidation-dehydration reaction rather than an applied pigment. The application or transfer mechanism of the image onto the cloth is still not known. . . . Available data from the 'blood' areas are considered and the results show these to be blood stains."[11] STURP's assertion is clear and backed up by every aspect of their nondestructive tests on the Shroud in Turin, Italy. Furthermore, their work has been subjected to the most rigorous peer review imaginable. McCrone has, on

27

the other hand, by his own admission been a "dissenter in the ranks."[12] Not only that, but he was a dissenter who insisted that he alone knew the truth about the cloth. STURP presented no hoopla, no mysterious miracle statements, no confusion—merely clear demonstrable statements of fact reviewed by peers and experts.

Finally, the fact that McCrone, like the other major Shroud opponents, spends much of his energy attacking the qualifications of STURP should be a dead giveaway that his case cannot stand on its own merits. Here's a sampling of McCrone's criticisms:

> I feel like Hughes Mearn's "little man who wasn't there" . . . forced to quit STURP for his unorthodox opinions. . . . I was completely ignored. . . . I think they were the wrong people for the job. . . . I seem to run into minds already made up. . . . no one in STURP has the specialized background in small-particle identification. . . . the problem with members of STURP is they want to believe it is real so badly that they are blinded to the science. . . .[13]

Perhaps most devastating to McCrone's case is McCrone himself. To begin with, his identification of the chemicals he claimed were painted on the Shroud was based strictly on viewing characteristics, which he believed only he had the expertise to determine. In other words, he thought the image "looked like"[14] a painting:

> Only the microscopist was able to observe the details necessary to lead to the correct conclusion. . . . only the microscopist was able to publish a definite conclusion and defend it with complete confidence. . . . only the ability to resolve and identify individual submicrometer particles and to observe their pattern of dispersal on the fibers and their manner of attachment to these fibers could lead to the correct answer. . . ."[15]

And what is "the" answer?

McCrone said, "The 'orange to red' pigment particles are red ochre, iron oxide, and red vermilion." He added, "No one untrained in the use of PLM (Polorized Light Microscopy) could have come to this conclusion."[16] Certainly it can be argued that to make a major scientific statement on the basis of what the image "looked like" in the face of all other scientific data seems highly subjective. It's interesting to note that the image over the entire Shroud is a straw-yellow color. *There is no red in it.*

As multiple sources indicate, STURP has never denied the presence of FE_2O_3 (iron oxide) on the Shroud, but FE_2O_3 has *nothing* to do with the image per se: ". . . amounts of iron . . . on the cloth are consistent with the retting process in common use in the preparation of linen."[17] The image is composed of straw-yellow fibers of dehydrated cellulose, not the red particles of iron that have been identified in three forms on the Shroud and that are separate from the image except in blood-image areas such as the scourge wounds. As one member of STURP put it, "If the blood on the image were the result of iron oxide and mercuric sulfide, it would show up far more distinctly on the Xray than the water stains, but quite the opposite is true. This represents only one of the many examples why McCrone's theory cannot be viable."[18]

More importantly, the single most significant conclusion of STURP was that the Shroud image cannot possibly be a painting. Two of STURP's members, Rogers and Schwalbe, state for the team: "The primary conclusion is that the image does not reside in an applied pigment. The reflectance, fluorescence, and chemical characteristics of the Shroud image indicate . . . some cellulose oxidation/ dehydration process."[19] Naturally speaking, some form of drying, aging (advanced decomposition) process has occurred on the image.

Furthermore, STURP has never claimed to have the only answer to the cause of the image or blood stains, choosing instead to leave the issue open for further study. This represents an excellent example of how STURP's unflinching attention to scientific credibility has paid off. Nowhere does

STURP succeed better than in laying to rest the theory that the Shroud was the work of a human hand. Perhaps these remarks by Meacham best explain the incredible gulf between STURP and the skeptics:

> Even if one ignored the very compelling evidence to the contrary and granted McCrone's interpretation of the iron particles and protein, all one could conclude would be that minute traces of a solution or ointment containing pure hematite are present in the body imprint. This is a far cry from proving the image to be a painting. As STURP responded to McCrone's first pronouncements, microscopic observations do not exist in a vacuum. McCrone *is* somewhat like Mearn's little man who wasn't there again today. He declined at least two invitations to discuss his findings in the multidisciplinary framework of STURP. He declined invitations to present his work at scientific congresses. He did not follow the STURP "Covenant" which he signed, to publish in peer reviewed scientific literature. And as he admits, he has not responded in print to the arguments of Heller and Adler, Pellicori, Riggi, and Schwalbe and Rogers on the physics and chemistry of the image. He has abandoned his earlier claims of a synthetic iron oxide (Post-1800) in the image and of a pigment enhancement of a genuine image. . . . the established facts are more than sufficient to refute the medieval clever-artistry hypothesis. A forger could have obtained a middle-east cloth, could have used some primate blood (and serum), could have depicted the body in flawless anatomical detail, and the pigment could have disappeared leaving a faint dehydration image—but that all of these unprecedented circumstances should have coalesced in the production of a single relic is virtually impossible to imagine.[20]

The bottom line for McCrone and all who follow with various painting-based hypotheses, is that the now heavily documented, independently confirmed, peer-reviewed work of STURP clearly has virtually eliminated *the* possibility that the Shroud image could be the result of an applied pigment. *All* of the electromagnetic spectrum, *all* of the chemical data, even *all* of the physics of the image mitigate against a man-made image.

Unfortunately, Mueller, Nickell, and others who have jumped onto the McCrone bandwagon seem blissfully unaware that for purely technical reasons the painting theory, regardless of the methodology, is a dead issue. Amazingly enough they continue to flog away at the now rotting carcass of this long dead horse.

Nickell, for example, touts a dusting/rubbing method which obviously would leave a heavy distribution of chemicals between the fibers of the cloth and on its reverse side. Body paintings and rubbings invariably contain pigment layers and distortion in three-dimensional projection, all of which are absent on the Shroud.

In addition, STURP member John Jackson, using the Nickell technique, found severe difficulties in its lack of distance information.

Although not strictly an action-at-a-distance hypothesis, another bas-relief based mechanism has been proposed by Nickell and involves contouring cloth to the bas-relief and "dusting" the deformed cloth surface so as to produce an image. . . . We conformed, as Nickell indicates, wet linen to the bas-relief so as to make all image features (eyes, lips, etc.) impressed into the cloth. We then "dabbed" the cloth with fine tempera powder . . . the shaded image seemed to contain more curvature than distance information of the face, in addition, we noted large quantities of powder falling through the cloth weave structure and accumulating on the reverse side. Accordingly we conclude that this mechanism is unacceptable.[21]

Keep in mind that this method was investigated despite the fact that it *failed to match the known chemical characteristics of the Shroud*. Nor was the technique known in medieval times:

Clearly, to be testable and viable, the hypothesis must derive from or at least not conflict with the known elements of 14th-century art. This it manifestly fails to do. . . . there is no rubbing from the entire medieval period that is even remotely comparable to the

Shroud, nor is there any negative painting. Nickell's wet-mold-dry-daub technique was not known in medieval times according to art historian Husband and even that technique fails to reproduce the contour precision and three-dimensional effect, the lack of saturation points, and the resolution of the Shroud image.[22]

Mueller, another virulently anti-STURP scientist, is the next person we will consider since he severely downplayed three-dimensionality. As he stated:

1. The celebrated "three-dimensional effect" begs the question as to whether the Shroud ever contained a full relief (statue or body). . . .
2. All of the extensive chemical and microscopic evidence is consistent with a hypothesis (based in part on the shroudlike rubbings from bas-relief sculptures done by Joe Nickell).[23]

With these few words, Mueller sweeps away the years of demonstrated work on both three dimensionality and image chemistry, brings out the same tired Nickell rubbing technique, and tries to refute all without the slightest demonstrable reference other than a "fair" negative which is perhaps the easiest characteristic to duplicate in an age that understands negative imagery. But as Dr. Jackson demonstrated, the Shroud image is three-dimensionally "consistent with a body shape covered with a naturally draping cloth and which can be derived from a single, global mapping function relating image shading with distance between these two surfaces."[24] In short, though none of the Shroud opponents would willingly concede this point, the three-dimensional effect is the Waterloo for all artistic theories. That same effect has been scientifically demonstrated and subjected to the best peer review. And it still stands.

Also, this same characteristic proves to be the acid test for all the image formation theories Dr. Jackson tried regardless of how well they met or failed to meet the other known Shroud image characteristics. A catalog of ruled-out theories includes the following: direct contact, diffusion, lab-induced radiation from a body shape, engraving, powdered bas-reliefs, electrostatic imaging, phosphorescent statues, hot statues or hot bas-reliefs.

The last theory, hot bas-relief, has been advanced as the solution to the Shroud question by a relative newcomer to sindonology, Father Robert A. Wild, S.J. In his *Biblical Archaeology Review* article, Father Wild incorrectly asserted that statue-scorching is rejected only because of the problem of burn through and that such a technique would be three-dimensional like the Shroud:

> Those who reject the "scorching" theory argue that a statue, when heated enough to scorch a piece of cloth will burn holes in the fabric where raised portions like the nose touch it. If the scorching theory is correct, we would have to reply that modern experimenters—and there have not been many—have simply not yet mastered a technique that was available to some medieval craftsman.[25]

Not only do these remarks show little understanding of the issues involved in confirming any Shroud hypothesis, but they do a great disservice to the many sindonologists who have attempted various scorching mechanisms since 1978. Excluding the members of STURP, who all have been involved in such research, I [Stevenson] have personally received materials from researchers all over the globe, including, but not limited to, Oswald Schuermann and Alan Whanger, plus researchers in France, Denmark, and even Japan, all of whom have done major scorch research for years. Even I have had to rethink seriously the entire issue of the "scorch theories." Nevertheless, statue-scorching is one scorch theory that cannot be accepted. It fails in regard to three-dimensionality, fluorescence, and a host of other difficulties. One researcher summarized the problems this way: "Jackson has done both theoretical and experimental work to address three-dimensional hot-statue hypotheses. He found that a simple isotropic radiation source could not yield the observed Shroud-image shading and resolution . . . (even allowing attenuation) the resulting directionality of the radiation would introduce an unacceptable distortion of the image. . . ."[26] The conclusion, *at least in so far as known forms of scorching are concerned,* brings the entire "scorch" theory into question.

POST-1981 SCIENCE AND THE SHROUD

There are, however, other specific areas of scientific research that can help provide identification of the man of the Shroud as well as deal with the major Shroud questions. Since science to this point seems to have ruled out the possibility of human artifice, we think it is safe to conclude that we are dealing with a genuine artifact—in other words, the Shroud is a real burial garment. Much evidence has been set forth to document this fact.

On the issue of a body, STURP commented, "If the blood images were made by contact with wounds, it follows that the cloth was used to enfold a body. We have evidence that the cloth was used in this way. . . . If we couple this argument with the testimony of the forensic pathologists, we can say more: not only was it a human form, but further, it was a human body."[27] William Ercoline demonstrated that the Shroud contained a three-dimensional body. More importantly, he provided a satisfactory explanation for some of the image's oddities and also provided corroborating evidence that the image projected from that body rather than had across-the-board contact with it. He concluded, "The Shroud image contains distortions which cannot be explained by anatomical variation, cloth stretching, or photographic perturbation. . . . These distortions seem to be consistent with those induced by draping a cloth over a full three dimensional body form. . . . the character of the distortions and some anomalies of the image seem to be best explained by a vertical mapping process."[28] Therefore, it certainly is not too farfetched to conclude that if this cloth contained a body with bloody wounds and that body left a three-dimensional human profile on the cloth, then it was most likely a human body—the body of a human being who suffered precisely as the Gospels state Jesus did. Nor would it be bizarre to conclude that, barring evidence to the contrary, the most likely person to have been in that cloth was Jesus. We discuss this probability further in Chapter 6.

Another interesting researcher to be considered in post-1981 Shroud literature is Dr. Alan Whanger. He uses a very detailed method of analysis called polarized image overlay technique. When two superimposed images are simultaneously projected onto a screen through polarizing filters, a third filter will allow a close-up comparison of details. The Whangers have repeatedly demonstrated that the Shroud image was known and used as a model for everything from icons to coins. Specifically, they isolated icons of Christ from the sixth century and coins bearing His image from the seventh and demonstrated 170 points of congruence for the coin and 145 for the icon. The significance of this research is that it only takes "45 to 60 points to establish the identity or same source of face images" in a court of law.[29] By their method the points of congruence between the artifact in question and the Shroud image itself can be clearly seen by everyone present. Some of the artifacts (for example, catacomb images of Christ) most recently studied in this fashion date as early as the first century, which lends tremendous credibility to Ian Wilson's theory concerning the years the Shroud was missing. (See Chapter 4.) These artifacts also provide corroborating evidence for the antiquity of the cloth beyond the fourteenth century. They have provided strong evidence to support theories concerning foreign objects such as coins/phylacteries on the facial image.

Recently Dr. and Mrs. Whanger traveled to Switzerland to visit the home of the late Dr. Max Frei (Dr. Frei's work is discussed later in this chapter and also in Chapter 4). As of this writing the Whangers have retrieved the remaining samples of Dr. Frei's botanical studies of the Shroud. These have in turn been passed along to Paul Maloney of the Atlanta International Center for Continuing Study of the Shroud of Turin (AICCSST) for further research.[30]

One point that drew flak in Shroud research has centered on the "coins on the eyes." Some have considered such research pseudo-science and have given it little if any credence. Many scientists themselves felt that since the 1978 photographs failed to reveal such data then the artifacts seen earlier must have been merely anomalies in the cloth weave. One sarcastically commented that he could even "see swans in the weave if he looked long enough."[31] However, Dr. Robert Haralick used the initial work of the Whangers and the late Father Francis Filas to demonstrate through digital image enhancement the following evidence:

> 1. the right eye area of the Shroud image contains remnants of patterns similar to those of a known Pontius Pilate coin dating from A.D. 29 [see Chapter 4];
> 2. the photographic negative of the Shroud image has qualities similar to three dimensional range data;
> 3. the face of the Shroud image is similar to the face on an icon of Jesus dating from the sixth century.[32]

Here from an independent researcher is confirmation not only of the coins, but also of Jackson's 3-D work and of iconography, both the Ian Wilson theory and the Whangers backup data. Though some in the past were quick to say that such research was about as significant as looking at a Rorschach diagram, that opinion is no longer valid. To begin with, as the Whangers' (who also found seventy-four points of congruence for the Pontius Pilate coin) pointed out in *Applied Optics:*

> Comparing the same area on the 1931 and 1978 photographs, this technique shows that the cloth is not in exactly the same position and drape for the two photographs and that threads over the eye area might have been stretched or rotated. This accounts for some apparent distortion of the letters and images in the 1978 photographs indeed making it more difficult to see them on these photographs.[33]

We know that the 1931 photos were taken with the Shroud stretched taut while our testing platform was specifically designed so as not to stretch or put tension on the cloth. Another interesting consideration is that perhaps this simple technique has given evidence concerning the image formation process. Since the Shroud must be taut in order to show the images of coins, perhaps the Shroud was taut when those images were first formed. Certainly if testable, this would be a strong piece of evidence against the German-Pellicori hypothesis, which states that the Shroud image was the result of "time lapse chemistry." In other words, chemicals on the body altered the cloth over several hundred years. It goes without saying that quickness to pooh-pooh this data now undermines the scientists' own work.

In the work of the late Dr. Frei, once again we find a variance in how significant various researchers feel his pollen finds actually are. Some argued that the pollens meant absolutely nothing. Others simply found fault with his methodology, particularly his controls and documentation. The major complaint seemed to be that the pollen could have been airborne, no matter what its country of origin. Frei responded:

> Groups A, B and C of plants on the Shroud from Palestine and Anatolia are so numerous, compared to the species from Europe, that a casual contamination or a pollen-transport from the Near East by storms in different seasons cannot be responsible for their presence. . . . The predominance of these pollens must be the result of the Shroud's stay in such countries. . . . Migrating birds or contamination with desert plants by pilgrims can be excluded because they had no possibility of direct contact with the Shroud.[34]

These comments concern only those pollens analyzed before Dr. Frei's demise. It is my understanding that the samples now being analyzed by AICCSST (Atlanta International Conference Center for the Study of the Shroud of Turin) could require years of further study. In addition,

Frei concluded that many pollens matched species found "almost exclusively" in microfossils from the Dead Sea. To his mind the preponderance of evidence mitigated against a medieval fraud. Consider the facts that this was Frei's field of expertise and that his work has been confirmed by Dr. Riggi, who also found "minute animal forms 'extremely similar in their aspects and dimensions' to those from Egyptian burial fabrics."[35] Meacham rightfully concluded, "pollen . . . is empirical data . . . ipso facto evidence of exposure to the air in those regions."[36] As to the concern that STURP only found one pollen, Frei's hand application of tape to the Shroud (which earned him much criticism from other researchers) ensured the transfer of particles that the nonpressure method of STURP obviously missed.

Another extremely important aspect of Shroud study after 1981 revolves around the two points we were most taken to task for in *Verdict:* the "scorch" theory and the resurrection connection. Let us begin with the scorch theory. In its summary report STURP stated the following:

> The primary conclusion is that the image does not reside in an applied pigment. The reflectance, fluorescence, and chemical characteristics of the Shroud image indicate rather that the image recording mechanism involved some cellulose oxidation/ dehydration process. It is not possible yet to say definitely whether these chemical modifications were produced by scorching or by some sensitized thermal or photochemical reaction. The fluorescent properties of scorches *may* eliminate them from consideration, but more detailed investigations are required to rule out scorch hypotheses generally.[37]

Much has been learned about the density shading and chemical properties of the image, but so far, there are no firm ideas about how the image may have been applied to the cloth. Again, Jackson's three-dimensional studies and the global consistency of the image suggest that some global mechanism was involved; however, nothing more specific can be concluded. Nonetheless, the choices are narrowed.

> Resolution considerations and the absence of gross distortion of the image in high profile-gradient regions argue against three-dimensional "hot-statue" hypotheses, although the remote possibility of contact or radiant thermal energy transfer from a flat model cannot yet be dismissed. *If* the image proves to be a chemically-induced cellulose modification instead of a scorch, it would be seen that the material transfer must have been accomplished by direct contact. (The superficial nature of the image eliminates a vapor diffusion mechanism.) Several contact-transfer models were considered, but none seems totally practical or convincing. . . . The *most* important outstanding problems pertain to the image transfer mechanism. Briefly stated, we seem to know what the image is chemically, but how it got there remains a mystery. The dilemma is not one of choosing from among a variety of likely transfer mechanisms, but rather that *no technologically-credible process has been postulated that satisfies all the characteristics of the existing image.* [38]

Here scientific objectivity begins to clash with the overall Shroud question. If all evidence points to a real burial garment and if the best explanation of that evidence appears to involve some sort of energy transfer, then to suggest an unknown form of "scorch" seems perfectly logical. In my [Stevenson's] opinion, STURP balked at this because of all people they know full well the ramifications. If they agree to a "scorch," are they not also agreeing to the Resurrection, just as many opponents have claimed? Given the possible ridicule of fellow scientists and the concern that such a revelation might call all of their work into question, I would expect STURP to tread cautiously around this issue. Instead of caution, however, what continually appears in print is denial. It would seem that STURP has succumbed to one of the two major human fears: fear of people or fear of failure. I hasten to add that while we agree that any known form of scorch causes fluorescing and the Shroud image does not fluoresce, we find that to be much easier to accept than a theory which has three or four problems and requires a mind-boggling series of happenstance even to postulate. Which theory requires more faith?

For obvious reasons, Habermas and I [Stevenson] concluded a "scorch" to be the most likely image formation process. Though this resulted in complaints that *Verdict* was "unscientific," some scientists such as Jackson generally agreed with us. Since that time, the scorch theory has led to more intemperate rhetoric than any other single issue, in spite of the fact that many of the scientists themselves have been quoted as giving theories that clearly would be interpreted as a scorch by anyone who heard them.

The party line currently seems to be that the scorch theory has been eliminated from consideration. Technically speaking, we agree. Any *known* form of scorching has been ruled out. Nevertheless, the current conclusions of STURP suggest that it's not that simple. For instance, the image is called a "more advanced stage of natural aging-type decomposition."[39] The process is described in this fashion: "This yellowing is due to the natural process of dehydration, oxidation and conjugation typical of *low-temperature* cellulose decomposition."[40] Additionally though the best lab results have come from "catalyzed-decomposition contact mechanisms" (German-Pellicori samples "baked" to simulate aging), they quickly added what we've said all along. The Shroud's three-dimensionality *alone* not only poses thus far insurmountable problems for contact, but also suggests a "projection" mechanism.[41] Chemist Alan Adler admitted that of the three working models even the two most promising theories are "energy transfers," which are also problematic.[42] One of these is Giles Carter's theory that the energy transfer mechanism was Xrays emanating from the body. Adler stated this was "fine chemically, fine physically yet bizarre biologically" and quipped that "the man would have been so radioactive that he glowed in the dark. Not to mention he would have been dead long ago from the radioactivity."[43] The other mechanism involved a high voltage, high energy transfer that Oswald Scheuermann, a respected physicist and sindonologist, has been experimenting with for several years. Using a dry cloth Scheuermann can produce an image very close to that on the Shroud.

> Images with virtually the same detail and physical and chemical characteristics as those on the Shroud can be produced on linen by means of radiation from high voltage, high frequency AC electrical currents. . . . the ionizing electrical energy spreads over the surface of any object in the electrical field, whether it be tissue, hair, cloth, leather, or metal. The sparks or ions then tend to be discharged as streamers (coronal discharge). . . . This helps to explain . . . why one can get detailed images on the Shroud of such objects as the Pontius Pilate coin over the right eye.[44]

But again the question seems to be how? Perhaps an unusual phenomenon such as ball lightning, but how does one duplicate such a thing? In addition, all of Scheuermann's samples which I [Stevenson] have seen to date seem to penetrate the cloth, something the Shroud images definitely do not do. Adler has suggested that the use of a larger, thicker model (at least five to six inches) would overcome some of the problems in Dr. Scheuermann's work, but that it would be extremely difficult to accomplish because of the amount of energy required, an estimated 50KV at 10 amps over a body-sized object.[45] (Reviewing these theories, scientist Igor Bensen suggested 50 watt-seconds/square centimeter for a power source of at least 1,100 kilowatts for $1/10$ second.) Dr. Scheuermann suggested a solution to this dilemma that might make some uncomfortable:

> Either there was a chain of coordinated processes of cause and effect due to laws that are still unknown or an inexplicable phenomenon of a supernatural kind left traces of a natural kind. . . . Consequently, it is high time now to completely record the primary aspect and add the phenomenon "resurrection" to the fact "corpse." . . . "Resurrection," even if inexplicable, must not be ex-

cluded as a point of reference or an action principle. . . . It has to be admitted that we know hardly anything as to how that resurrection is to have taken place; but that does not exclude that it could have left palpable traces—despite many a theological opinion—not only an empty tomb and all the attendant circumstances, but also a very informative image.[46]

Once again, the evidence seems to point to the empty tomb and the Resurrection.

CONCLUSION

In fairness to those STURP scientists who may also believe that the image was caused by the Resurrection, we have to consider politics. In Turin a select group of people in essence controls the destiny of the Shroud. When *Verdict* was first published, some in this group took the position that there was no further need for testing since the Shroud had been "proven" authentic. As the former spokesman for the team, I can attest that very explicit directions were given to each STURP member as to what could and couldn't be said in public. Furthermore, despite the fact that everyone supposedly had the liberty of a "personal opinion," such liberty was for all intents and purposes sacrificed for objectivity/credibility. In a classic example, I was told that as the spokesman, I no longer had that liberty. Admittedly this occurred after a series of media misquotations (all by STURP members) had ruffled a few feathers in Turin. Given the alternatives, some of the scientists may have felt more concern over the consequences than courage of their convictions.

Again the issue of identity seems to offer an out and a problem at the same time. If this cloth held the crucified body of Jesus of Nazareth, then perhaps the Resurrection is involved. Obviously there is no known way to duplicate that feat, and therein lies the rub, not to mention the eagerness of opponents to cry, "Miracle! Miracle!"

On the other hand those who pursue the totally natural

avenue continue attempting to develop the Pellicori-German model. The primary problems with this model are three-dimensionality, superficiality, capillary-flow, and the ability to produce *all* known points through image contact. Though German and Pellicori are confident that given the proper environment—specifically a humid one—the once stiff cloth would sag sufficiently to produce the proper 3-D gradient and contact pattern and that the right body oils would only produce a superficial stain and would therefore not evidence noticeable capillary flow, they have so far failed to produce such an image in any of their laboratory tests.

In past Shroud research, the major failing has been not cooperating to coordinate the methodology, data, and results. Also entire fields of expertise have been ignored or simply not consulted. Finally, little if any of what was learned ever received widespread dissemination. (Most of these comments specifically target the so-called "secret" commission.) STURP initially did a fairly good job of avoiding these errors both before and after Turin. However, for whatever reasons, STURP became somewhat parochial in later years and has (in my [Stevenson's] opinion) failed to capitalize on the excellent results it did achieve. For example, some members of STURP seemed overly concerned about sensationalistic news reports. After one such report, a STURP member inaccurately concluded that "the credibility of STURP is in ashes."[47] In reality, the incredibly well-documented and peer-reviewed articles by STURP have met with respect, stimulated much discussion, and led to further research in a variety of new fields. Also STURP has by its own admission had an incredible fear of the religious issue and tried to avoid it at all costs. In my opinion, a far wiser course of action would have included biblical and archaeological experts to deal with such issues as the identity of the man, Jewish burial customs, and textile and coin experts.

Likewise, in *Verdict* we made some mistakes, many of

which we already mentioned. The primary one was underestimating the way a book written for public consumption could be misinterpreted and twisted. Second, in our excitement, we were perhaps too strong in our espousal of the scorch theory as we understood it at the time. Also we were perhaps premature in shooting for the definitive book.

Where do we stand now? Scientifically speaking, the Shroud is not a painting of any type. It rather seems clearly to be a genuine burial garment, stained with real blood and containing an image of the male body it once contained. Chemically, that image is composed of dehydrated-oxidized cellulose of the linen itself.

The recent carbon-14 dating has raised more than a few concerns. Touted far and wide as proof that the Shroud is a hoax, this late addition to the Shroud data bank is not at all what it is cracked up to be. In short the C-14 data flies in the face of *all* the other data and yet is expected to stand by virtue of its name alone—in spite of the fact that most scientists will readily admit that C-14 is not infallible. As we shall see in the next chapter, the dating as it has been presented to the public (with limited and secondhand facts at best) is severely flawed and in fact proves nothing.

On the other hand, multiple fields of research indicate scientific evidence, including pollen, coins, mites, and textile data, to support the Shroud's longevity and its Middle Eastern origin. Photographic research confirms that it was known and copied long before its appearance in medieval France, and possible pigment contaminants may also confirm that.

Though the cause of image formation is not yet known, only three have any semblance of validity. One, the German-Pellicori natural latent chemistry model, has no known precedent, has defied reproduction and seems to violate three-dimensionality, superficiality, capillary-flow, and the detail of the image. The second, Dr. Carter's theory— namely that the victim's bones emitted X rays that created the Shroud's image—seems bizarre from a biological standpoint, which would contradict or at least compromise the otherwise straightforward chemistry of the image. Finally, the high voltage, high energy transfer approach is also without precedent and has defied reproduction thus far, but it seems promising in our opinion.

What does it all mean? That's the central question this book will address.

3

CARBON 14

Is the Shroud a Medieval Object?

The hottest current issue in the Shroud story is the already heavily debated carbon-14 testing. The media reporters are bursting with the news that the Shroud has been dated by the controversial C-14 process. On the basis of those reports, many are writing the Shroud off as a medieval artifact. To them it has become just a scientific curiosity. Others, apparently ignorant or perhaps biased about the wealth of data against human artifice, have claimed that the Shroud is a forgery.

Is C-14 a valid method of dating an article such as the Shroud? What range or margin of error must be allowed in dating the cloth? If in fact it does not date two thousand years old, does that finally settle the major questions for most scientists? On the other hand, does a younger date completely eliminate any possibility of authenticity? Who conducted these tests that are now in question? What methods did they use? Was adequate attention given to their controls and protocols? Who supervised their work, and has it met with the same level of successful peer review that made the work of STURP such a milestone in Shroud studies? What results did they in fact get, and are those results reliable? These are the major issues concerning the C-14 dating of the Shroud of Turin.

Even before STURP's first journey to Turin in 1977 to propose testing the cloth to a panel of appointed authorities and sindonologists, plans were included for dating the cloth. Dr. Jackson went so far as to contact Dr. Libby who is credited with the development of modern carbon dating. Dr. Walter McCrone, who joined STURP in Turin, proposed a dating procedure at a cost of approximately $50 thousand. Not convinced that his proposal met with a favorable response, McCrone called on the late King Umberto II, last surviving monarch of the royal house of Savoy and legal owner of the Shroud. The resulting fracas nearly capsized the entire STURP expedition before it got under way. However, careful distancing ensured that STURP testing would be proposed independently of the then *persona non grata* McCrone. Much later we learned that McCrone and his associates were not even properly equipped to conduct the dating. Nor were they experienced in the field.

After STURP arrived in Turin in October 1978, I [Stevenson] was practically accosted by Dr. Harry Gove of the University of Rochester who interrupted my press conference to question what made me an "expert" on carbon-14 dating. I had at no point claimed such expertise. The issues surrounding C-14, as well as the media's constant claim that the church was refusing the test because it had something to hide, had necessitated a statement of STURP's official stance on C-14. As team spokesman, I had been quoted delineating the caveats for such testing. Gove didn't agree with the caveats at all. When the dust settled, he became one of the representatives of several labs to propose a formal dating plan for the Shroud. As we shall see later in this chapter, however, perhaps even Gove would agree the STURP caveats were well-advised after all.

Carbon-14, also known as radiocarbon, is radioactive and has a documented half-life of roughly 5,730 years. Since living organisms can absorb C-14 and dead ones cannot, the dating theory of radiocarbon requires measuring the residual C-14. Due to the fact that C-14 decays at an exact and constant rate, an approximate age can be determined. C-14 has been somewhat controversial since its development, and experts have often been hotly divided over its reliability. At one point some even suggested that those pushing for a Shroud dating would use the cloth as a "guinea pig" for testing new methodology. While I certainly would not question the sincerity of all C-14 researchers, such use of the Shroud was indeed a real concern. Now that very concern overshadows all the current media statements on C-14 dating.

LABORATORY SELECTION

One thing that really affected the dating issue was the "on-again, off-again" secrecy hang-up of the Center of Sindonology operation. Before leaving Turin, Archbishop Ballestrero publicly announced that carbon-14 testing had been approved in principle with certain very reasonable stipulations and that proposals that met those guidelines would be accepted and fairly evaluated. This was one of only three things that I *could* state publicly after Turin without compromising the data reduction—including analysis, discussion, and publication and peer review of the testing methods and the obtained results—that would be ongoing for three years. Notwithstanding that announcement, STURP and Professor Luigi Gonella, a representative of the archbishop, hotly protested the distribution of *Verdict* on the grounds that it would hinder the approval of carbon dating. Gonella, whom I still consider a personal friend, even wrote me an extensive letter arguing the point as if I had not been present or had a faulty memory. In retrospect, some may have truly believed that *Verdict* was strong enough to negate the need for C-14 in the minds of the Shroud's custodians. The truth of the matter is that, for whatever reason, the Shroud question is touchiest with those who control its destiny. They move in "strange and mysterious ways," ostensibly to protect it, but the end result is that outsiders often feel the custodians have something to hide (see Chapter 12).

The gist of Turin's dating stipulations presented in 1978 was as follows:

1. The laboratories selected to do the dating must agree on methodology so as to provide an equal comparison. (Later proposals suggested alternate methods to increase objectivity on the date received; unfortunately, however, the alternate protocol was dropped.)

2. They must also agree to conduct a double blind study. (Typically a scientific double blind ensures objectivity by requiring the lab to test at least two unidentified samples simultaneously—one of a known date. This too was apparently violated.)

3. They must first successfully date a sample of known origin. (During this test one of the selected labs was off by over a thousand years.)

4. They must (as we did) first brief the archbishop or his representative on all results. (Though the wisdom of this point was questioned in *Verdict,* I [Stevenson] stand by it. We were asked to do this as a courtesy, and we agreed. Apparently, so did the C-14 labs.)

The C-14 situation progressed significantly. To begin with, Dr. Gove and his associate were deleted from the C-14 testing (although we understand that he worked with Paul Damon, C-14 expert at the University of Arizona who headed their dating work there on the Shroud), reputedly for having a different orientation from the selected labs which use the gas counter method.[1] The samples were received by three laboratories, the University of Arizona, the Federal Polytechnic Institute in Switzerland, and Oxford University in England.[2] The results began to leak first from Oxford and then from multiple sources. Finally, in exasperation, the representative for Archbishop Ballestrero announced that the dating was completed and the age was medieval. But serious questions about both the dating procedures and the stated results have been raised from many quarters.

METHODOLOGY

To begin with, let's understand the chosen methodology. Unlike the Libby method, which requires pieces of significant size, the selected process uses an accelerator to do mass spectrometry to determine age. This method requires substantially less material for analysis. The pretreated, chemically modified sample (converted to graphite) is ionized and passed through an electric field to strip electrons from its atoms, leaving highly charged individual atoms. These in turn are accelerated and bent (the bending is a function of atomic weight and imposed magnetic field) along different paths specific to each atom—even to its isotopes. This step occurs in a cyclotron which detects these accelerated atoms much like a centrifuge. Only atoms with the masses of C-13 and C-14 are detected. Filtered beams (filtering removes nitrogen 14) of the remaining carbon atoms strike detectors that count the C-13/C-14.[3] Most labs claim an accuracy of +/− 200 years. This new technique would only require a few centimeters of material, a piece no bigger than the nail on your little finger. Even if they had used pieces of a large fragment that was removed in 1969, many tests could have been done simultaneously. However, the use of this larger fragment would have been extremely ill-advised since it would introduce too many unknowns into an already difficult situation. As Meacham accurately described it, "Certainly most archaeologists would have rejected the use of samples subjected to a long separation from the object to be dated and held under unknown conditions of storage and handling."[4] Unfortunately, as we shall see, the particular sample selected may have been an equally serious error.

According to the *Los Angeles Times,* the entire dating "process [was] being supervised by the British Museum, Pontifical Academy of Sciences and a representative of the Archbishop of Turin."[5] While the museum claims it was in fact not supervising the dating but was merely the institution selected for the C-14 symposium, it was definitely responsible for the certification of the Shroud samples and the statistical analysis of the data itself. Even though the labs were given three cloth samples to conduct the blind study (they were not told, of course, which came from the Shroud), Michael Tite of the British Museum also noted, "A laboratory *could* if it wanted to, distinguish the shroud sample from the others, *so the blind test depends ultimately on the good faith of the laboratories*."[6] To my horror, I discovered that the labs openly admitted they knew when they were dating the Shroud: "He [Paul Damon] was looking at a quarter-inch-square piece of the Shroud of Turin."[7] The significance of this statement will be discussed in detail later in this chapter.

I want to make it clear from the outset that if we are to arrive at a solid conclusion concerning the age of the Shroud, C-14 is not nor should it be *the* acid test of the Shroud's possible authenticity. Meacham put it extremely well at the 1986 Hong Kong Shroud Symposium:

There appears to be an unhealthy consensus approaching the level of dogma among both scientists and lay commentators [that C-14 dating will] settle the issue once and for all time. This attitude simply contradicts the general perspective of field archaeologists and geologists [notice these are the ones most likely to need accurate dating on a regular basis] who view possible contamination as a very serious problem in interpreting the results of radiocarbon measurement . . . I find little awareness of the limitations of the C-14 method, an urge to "date first and ask questions later," and a general disregard for the close collaboration between field and laboratory personnel which is the ideal in archaeometric projects . . . statements quoted (from Shroud researchers both pro and con) reveal an unwarranted trust in radiocarbon measurement to produce an exact calendar date. . . . I doubt anyone with significant experience in dating . . . would dismiss . . . the potential danger of contamination and other sources of error. No responsible field archaeologist would trust a single date, or a series of dates on a single feature, to settle a major historical issue. . . . No responsible radiocarbon scientist would claim that it was proven that all contaminants had been removed and that the dating range was . . . its actual calendar date.[8]

If space permitted, I would reproduce Meacham's entire article, for it masterfully delineates the problems and issues currently facing the Shroud dating laboratories.

Remember this comes from a scientist who, though recognizing C-14 "is not an infallible technique, and . . . contamination . . . is always to be taken seriously," nevertheless "excavated and prepared and submitted . . . more than 70 samples . . . and had liaison with major C-14 laboratories at Oxford [a selected lab], Canberra and Teledyne"[9] in his own archaeological work.

The *McGraw-Hill Encyclopedia of Science and Technology* also has some important facts to add concerning C-14 dating relevant to the Shroud. To begin with, it points out several critical forms of "variation" that are problematic to *all* C-14 dating. These include secular variation and the DeVries effect and they result "in the *necessity to calibrate conventional C-14 dates.*"[10]

Secular variation refers to a general long-term variation in C-14 dating in which the radio-carbon years and calendar years are not equivalent. This form of variation exhibits a sine-wave function of 150 to 800 years in deviation. The causes of it are not yet totally understood. Nevertheless, in the case of the Shroud, secular variation alone could cause the C-14 testing to give faulty data.

The *DeVries effect* is a high frequency variation in dating which causes anomalies in the dating process. As a result of this effect, an article can reflect "two or more points in time" for a single artifact being dated.[11] Furthermore, neither the scientists nor the current store of data are internally consistent on artifacts that date from before A.D. 1000.

Due to secular variation and the DeVries effect, articles "between about A.D. 1300 and the later part of the first millennium B.C. . . . *register too young.*"[12] There is also "a lack of complete agreement concerning the frequency and magnitude of relatively rapid periods of oscillation before A.D. 1000."[13] If that were not enough in the way of caveats, the article goes on to say that "variations equivalent to up to

52

several hundred years can result." Therefore they conclude, *"C-14 has lost a considerable amount of its significance."*[14]

We by no means want to imply that C-14 is useless or should not have been used. Quite the contrary, we believe it should have been done, but under totally different conditions and protocols than were used. In addition we do not feel that C-14 alone will ever *settle the matter*.

More germane to the issue is the dry run of C-14 testing, which was detailed in the journal *Radiocarbon* in 1986. Scientists used C-14 to date an Egyptian Bull Mummy linen (the wrappings from an ancient Egyptian burial) as well as two Peruvian linen cloths. The results of this testing using the new accelerator method was extremely revealing. First of all, it underscored the fact that the method is somewhat wanting in accuracy. On the Egyptian Bull Mummy linen, the dates ranged from 3440 to 4517 B.P. (before present)—a span of 1100 years. Although the known age of the cloth was 3000 B.C., the closest date they could get using C-14 was 2528 B.C., a date which required a calibration of 472 years to correct it. That should raise plenty of eyebrows. The second sample, one of the Peruvian cloths, was not much better, with a span of 450 years and the closest date 250 years off. Finally, the third, also a Peruvian cloth, had a span of over 1100 years and the closest date less than 100 years off. This Peruvian cloth was a much easier target to hit because the date was "guesstimated" between A.D. 1000–1400. That range gave the testers a built in window of +/− 200 years to start with!

After the tests on these three samples were run, the farthest dates were 1549 years, 709 years, and 439 years off respectively. To allow that margin of error on calibration alone would be ridiculous. Moreover, even admitting that errors of contamination would radically affect the test results still underscores the inherent weaknesses of this dating method. In fact, when the testers accredited these poor results to contamination during pretreatment and reran the tests with significant improvement, the oldest cloth still showed an error of nearly 1,000 years. Most importantly, it was 1,000 years *on the young side!*

The significance of all of these dates is that they clearly demonstrate that serious anomalies not only exist but that even the calibration techniques used to correct them are not an exact science. For example, let's look at the calibrated results themselves. The three samples gave the following date ranges after calibration: 3255–2827 B.C. (on a 3000 B.C. cloth), A.D. 1400–1668 (on an A.D. 1200 cloth), and A.D. 1289–1438 (on an A.D. 1000–1400 cloth).[15] These results confirmed what the experts had said concerning C-14 dating and its problems. Admittedly the calibrated results were much improved, but being over 400 years off on a known sample seems significant. Indeed, these results confirmed what the experts had said concerning C-14 dating and its known drawbacks. I must point out, however, that the article in *Radiocarbon* very glibly understated these problems and, in fact, concluded the following:

> Overall, there is *good agreement* between the results obtained and the expected historical dating of the samples. . . . A coherent series of results can be obtained when several laboratories undertake separate blindfold measurements of the same sample. . . . there are *no special difficulties* in dating textiles by C-14 using small sample techniques . . . the distribution (span) of the results . . . *lends added emphasis to the need for the dating* of any important relic such as the Shroud of Turin *to be shared by several laboratories* if the results are to have *maximum credibility.* . . . as a further check, *exchange of pretreated samples* . . . might be desirable.[16]

You need to understand that the number of labs determined for conducting C-14 tests on the Shroud was reduced to three from the seven proposed; one of the three selected labs was the lab which had the most "outlying results"; one of the protocols or methods of testing was totally eliminated; and the samples were sent in such a fashion that Tite, spokesman of the British Museum, admitted the test was not truly a blindfold test. Furthermore, the two labs that in essence developed the accelerated method were eliminated from the testing.

DATES OR DISCREPANCIES?

As we were preparing this manuscript, articles began appearing everywhere stating that the Shroud was dated with 95 percent accuracy between 1260 and 1390. The worst part of it all was that many articles added that the Shroud was obviously a forgery. Nothing could be further from the truth. Even if the dating was not fraught with problems, the Shroud has been *demonstrated* to be a genuine burial garment and not a human endeavor. Certainly had the date been reported to be first century the opponents to authenticity would have raised an array of concerns, or merely claimed that the "artist" used an ancient cloth. But the mood of the day seemed to be to accept the dating without question and to springboard to an unwarranted conclusion. Nevertheless, even the scientists involved in the C-14 testing have made comments that contradict such a facile reception of the medieval date. For example, the Oxford lab has stated, "At least 1 in 5 dates are contrary to expectation. . . . A major source of error in the dating procedure was in . . . their [the six labs doing the pretesting, namely, Arizona, Bern, Brookhaven, Harwell, Oxford, and Rochester] method of pretreatment of samples, i.e., in removing contamination. . . . Before AMS (the method used on the Shroud) is accepted as the final arbiter of chronology, criteria are needed to decide if and when an AMS date is unacceptable."[17] It's interesting in the light of these comments that Oxford, with very little experience in dating cloth, dated the Shroud and was among the first to leak the reports that claimed the Shroud was a fake.

It seems incredible that the Oxford lab could so quickly pronounce the Shroud a fraud on a single dating in a field in which the lab has limited experience, especially given the caveats they themselves raised. But they are not the only enigma in the Shroud C-14 dating. Dr. Willy Wolfi of the

Zurich lab, whose testing of the Egyptian Bull Mummy was so far off, stated "One single date, is no date . . . for the particular case discussed here [i.e., an Egyptian cloth] it is obvious that the number of *64* investigated samples is still too small to properly understand the observed disparity between radiocarbon dates and historical chronology."[18] If sixty-four samples from an Egyptian cloth were insufficient, how can such accuracy now be claimed in regard to the Shroud when only one sample was tested?

When discussing the Shroud testing, Dr. Gove himself, in a strong letter of protest to the British Museum, said in part, ". . . there are many people who are overly suspicious of this entire operation. . . . I am astonished you would permit the British Museum to risk having its reputation called into question in what has become a somewhat shoddy enterprise."[19] In addition, the C-14 results have yet to be published in acceptable scientific journals, much less subjected to the same intense peer review and criticism that were both a blessing and a curse to STURP. Initial reports indicate the following discrepancies:

1. The samples were all taken from the bottom of the Shroud, a mere two to three centimeters from a repair site due to the 1532 fire. This site selection created serious problems for the dating procedure. For example, if, as some sindonologists have suggested, the dating zone (or test sample) was actually an added strip of cloth and therefore not part of the original Shroud, we have no knowledge of its history and testing it would have resulted in an inaccurate age for the Shroud. Furthermore, we know for a fact that the Shroud was heavily handled throughout its history and that it was damaged by fire and repaired with strips of cloth during the Middle Ages. Each of these factors adds an unknown variable of contamination to the dating equation, making a definitive C-14 dating extremely difficult, if not impossible.

2. No testing or measurements were done to ensure that

the fire damage in no way altered the cloth due to isotope exchange, which occurs at 300° even though the Shroud was in a fire of at least 960° and was also subjected to super-steam vapor when doused with water during the fire. When the Shroud was burned in the 1532 fire, carbon molecules from its silver casing, the case's silk lining, and its framing materials would have begun to mix with the Shroud's carbon molecules. This would have occurred at any temperature over 300°F. Dousing the Shroud with water would have also caused additional molecular exchange. By not checking out these factors and including them as part of the dating equation, the labs left themselves open for a faulty date.

3. Only one type and amount of solvent was used to cleanse all three samples, though stronger solutions may have removed additional contaminants from the cloth and thereby resulted in an older date.

4. The small counter method (gas), which is considered much more reliable and effective for testing cloth samples, was eliminated. (Remaining gas can even be redated.)

5. A true scientific blind study was never conducted: a) All labs involved in the dating were present at the removal of the Shroud samples, so they knew which samples were which; b) The linen was left intact with its unusual weave (3–1 herringbone twill with a "Z" twist), obviously recognized by the labs during the tests (it has been reported that some labs even found fibers of the red silk backing cloth during their preparations); c) The date of the "dummy" cloth was published and available to all the labs; d) The "dummy" cloth was of a totally different weave from the Shroud.

6. The textile expert present at the removal of the test samples has not made detailed public statements or published a report concerning the location, examination, or extrication of the samples for C-14 dating. This is a critical oversight, especially in light of reports that some stray

threads on the sample were merely snipped off, not unwoven to help prevent contamination. I [Stevenson] have received several letters concerning a video of this procedure. All the writers stated that it "appeared" to them that the test samples were from the side strip—a highly contaminated portion of the Shroud. One of these observers also confirmed the reports that stray threads on the sample were merely "snipped off."

7. There was no publications or peer review of the method and the results before boldly proclaiming the date results to the public.

8. The labs' interpretation of the dating results was prejudicial. The labs stated they had "proof of forgery," which certainly undermines their professed objectivity in the light of the other published, peer-reviewed technical data on the Shroud that have not yet been successfully refuted.[20] Indeed, this data have been largely confirmed by others in their respective fields of expertise.

9. Potentially the most damaging single piece of evidence to controvert the 1988 test results comes from the reported disclosure that there was a secret dating of the Shroud conducted at the University of California nuclear accelerator facility in 1982. Separate ends of a single thread were dated, with one end dating A.D. 200 and the other A.D. 1000.[21]

At least two conclusions can be drawn from this data. For one, the wide divergence in dating—even on the same thread, much less between the different samples for the 1982 and 1988 tests—should be alarming for those who conclude that the 1988 carbon dating was definitive.[22] For another, the plus or minus factor for C-14 would place the end of the thread dated earlier at about the time of Jesus. At any rate, the 1982 test results should at least lessen dogmatism over the conclusiveness of the 1988 dating.

10. The final straw to be added to the back of this horribly overloaded camel is best reflected in the words of Wolfi of Zurich: "The C-14 method is not *immune to grossly inac-*

curate dating when non-apparent problems exist in samples from the field. The *existence of significant indeterminate errors occurs frequently*."[23] Keep in mind that this man's lab was the same lab that had the extreme outlying results during the dry run C-14 tests.

Given all of the above, where do we stand with C-14 in regard to the question of the C-14 dating of the Shroud? At the very least, the first round of C-14 testing has allowed the widespread publication and interpretation of data that have raised serious questions yet to be answered. At the worst, it has introduced inaccurate data that have been permitted to jeopardize the search for sound answers to the questions surrounding the Shroud's authenticity. In both instances, the 1988 C-14 tests did little to advance scientific study on the Shroud.

CONCLUSION

Whatever the final verdict on the initial C-14 testing, presently it has only added a serious degree of confusion at a crucial turn in Shroud studies. Having built up the dating as the "be all and end all" of sindonology, Turin authorities are now faced with the extremely disappointing results. Moreover, they appear to have accepted very questionable data without question. Fortunately, however, efforts are even now underway to petition Turin and the Vatican to seek a more scientific "second" opinion. If all these tests had produced different dates, controversy would have raged for years while the main issues were pushed aside. Since all the tests apparently have produced a medieval date, even C-14 experts as diverse in opinion as Gove (who rejects the Shroud's authenticity) and Meacham (who accepts the Shroud's authenticity) are beginning to shout "Foul!" over the protocols alone.

Also no one has taken into account the bizarre history of the Shroud itself and what impact that might have had on the dating. Meacham spelled it out this way:

For the Shroud, there is a 600-year history in a number of different environments and unknown handling situations, and a possible further 1300-year existence during which the object could have been in contact with virtually any natural or man-made substance in the areas it was held. To measure Shroud samples, one must therefore consider every possible type of contamination and attempt to identify and counter them all.[24]

The bottom line for the age of the Shroud is the same as the bottom line for the Shroud in general—we must view the Shroud's age in its entirety with every possible piece of relevant data taken into account. Then when all of the evidence is in, we can make an educated guess as to the most likely age of this cloth. As with the Shroud itself, no one piece of data is enough, but the data as a whole are overwhelming. Since C-14 alone is not enough, and the current C-14 test is so debatable, let's move on to discuss other considerations about the age of the Shroud—considerations that have been tested, retested, and thoroughly reviewed.

Before we do, however, one final remark on the 1988 C-14 tests is in order. Although we, and many other sindonologists, have serious questions about the results of these tests, we do not question the overall validity of C-14 as a test for age. Certainly it has its weaknesses and pitfalls, but when properly used, it can be a helpful dating tool. Our concern is over the recent use of C-14 to date the Shroud. In this instance, it appears that flaws in preparation and experimentation have resulted in a flawed conclusion, as the other tests for age strongly indicate.

4

OTHER TESTS FOR AGE
Their Reliability and Their Results

Given the problems surrounding the C-14 dating and realizing that the resulting controversy may well continue for years, other methods and scientifically credible techniques to arrive at an approximate age for the Shroud must be explored also.

Unfortunately, STURP had no one truly qualified in archaeology, history (although there was an open liaison with Ian Wilson, an art historian and well-known Shroud researcher), textile analysis, and biblical research—the very fields most likely to have provided good evidence for the Shroud's longevity. Into this gap came Max Frei, Ian Wilson, Bill Meacham, Francis Filas, Al Whanger, and a host of others to whom we now turn.

SCIENTIFIC RESEARCH

Let's examine the first scientific statements made concerning the origin of the Shroud. In 1969 experts from various fields were called in to examine the Shroud in preparation for a television exposition. This group eventually became known as the secret commission, primarily because its efforts were unknown to the public until they were leaked to the press. Most of their efforts still are not widely known, and it was years before any effort was made to translate their findings. One of that group, a textile expert, Professor Gilbert Raes, later concluded in part that the

61

Shroud was consistent with cloth woven in the Middle East. The key factor in his conclusion was not the weave but the discovery of minute fibers of cotton interwoven in the cloth. Cotton was not grown or widely used in Europe in the Middle Ages; however, it had been used in the Middle East for centuries. To the best of my [Stevenson's] knowledge, Raes was one of the only textile experts to have "hands on" experience with the Shroud, but he was not the last to place its origin outside of Europe.[1] Thus, the documented history of the cloth is well established by the controversy surrounding it. After all, from the first public display of the Shroud in medieval France, the Shroud's whereabouts has been heavily documented precisely because its authenticity has been so hotly debated. Therefore, any individual factor that takes it outside of medieval France, automatically increases its longevity. For example, the cotton found on the cloth raises greatly the probability that the Shroud was woven in the pre-medieval Middle East. Other factors, such as pollen, coins, and cloth weave, also point to a much older and non-European origin for the Shroud.

In fact, several areas of research contribute significantly to the establishment of a reliable age for the Shroud. These other areas include the following:

1. Identification and origin of pollen and mites
2. Identification and dating of artifacts such as coins or phylacteries on the image
3. Verification and origin of archaeological details
4. Cloth/weave comparison and analysis
5. Historical verification

Though any or all of these methods might seem without merit to a chemist or a physicist, they are nonetheless a vital part of normal historical identification. Certainly all of these would be essential factors to an archaeologist, and whatever else is certain about the Shroud at this point, it is most certainly an archaeological artifact. For example, if an individual work of art were discovered and previously unknown, similar techniques would be used to make the case for its origin and manufacture. More importantly, these methods would be especially critical when the history of the artifact is cloudy or unknown.

Pollen

Perhaps the most significant work on the identification and origin of pollen on the Shroud was done by the late Dr. Max Frei, who founded the scientific department of the Zurich Police and whose doctoral thesis was on the flora of Sicily. Dr. Frei was present with STURP during the 1978 studies, primarily because he had previously identified key pollens that definitely placed the Shroud in both Palestine and Turkey at some time in the past. Though many pollens on the Shroud could be attributed to those areas, such as in the famous cedars of Lebanon, Frei only selected those pollens that are still unique to each specific area. In my [Stevenson's] opinion, the significance of the pollens cannot be overestimated. For example, certain desert halophytes that he found on the Shroud led Dr. Frei to say:

> These plants are of great diagnostic value for our geographical studies as identical plants are missing in all other countries where the Shroud has been exposed to the open air. Consequently a forgery, produced somewhere in France during the Middle Ages, in a country lacking these typical halophytes, could not contain such characteristic pollen grains from the desert regions of Palestine.[2]

The pollen analysis confirmed in scientific detail the history that Ian Wilson had developed from scattered references and artistic comparisons. According to Wilson, at some time in its history, the Shroud was exposed to the open air in Palestine and Turkey—precisely where it should have been if it and the Mandylion cloth are, in fact, one and the same. It is certainly doubtful that a medieval forger could have known, let alone produced, a cloth with just the right pollen spread.

In 1978, compared to the extremely detailed and orchestrated approach of STURP, Dr. Frei's methods seemed a little haphazard. In particular, his somewhat heavy-handed application of sampling tape earned him scorn from a few of his fellow sindonologists. In fact, however, STURP's meticulously applied tapes yielded few if any pollens, which led many STURP members to doubt Frei's earlier work.

Later scholars have helped to vindicate and confirm the wisdom of this man whose criminal expertise was respected throughout Europe. Apparently the hand application of tape was much more likely to contact the pollens that almost certainly would have settled deeper into the fibers and crevices. The purely surface roller method used by STURP barely disturbed the cloth, nor did it penetrate to the level of the pollens. Werner Bulst, in a response to the late Dr. Frei, made the following observations:

> . . . [of] Pollens from 58 species of plants . . . less than one third grow in France or Italy. . . . [This] astonishing . . . small number of European species can be explained by the history of the Shroud in Europe, for, normally kept in a closed reliquary, the Shroud was protected from pollen contamination. Only on special occasions was it exposed in the open. . . . The spectrum of non-European species is highly astonishing. . . . There is only one place where all of these plants—with the exception of three . . . grow in a very small radius: Jerusalem. . . . This cannot be an accident. . . . pollens could have been carried to Europe on winds. . . . but a transport of pollens from the Middle East is highly improbable.[3]

In addition, the three isolated plants apparently are found in the Edessa and Constantinople areas where history again would suggest that the cloth received very little, if indeed any, open exposure.

Bulst's most impressive statement also clearly demonstrates the weakness of the argument that Middle East pollens are insignificant.

> Pollen grains can come upon the Shroud only when it is exposed in the open. It would have been a stupendous miracle if, precisely in

the few days when the Shroud was being exposed, storms would have brought pollens over a distance of 2500 km. and—even more miraculous—if those winds were carrying many more pollens from the East than from the European environment. Moreover, the pollens on the Shroud are from plants which bloom in different seasons of the year. Therefore the same improbable "accident" must have happened repeatedly.[4]

It should be pointed out that pollen analysis is acceptable evidence in a court of law and therefore certainly empirical data as to the Shroud's longevity and non-European origin. Furthermore, with the remaining samples from Dr. Frei's lab, which were generously donated to ASSIST (Association of Scientists and Scholars International for the Shroud of Turin) by his widow, much more can yet be learned from the folds of this cloth.

Mites

Another interesting aspect of the microscopic material found on the Shroud is the discovery of mites by Professor Giovanni Riggi. During his analysis of samples vacuumed from between the Shroud and its backing cloth in 1978, he isolated and identified a mite peculiar to ancient burial linens, specifically Egyptian mummy wrappings.[5] If the Shroud was a creation of the Middle Ages, then its forger must have ordered the mites to go with it.

Artifacts

Artifacts visible in the Shroud image areas are the next consideration. These include "coins" over the eyes, a possible phylactery upon the forehead (which logically should have a corresponding "prayer box" on the arm), and other "clothes," such as a modesty cloth or "bands" at the head, hands, and feet. In 1978 Eric Jumper, John Jackson, and I [Stevenson] co-authored an article which appeared in *The Numismatist* and postulated the theory that 3-D objects visible on the eyes might in fact be coins. Working with Ian

65

Wilson, we suggested the lepton of Pontius Pilate because the size, shape, and markings seemed uncannily accurate.[6] The sample of the lepton I ordered and purchased for STURP was fairly well preserved, but I do not currently know its whereabouts. Though we asked for suggestions and admitted the research to that point was "inconclusive," we were in no way prepared for the hailstorm that followed.

To begin with, many lambasted *The Numismatist* for even including an article on the Shroud. Others suggested that we took great liberties in supposing that the use of coins was compatible with early Jewish burial customs. There were also some who made helpful suggestions for additional research. The final blow seemed to come when the 1978 photographs failed to reveal the same details over the eyes as was seen on the earlier photographs.

While at least one of my co-authors on the article may have changed his view, I retained an interest that has been somewhat vindicated by independent research.

First, the late Father Filas proceeded to find coins that matched the initial lepton, right down to a peculiar misspelling. The coin's inscription contained the letter sequence UCAI. The correct spelling should have been UKAI. Father Filas found several extant copies of the lepton with this spelling error. Apparently, the die used to make the coin was misstruck in the same way as a twentieth-century three-legged buffalo nickel. And it was used until the error was finally detected. Josh McDowell and many others who were suspicious of the Shroud's authenticity criticized Shroud supporters asserting that "the coin striker would have had to be either drunk or ignorant" to mint a coin with such an error.[7] It seems they forget that Romans, like the rest of us, made mistakes occasionally, even honest ones.

Second, Father Filas submitted that research to Dr. Haralick who independently confirmed the presence of the "coins" (see Chapter 2).

Finally, a separate 3-D analysis also confirmed the identification.[8] It is most interesting to me that the 3-D photos of

The Shroud face compared to an eleventh-century icon. Some scholars have discovered up to 170 points of congruence between the Shroud image and early Christian icons, dating as far back as the 6th century. Current research suggests that such icons may be found back to the 2nd century.

Armenian artist Aggemian painted this likeness of Jesus in 1935, basing it on the face of the Shroud of Turin.

Italian artist Giovanni Battista della Rovere painted this depiction of the Shroud in the 16th century. In it he imagines how the cloth was draped over the body to permit the creation of the image.

The cathedral in Turin, Italy, that houses the Shroud.

The altar where the Shroud is stored.

When the Shroud is not on public display, it is wrapped in red silk and placed in an ornate silver-lined casket for safe keeping.

The Shroud on public display in Turin in August 1978.

The arrival of a truckload of scientific instruments at the Rennaissance palace of the Savoys in Turin, just prior to STURP's testing in late 1978.

The X-ray fluorescence exam conducted by STURP in 1978.

John Jackson, physicist and one of the leaders of STURP, and Robert Bucklin, former deputy coroner of Los Angeles County in California, studying Shroud photos at the Baylor University bio-stereometric laboratory.

Don Devan, from Information Science Inc. in Santa Barbara, California, examining the Shroud with a microscope.

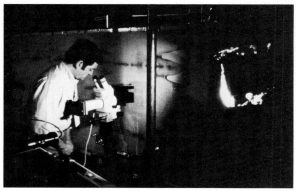

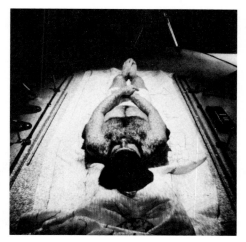

STURP scientists used a Shroud mock-up and a volunteer selected to fit it to reconstruct the original position of the man buried in the Shroud. Experiments of this kind helped scientists to determine the burial victim's height and weight.

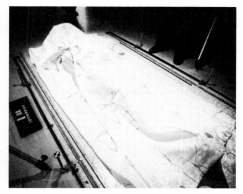

Due to the preciseness of the Shroud image's three-dimensional characteristics, scientists were able to construct this fiberglass and cardboard statue of the man who was buried in the Shroud.

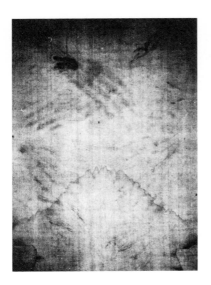 

An ultraviolet fluorescence photograph of the hands and legs of the image (above left) and the upper right corner of the close-up of the wrist wound (below) show the odd flow of blood running down the victim's arm. This might be the result of blood moving around an arm phylactery or prayer box, commonly worn by first-century Jews.

Pathological and archaeological studies confirm that crucifixion victims were nailed through the space of Destot—a tiny spot between three bones in the wrists. Nails driven through this space would sever or damage the median nerve which flexes the thumbs, thereby causing the thumbs to draw tightly to the hands. Thumbs are not visible on the Shroud image.

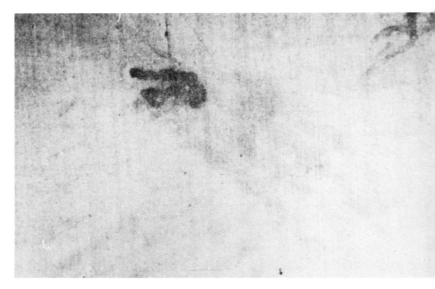

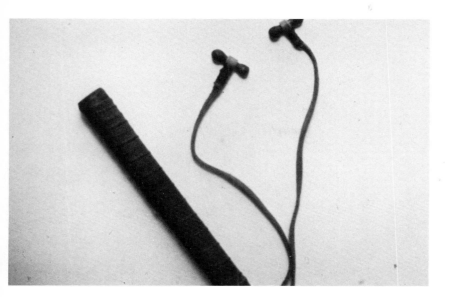

Reconstruction of a Roman flagrum (above), a brutal two- or three-thonged whip that was used as a means of punishment in the first century. The Gospels record that Jesus was scourged—whipped with a flagrum—before being crucified. The man buried in the Shroud was also scourged with a flagrum, as the dumbbell-like marks covering most of his body clearly show. This photo (below) is of the image of the man's back.

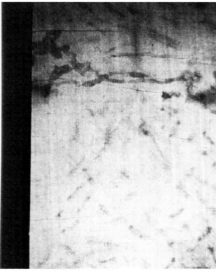

In these pictures, the scourge marks on the victim's back and backside of his legs and feet reveal the extent of his injuries as caused by the flagrum. There are between 90 and 120 such marks on the victim's front- and backsides, indicating a severe scourging.

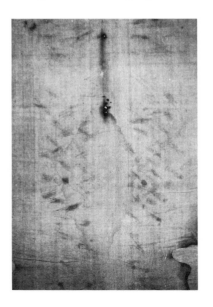

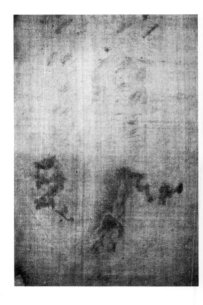

the "coins" actually reveal more clearly the letter shapes which match the Pilate coin inscription. Also, the earlier photographs were apparently taken with the cloth stretched tautly on a board. In the 1978 photos, the Shroud was only loosely held to the testing platform. This difference is significant in that the minute details visible on the earlier photographs would likely be hidden in the crevices of the Shroud when loosely held.

Personally, I spent some time with Jewish scholars in an attempt to clarify the burial custom controversy. Once again, however, the results were inconclusive. While some felt that nothing precluded the custom, others felt there was relatively little to support it either. Though no clear custom can be established, coins have been found in skulls in the Middle East dated in and around the first century A.D. Alternate theories can be advanced to explain this archaeological fact, but no one knows for certain in the absence of either a written record or eyewitness testimony.

The primary significance is that *if* the coin is in fact the Pilate lepton, it is strong corroborating evidence that both the image and the cloth date to the first century. And with this form of dating, the margin of error is substantially less than with C-14. In addition, the overlay technique of the Whangers confirmed the presence of not only coins but also phylacteries. When the 3-D photographs revealed that the "box" on the dead man's forehead was apparently an artifact, Wilson and a Jewish cadet at the Air Force Academy both suggested a tephillin—a Jewish phylactery or prayer box which contains a portion of Scripture. When I later discussed this possibility with Eleazor Erbach, an Orthodox Rabbi from Denver, he not only confirmed its size and shape, but also suggested that the broken blood flow on the right arm might have been caused by the corresponding arm phylactery.[9] If indeed these artifacts are what they appear to be, then not only do they add to the case for longevity, but they also mitigate strongly against forgery. Additional researches by Whanger and Haralick seem to support the notion of other clothes, such as a modesty cloth in the groin area or "bands." But these are much more elusive from a technical standpoint, and they do not add much to the overall case for authenticity. Given that some of the scientists do not consider these studies validated even now, further expert testimony is needed.

Archaeological Peculiarities

One facet of age determination that has been little developed is verification of archaeological details and peculiarities. For example, researchers have often observed that all medieval artists have depicted the nails in the hands of the crucified Jesus, not in His wrist. Meacham noted, "The nail through the wrist is a solid historical indicator. After all, all of the evidence says that this is a crucifixion victim. So that puts the Shroud in the years of crucifixion—a date from 150 B.C. to A.D. 350. You can't do much better than that even with C-14."[10]

Another indication that mediates against the medieval date is the length of the dead man's hair. As Noel Currer-Briggs pointed out, "The fourteenth century was not alone in disapproving men with long hair. . . . [Medieval] contemporary iconography depicted Jesus with fairly short hair."[11] He even intimated that this may have incited the medieval inquisitors to attack the Templar Knights. The Templars were the same group art historian Ian Wilson suggests became custodians of the Shroud after it disappeared from Constantinople. What other indicators would a trained historical or scriptural expert come up with given a detailed firsthand study of the cloth?

Textile Studies

Textile comparisons also testify to the longevity of the Shroud. John Tyrer, a chartered textile technologist who has worked in that field for twenty-five years, discovered in his research that while Middle East linens similar to the

Shroud exist that date as far back as 3600 B.C., not much medieval linen has survived. Additionally he determined, "It would be reasonable to conclude the linen textiles with 'Z' twist yarns and woven $^3/_1$ reversing twill similar to the Turin Shroud *could have been produced in the first-century Syria or Palestine.*"[12] Tyrer even suggested that textile analysis alone would aid in dating the cloth. He also confirmed what early Shroud researchers have suggested concerning the longevity of linen. Furthermore, he added that textile analysis might offer important clues to the effects of yarn variations on image-formation and to cloth draping. Tyrer concluded, "The Shroud is probably the most remarkable 'Standard Sample' for the interpretation of the history of textiles that has come down to us."[13]

History

Another area pertaining to the age question is historical research that has come out since 1981. Even given the excellent coverage of magazines such as *Shroud Spectrum International,* it is a gargantuan task to remain current on the historical research being done on the Shroud. Some of the most exciting work has come from authors who have provided further evidence for the Wilson theory of iconography—the Edessa connection. In *Shroud Spectrum International* alone, articles from Fossati, Crispino, Pfeiffer, and Barber delved into the iconographical connection. With the exception of Pfeiffer, a synthesis of these articles suggests mounting evidence in support of Wilson's reconstructed history. In addition, these other researchers are filling in a few of the gaps in Wilson's work. Fossati, for example, disclosed that the Holy Face of Edessa (one of several Mandylions) found in the Vatican is actually painted on herringbone fabric which seems "similar" to the Shroud.[14] He went on to make the obvious suggestion that detailed studies of these icons could provide supportive details for sindonology. Rex Morgan and Noel Currer-Briggs also offered corroborating historical evidence that the image was both known and used as a basis for the paintings of Christ from as early as the first century.

Concerning his work, which involved comparing the earliest known paintings of Christ found in the catacombs and alleged to be made by eyewitnesses, Morgan cautiously concluded:

> If other researchers, by examining these reproductions of the earliest portraits of Christ, if that is what they are, can agree to any extent that they portray the same man as the Shroud of Turin image depicts, *then we can take the date of the existence of the Shroud back to the time of Christ.* . . . If the congruent features are sufficiently convincing, and I suggest . . . they are, then this discovery must add weight to the already considerable weight of evidence for authenticity.[15]

If these early art works, some of which are believed to be first century, could be subjected to the overlay technique developed by Dr. Whanger (see Chapter 2) and have the same level of congruence, it would again provide strong corroboration for the Shroud's existence before the Middle Ages. Furthermore, in a recent conversation, Morgan told me [Stevenson] that he has now acquired an original photograph of the Templecombe image that is of a much finer quality than that which was published by Wilson and which again lends credence to the iconography theory (see Chapter 5).[16] The Templecombe image is the surviving link between the Shroud of Turin, a painted copy of the Templars' "treasure," and the "miraculous image of the Savior." It is strikingly similar to the Shroud in color and imagery. Its discovery strongly suggests that the Templars had the Shroud in their possession—again raising serious questions over positing a medieval origin for the Shroud. Morgan's book, *The Holy Shroud and the Earliest Paintings of Christ,*[17] brings out much evidence for a professional historian to follow up in detail.

70

Currer-Briggs after providing intricately detailed historical research for *The Holy Grail and the Shroud of Christ,* in
which he strongly bolsters Wilson's Templar connection
said:

> There is simply no genius of this caliber known to art historians
> capable of creating such a masterpiece at this period. . . . Highly
> intelligent and cultured men and women who saw it in the twelfth
> and thirteenth centuries believed that it was genuine . . . that the
> image of Christ . . . was not made by human hands. . . . They should
> have known the difference: there were enough representations of
> Christ's head in paint and mosaic for them to be able to tell. . . . [To
> them] it was the genuine Shroud of Christ.[18]

The only medieval voice alleging forgery appears to be
Bishop Pierre d'Arcis, who claimed that the image was
"cunningly painted." But he never turned up the artist who
allegedly painted it, and the reigning Pope subjected the
Bishop to "perpetual silence" on the matter—a peculiar de-
mand that raises questions concerning d'Arcis' motives, or
at least as Ian Wilson states, leads to the conclusion that
there was "more to the affair than any of the documents tell
us."[19]

CONCLUSION

It should be readily apparent by now that the issue of the
age of the Shroud is much the same as the overall question
of authenticity. To arrive at any reasonable conclusion, all
of the facts must be evaluated. As I [Stevenson] prepared my
sections of this manuscript, the one thing that repeatedly
amazed me was the wealth of articles on the subject of the
Shroud that I had never seen. It is perhaps little known that
in Esopus, New York (a scant fifteen miles from where I sit),
there is a well-stocked library dedicated to the Shroud.
Many of the writings there have never been translated and
date back generations. Who knows what lost historical details exist on those pages—details that could unlock the
missing years of the Shroud entirely?

71

For now, we must summarize the case for the age of the Shroud: (1) It was known, copied, and revered as the image of Christ, perhaps as far back as the first century; (2) it obviously came from the Middle East and has cotton, pollen, and mites from that area imbedded in its threads; (3) artifacts from coins to hair style point to an early origin; (4) it accurately displays a form of capital punishment not practiced since A.D. 350; (5) the data as a whole match a historical path that is continually gathering support; after all, a cloth from the Middle East which was also exposed in both the southern steppes of Turkey and the area of modern Istanbul is much too close to the path Wilson postulates for mere coincidence.

Individually, none of these points would carry the day. But together they merit much more consideration than some scientists have given thus far. The bottom line for many scientists seems to be that too much speculation is still involved. Nevertheless, we must add at this point that the human artifice theory is no longer feasible on scientific, historical, archaeological, or biblical grounds. To imagine the genius necessary even to conceive, much less produce, such a level of historical detail seems beyond all reason. Just how well does all of this evidence match the historical traces of the Shroud? We'll examine that in detail in the next chapter.

5

THE WITNESS OF HISTORY

Though in the past some would have been inclined to say that the Shroud's weakest link is its history, research indicates that the pre-medieval knowledge of this cloth is more than we ever imagined. Not only was the Shroud known, copied, and revered to such an extent that its history can be established, but the logical, traceable historical path matches known and accepted scientific data. In this chapter we will reconstruct Ian Wilson's historical theories and their surrounding supportive evidence.

Perhaps the most unusual and fascinating piece of historical support is found in the novel, *The Scrolls of Edessa*, by Robert Wise. Why cite a novel at this critical juncture of historical research? Precisely because Bishop Wise, a conservative reformed theologian and not a sindonologist, used only historical sources to trace the Shroud's history and arrived at the same conclusion regarding the Shroud's "missing years" as did several renowned sindonologists. Although as a novel *The Scrolls of Edessa* is not historically authoritative in itself, its reliance on historical sources and sound historical method makes it a viable reference for filling in details of the Shroud's past.

In the introduction to his excellent work, Wise wrote:

Eusebius has long been recognized as one of the most important and reliable of the early church fathers and historians. Around 325

73

he wrote in his *Ecclesiastical History* of the correspondence between Jesus and King Abgar V of Edessa. He noted that he had himself personally translated the Syriac documents into Greek. . . . Eusebius reports that Abgar V sent a messenger to Jesus imploring Him to come and heal him of an incurable disease. Jesus declined, but promised to send a disciple. Ultimately the Apostle Thaddeus came, bringing the Shroud with him (although this last event is not recorded by Eusebius). This little-known encounter between Abgar and Thaddeus is one of the remarkable stories of Christian tradition.

Further details of the history and tradition surrounding the Shroud's journey to Edessa are recorded in The Doctrine of Addai, now in the Imperial Library in Leningrad, Russia.[1]

(An interesting side note: when we were in Turin for the 1978 testing, an article appeared in *La Stampa* stating that the Russians claimed the Shroud was rightfully theirs because of that very document.)

From these little known documents, Wise wove a plausible story about the missing years of the Shroud. Using only the historical and legendary references, he arrived at basically the same conclusion as did British historian Ian Wilson in his book *The Shroud of Turin.*[2] And significantly a major thread of the novel is the agony of Thaddeus over the use of the Shroud as a witness to the resurrection of Jesus Christ.

Those who believe the Shroud is a forgery are quick to point out that the Gospels make no mention of an image. Even Shroud enthusiasts are likely to quail when reminded that the "witnesses" did not mention such an image. It has been said numerous times that the Gospel writers would not have left something that important out of their accounts. However, many Shroud researchers have come to know that "it was extremely risky to publicly display the Shroud with its figurative imprints and one understands the almost absolute reticence, during all the first millennium, to explicitly mention the existence of an image on the Shroud."[3]

An alternate explanation for the lack of mention is the

primary natural formation hypothesis of German and Pelli-cori. Their theory absolutely requires that the Shroud had no image when it was first discovered because it is a "time dependent theory" (see Chapter 2). In short, the very forma-tion process itself required an extended time period for image development, perhaps even hundreds of years. This, argue German and Pellicori, would explain the lack of an early history for the Shroud.

This overall attitude, however, fails to take into account the following facts:

1. All of the eyewitnesses and most of the disciples were Jews to whom images were absolutely anathema.

2. Burial garments were considered unclean and should have been destroyed by law.

3. The conversion of John after he went into the tomb "and he saw and believed"—is one of the most powerful statements in the New Testament. It has led to a great deal of speculation as to what inspired him. (Most conclude it was an empty mummy wrap, which is totally inconsistent with Jewish burial customs.)[4]

4. The disciples were such sticklers for the law that even Paul had to correct them concerning their liberty in Christ.

5. Many historians agree that Jude Thaddeus preached the gospel in Edessa and was martyred there for the faith. Several at least allude to the Doctrine of Addai and other legends that connect Jude with a "miraculous image of the Saviour."[5] The connection is displayed in many of the churches dedicated to St. Jude, which have a portrait of the apostle carrying an image of the Savior in his arms. That portrait is clearly based on the Shroud image.

6. This same Jude was in some way related to Jesus. Some believe he was a half-brother or cousin.[6]

7. The Wilson-Iconography theory provides a reasonable historical track of the cloth and image all the way back to the time of Christ.[7]

Not only do these facts indicate that a second look is in order, but as we shall see, there are numerous early references to an image on the burial linens of Christ that further corroborates what the other facts indicate.

THE CLOTH OF EDESSA

Given all of the above, we can postulate a very logical progression of events. The Shroud did have an image. And although that image was problematic to the Jews, the cloth was kept precisely because it bore an image, and it was given to Jesus' family. Knowing the affinity of Gentiles for images, one member of Jesus' family, Jude Thaddeus, took the Shroud with him as a tool to share the gospel. The question is: Does the known evidence support such a theory?

Ian Wilson presents a detailed case that the Shroud was first brought to Edessa by Thaddeus and that Edessa became one of the first Eastern cities to convert to Christianity. Later the cloth disappeared during a period of persecution of the new church, only to be uncovered nearly five hundred years later—sealed in a wall of the city. Again nearly five hundred years passed and the Shroud was surrendered to superior forces from Constantinople. In 1204, it was stolen by French Crusader Knights when they sacked the city of Constantinople. Consequently, the cloth disappeared once again. Finally, the Shroud as we know it today, turned up in Lirey in the family of a French Crusader Knight who claimed it was a "spoil of war."[8]

If we allow, for sake of argument only, that all these events did occur, then the historical chain of events becomes clearer. First of all, when this image was uncovered in Edessa after a serious flood destroyed a portion of the walls in approximately A.D. 525, it was believed without question to be the cloth of the Edessa legend. The earliest records of this story date to the second and third centuries. Also the cloth and its image *acheiropoietos* ("not made with human hands") eventually became so famous that artisans from all over the world came to paint copies of it from at least the sixth century onward. In 1978 I [Stevenson] was shown a copy of a Russian icon that was believed to be at least

76

twelve hundred years old. The influence of the Shroud was unmistakable. Furthermore, recent research has confirmed the knowledge of this likeness from as early as the second century. As the knowledge of this image grew, it began to attract attention until A.D. 944 when it was handed over to an army from Constantinople. Having laid siege to the city and demanded its surrender, General John Curcuas agreed to release two hundred Moslem prisoners, grant a perpetual peace treaty, and pay twelve thousand pieces of silver in exchange for the Shroud. In spite of such a princely ransom, the Moslems attempted to pass off a fake before finally releasing the true relic.[9] The point of all this is that it hardly seems likely that either side would have gone to such lengths to acquire/retain a painting. They could merely commission another. How would a bishop have recognized the real from the fake unless in fact it had been well-known throughout his known world at that time?

With all these things in mind, how do we link the cloth of Edessa with the Shroud of Turin? One of the most incontrovertible pieces of supportive evidence for Wilson's theory is the pollen analysis of Max Frei (see Chapter 4). It is especially convincing in that it strongly suggests both longevity and authenticity. After all, it is possible, though not very likely, that a forger could have been wise enough to order a cloth from Palestine, even that he might have ordered an "old" cloth from Palestine. But to suppose he could have ordered a cloth woven in the Middle East and then specified that the cloth must be exposed to open air in the areas of both Turkey and Istanbul to ensure the proper pollen spread boggles the imagination. Anyway, the existence of pollen would not be discovered for at least another six hundred years. Moreover, the historical path of the Shroud would not be reconstructed for nearly eight hundred years.

Religious relics were forged frequently with no such sensitivity to detail. Many churches claimed ownership of the same relic, and in the case of the Shroud itself, notoriously poor copies were held in esteem in various places. To imagine that with this relic and only this relic there was sudden inspiration of heretofore unrecognized and unheralded genius is truly clutching at straws.

We also have evidence pertaining to the Shroud's image. First of all, it is described as " 'a moist secretion without coloring or painter's art' " and that it "did not consist of earthly colors."[10] Certainly this would be an accurate description of the Shroud. More importantly, a sixth-century text describing the cloth clearly states that it was "doubled in four."[11] If the Shroud is doubled in four, only the face remains visible. This could account for the image that has been so heavily copied, as well as accounting for numerous references in which the Mandylion appeared only as a face. It would certainly make sense since the Shroud was a burial garment. After all, burial garments were considered terribly unclean. To postulate that it was folded so that only the face was visible would seem the most reasonable way to disguise it and still maintain its effect. There are even some creases in the Shroud that would seem to support this supposition.[12] Even today many consider the face extremely moving.

There are also scattered references to the image having much more to it than just a face. For example, an eighth-century sermon by Pope Stephen III related to the Mandylion saying, " '[He] stretched his *whole body* on a cloth, white as snow, on which *the glorious image of the Lord's face and the length of his whole body was so divinely transformed* that it was sufficient for those who could not see the Lord bodily in the flesh to see the transfiguration made on the cloth.' "[13] A later record, written by a monk in 1130 described, " 'a most precious cloth with which he wiped the sweat from his face, and on which shone the Savior's features miraculously reproduced. This displayed to those who gazed on it *the likeness and proportions of the body* of the Lord.' "[14] A twelfth-century Vatican version read, " 'I send you a cloth on which know that the image not only of my face, but of *my whole body has been divinely transformed.*' "[15]

From the thirteenth century, yet another account survives: "'For it is handed down from archives of *ancient authority* that the Lord prostrated himself full length on *most white linen,* and so *by divine power* the most beautiful likeness not only of the face, but also of the *whole body* of the Lord was impressed upon the cloth.'"[16]

An additional confirmation is the sudden appearance of a full-length head-to-head representation of Christ in art from around the eleventh century. From about 1025, the traditional mummy wrap concept associated with the burial of Christ disappears. Many churches began to follow a strange scenario that Robert de Clari detailed from Constantinople. After giving the same basic type of description of the cloth that we've seen thus far, Robert de Clari said that the "sydoine . . . stood up straight every Friday so that the figure of Our Lord could be plainly seen there."[17] Wilson discussed those churches that during Holy week would raise an image of Christ's body to simulate His resurrection from the dead. Certainly it would again make a great deal of sense that the new keepers of this "miraculous image" would have examined it in greater detail and uncovered the full-length figure. Finally, an interesting account of the "keeper" of the relic collection at Constantinople described, "the burial sindon of Christ: this is of linen . . . material, still smelling fragrant of myrrh, defying decay, because it wrapped the mysterious, naked dead body after the Passion."[18] Again each item is significantly tied to what we now know as the Shroud of Turin.

These references seem most significant in that they mention older documentation, the color of the then much younger linen, that it was clearly no painting, that the image was attributed to a miracle of "power," and that it was a full-length image. All of Wilson's opponents argue that the Shroud and the Mandylion were not the same, primarily because of the belief that the Mandylion was a facial image only. However, as we have seen, there was widespread knowledge that the entire body was represented. With that knowledge, the main objection to Wilson's theory runs aground.

CONCLUSION

All of these references taken together on an object of less significance would be readily acceptable in helping to identify that object. After all, many entirely new archaeological discoveries have been made based on a mere mention in the Bible. Often whole towns for which we have absolutely no external historical record are found. Even the allowance that some of the early internal documentation (such as the letter of Christ to Abgar) is apocryphal, should not in itself affect our acceptance of the data. After all, traditions and even history itself began in oral repetition handed down from generation to generation. We are all familiar with the very recent success of *Roots,* in which Alex Haley traced his family back to the very village of his heritage with a few poorly remembered words that had been handed down for over two hundred years. To put stock in multiple source references to an image independently confirmed by other means seems to me [Stevenson] not at all unreasonable.

The very mention of the early existence of an article nearly identical to what we now know as the Shroud, if it came from a reliable source, would be grounds at least to question any radiocarbon date that was too far removed from those early dates. We have, in fact, a variety of reliable sources that match a reasonable history of the Shroud's missing years. Once again, we have a knowable, traceable, testable theory for the Shroud's presence and influence prior to the Middle Ages. The theory goes beyond speculation when point after point is independently documented by separate researchers. We have then, in short, one more crucial support for the Shroud's longevity and at the same time an equally important reason to reject the initial round of C-14 testing. What is most significant about this evidence is that it comes from the very field once thought to be most devastating to the Shroud's authenticity!

Knowing that the Shroud's whereabouts are heavily documented from 1357 onward, we are left to postulate how so many things—history, art, legend, pollen, and religious tradition—can possibly line up by coincidence alone. Since much of what we now know was only uncovered in Wilson's research, it seems ludicrous to suspect that someone could have contrived it all. How, indeed, could an unknown, medieval forger contrive to order a cloth woven in the Middle East and taken through Turkey so it would match the pollen, legend, and scattered history of the Shroud of Turin? Nor would anyone have had the detailed knowledge of the art, religious traditions, and legends of countries and cultures half a world and at least a thousand years removed from the Shroud's European debut.

Don't forget that the lack of an unbroken historical tradition was the main target of early Shroud opponents. It seems obvious that, like the scientific testing itself, the history of the Shroud of Turin could only *begin* to be pieced together at a time such as the twentieth century when the technology exists to trace so many tenuous threads back to their original source. I might add that *if* the Shroud is a medieval forgery, then even the great art masters will pale by comparison to this forger's work. For not only did the forger create a masterpiece, but he did it in such a way that it would match a historical and an artistic tradition that would require years of super-sleuthing, an army of translators, and a team of researchers even to begin to put it all together. Furthermore, he had to convince countless historians that they at last had a reasonable explanation for the problematic similarities between the Shroud and some "lost" miraculous image. Finally, he did all of this with assuredly almost no access to or knowledge of the majority of the data. Nor does any of the data include the tremendous knowledge of ancient Jewish burial customs and pathology which we will discuss in the next chapter.

Besides, even if we postulate against all this evidence that the Shroud is a man-made copy of an earlier lost image, we are still left with the scientific data which clearly demonstrates that the Shroud is not the creation of human hands. Therefore, the most logical and evidentially satisfying conclusion is that the Shroud was the inspiration for all the image imitations, not one of those imitations.

6

THE BURIAL CLOTH OF JESUS?

If, as we have argued, the Shroud is quite possibly a pre-medieval artifact, is perhaps even from the first century, it raises the question that everyone wants answered: Is the Shroud of Turin the burial garment of Jesus? For many people, this is the major question behind recent interest in the Shroud. Even when the press questioned the scientists in the October 1981 meeting at New London, Connecticut, both publicly and privately, the primary concern was whether there was any possible connection between the Shroud and Jesus.

The earlier scientific testing had revealed that in all likelihood the Shroud was an actual archaeological artifact. Even after testing many different models to explain how the Shroud image could have been crafted by human hands, the scientists concluded that the cloth apparently had held the body of a crucified Jew.

But now we appear to have a few options. In spite of the prior scientific findings, those who accept the carbon dating results released in the fall of 1988 will view the Shroud as something other than the burial garment of Jesus. Perhaps this cloth will still be seen not as a fraud but as an authentic piece of medieval art. But if it is not a first-century object, the question of who may have been buried in the Shroud is basically moot, at least in terms of historical relevance for Christian apologetics, and this chapter is simply misplaced.

But for those who question the dating procedures, the possibility that the Shroud wrapped either the dead body of Jesus Christ or another Jewish crucifixion victim is still open. In other words, since the Shroud is still possibly an original object of archaeological interest rather than a later creation and since research reveals that it wrapped the body of a crucified Jew, our options are that it wrapped either Jesus or some other crucified person. We will continue to address this last set of options.

In order to discover whether the Shroud of Turin is Jesus' burial garment, we need to know if the New Testament Gospels are reliable historical sources. As we pointed out in *Verdict,* we can only hope to learn whether the man in the Shroud was Jesus if we know that the Gospels are reliable, especially in their reports of the events leading to Jesus' death. Because we treated the reliability of the Gospels in our previous book, we will not repeat that argument here.[1] Instead, we will assume historical veracity and, initially, observe the major similarities between the gospel accounts of Jesus' passion and the findings on the Shroud. Next, we will look at the question of identification. Last, we will consider some of the scientific researchers who recently have declared their belief that the Shroud is Jesus' burial garment.

JESUS AND THE MAN IN THE SHROUD

Even to one casually acquainted with the New Testament Gospels, there are numerous similarities between Jesus and the man buried in the Shroud. Of course, this is *not* the same as an identification. An artist or a forger could attempt a duplication. But if there are many similarities, including some an artist or forger would likely miss or be unable to reproduce, and if there are no differences, then the probability that Jesus was the man buried in the Shroud increases dramatically.

The Gospels relate that Jesus was subjected to numerous punishments before His crucifixion. At Pilate's order He

84

was scourged by Roman soldiers (Matt. 27:26; Mark 15:15; John 19:1). There are various ideas of exactly how this beating was actually performed, but it was a serious administration of great bodily punishment, not superficial blows. Pilate apparently hoped that the Jews would regard the scourging as sufficient punishment for Jesus' alleged blasphemy, for on at least two occasions after the scourging, he tried to reason with the Jews to let Jesus go. But Pilate was unsuccessful (John 19:1–16).

The man in the Shroud was also beaten severely. Most researchers have discovered 100-120 scourge marks, and Guilio Ricci counted over 220 on virtually every portion of the body.[2] A flagrum, a whip-like instrument with a handle and several leather strips ending in pieces of metal or bone, was used by the Romans to inflict great pain.

The victim was often stripped and bent over to make a better target. Usually the force of the blows would knock down the victim and steadily weaken the body. Scourging was so painful that the subject twisted, turned, and even rolled on the ground in response to each blow.

In the case of the man in the Shroud, there is evidence that the flagrum may have had three dumbbell-shaped, perhaps sharpened lead tips. These tips sliced through skin, into small blood vessels, nerves, and even muscles. Either two men did the whipping, or one scourger moved from side to side, which would account for the different angles of the wounds.

The Gospels also record that Jesus was clothed with a robe and crowned with thorns (Matt. 27:28–29; Mark 15:17–18; John 19:2), largely to mock His claims to kingship. The Roman soldiers even knelt before Him and pretended to worship Him.

Likewise, the man buried in the Shroud was pierced throughout the scalp with a number of sharp objects. Blood from these wounds is visible in the hair on top of his head, on the sides of his face, and on his forehead. On the reverse portion of the image, blood is especially visible throughout

85

the hair at the back of the man's head. Because these wounds differ from the ones inflicted by the flagrum, they must have been caused differently.[3] A crown of thorns fits their characteristics quite well.

Jesus was also repeatedly hit on the face and head, including being struck with a rod or staff and spat on (Matt. 27:30; Mark 15:19; Luke 22:63–64; John 19:3). The man in the Shroud has multiple bruises about the eyes and cheeks and a twisted nose. Interestingly, in the three-dimensional photographs, a ridge is visible across the right cheek, nose, and left cheek, a ridge that may well have been made by one blow with a long, slender instrument.

Following these beatings and similar mistreatments, Jesus was forced to carry His own cross to the crucifixion site (John 19:17). But since He was apparently unable to complete the journey, a man named Simon of Cyrene was made to carry the cross for Him (Matt. 27:32; Mark 15:21; Luke 23:26).

The Shroud reveals a similar scenario. The man has large rub marks on both sides of his upper back in the scapular region. This came *after* the beating as is evidenced by the blood from the scourge marks, which is smeared at these points. The most likely cause for these rub marks is either a heavy object that was carried across the man's shoulders or the up-and-down motion of his body while he was suspended on the cross. Perhaps both are true.

Additionally, both knees have contusions. The left knee is cut particularly badly. Again, two conclusions are likely. These cuts and bruises could have been caused when the man repeatedly fell to the ground during the scourging. They could also have been caused when he fell under the weight of his cross. While the Gospels do not report this event about Jesus, it is a possible explanation for the fact that Simon of Cyrene was forced to help Him.

The Gospels assert that crucifixion in Jesus' case meant being nailed to a cross through the hands/wrists and through the feet (Luke 24:39; John 20:25–27). The man in the Shroud was also pierced through both wrist areas just below the palms. The exact locations of these wounds will be discussed in the next chapter, but there is little doubt among forensic pathologists that the man in the Shroud was crucified as Jesus was.

The Gospels agree that due to the beatings and the crucifixion itself, Jesus did not survive: He died (Matt. 27:50; Mark 15:37; Luke 23:46; John 19:30). The man buried in the Shroud shows sufficient evidence of death (see Chapter 7).

One of the most interesting occurrences of Jesus' execution is recorded in the Gospel of John. In order to hasten death, normal crucifixion procedure involved breaking the victim's legs (John 19:31–32). This process is confirmed by the discovery of the skeleton of a first-century crucifixion victim (Yohanan), whose legs were broken in just this manner. When the soldiers came to Jesus and found Him dead, they did not break His legs. Rather, a Roman soldier pierced Him in the side of His chest with a spear, causing blood and water to flow from the wound (John 19:33–35).

Likewise, the man in the Shroud was stabbed in the chest, and the image shows no signs of broken legs. A stream of blood and watery fluid that flowed vertically down from the 1¾- by ⁷/₁₆-inch cut, located between the fifth and sixth ribs, is also apparent on the Shroud. The fluid is likewise visible in a horizontal flow across the lower back in the reverse side of the image.

Crucifixion was generally reserved for war captives and those involved in civil rebellion. Because of the nature of the crime and the embarrassment of the punishment, victims were usually given only the simplest of burials. Often the body was not even claimed, but was thrown in a common pit. However, the Gospels explain that Jesus' body was not only claimed, but was given a private and individual burial in new linen by Joseph of Arimathea, a rich man who used his own tomb for this purpose (Matt. 27:57–60; Mark

15:42–47; Luke 23:50–53; John 19:38–42). Yet the hurried burial was incomplete before the beginning of the Sabbath (Mark 16:1; Luke 23:55–24:1).

Once again we perceive similarities with the man buried in the Shroud. His body was also taken and given a fine, individual burial in linen wrappings. There is also evidence that his burial may not have been complete.

The comparison between Jesus' crucifixion and burial and that of the man revealed in the Shroud of Turin is remarkable, to say the least. Even a cursory review of the similarities led many to this conclusion. The man of the Shroud was beaten, crucified, and buried as the Gospels say Jesus was.[4]

THE IDENTIFICATION OF THE MAN IN THE SHROUD

We must now consider the possibility that the Shroud of Turin is the actual burial garment of an unknown, crucified Jew. Some of what science can tell us about the Shroud has been set forth earlier. But having no tools to perform such a historical investigation, science is unable to reach any specific conclusion in this matter. It remains for historians and archaeologists to try to ascertain who was buried in it.

History and archaeology tell us much about Roman methods of crucifixion and Jewish burial techniques. When the knowledge from these two disciplines is coupled with the similarities between the extraordinary events surrounding Jesus' crucifixion and that of the man buried in the Shroud, a tentative conclusion is possible. We must judge the probabilities that two men could have been crucified in just the same way in so many unordinary circumstances.

Several Shroud researchers have used and advocated the method of basing probabilities on the irregular points that are shared between Jesus and the man buried in the Shroud. Depending on which common aspects are used and how they are evaluated, researchers have reached various conclusions.

After studying the irregularities held in common between the Gospels and the Shroud, Francis Filas, late professor of theology at Loyola University in Chicago, concluded that there is 1 chance in 10^{26} that the man in the Shroud was not Jesus.[5] Vincent Donovan's conclusion was much more conservative, but still estimated only 1 chance in 282 billion that the two men were not the same.[6] Engineer and Jesuit Paul de Gail arrived at an even higher figure than Donovan's in spite of the fact that his work was done in 1972, some six years before the major scientific investigation.[7] The lowest figure was given by Professors Tino Zeuli and Bruno Barbaris of the University of Turin's science faculty. In 1978 they concluded that there is 1 chance in 225 billion that the two men were different.[8]

Although statistical studies can be rather subjective in method they are regularly used in scientific study and are not simply arbitrary guesses. Both the smallest figure of 1 in 225 billion and the largest of 1 in 10^{26} practically conclude that the Shroud is the burial garment of Jesus. Why do so many researchers agree on identifying the two men? We will not reproduce here the basis for the probability we presented in *Verdict,*[9] but we will briefly note the major irregularities that both the Gospels and the Shroud reveal.

1. Both the Gospels and the Shroud plainly concern cases of crucifixion. While it is true that many persons were crucified in ancient times, the number is small in comparison to those who died by all other means combined. In other words, if the Shroud belonged to some person other than Jesus, it would probably have been that of a noncrucified individual, but that is not the case. The probability of identification is increased, though only slightly, by the fact that both victims were males. Occasionally, some females were crucified—hence, a small increase in probability.[10]

2. It is also unlikely that a random burial shroud, espe-

cially one surfacing in western Europe, would bear the image of a person of Semitic origin. Yet T. Dale Stewart of the Smithsonian Museum of Natural Sciences pointed out that the features of the man buried in the Shroud indicate that he was Caucasian and possibly Semitic. Former Harvard University ethnologist Carleton Coon concluded, "Whoever the individual represented may have been, he is of a physical type found in modern times among Sephardic Jews and noble Arabs."[11]

3. The scourging and beating of Jesus at the hands of His enemies was unusual treatment for those marked for crucifixion. We are told that Pilate hoped in vain to satisfy the mob by punishing Jesus in these other ways, but the people demanded His crucifixion, rejecting the suggestion that Jesus be set free (John 19:1–16). Therefore Jesus was both seriously beaten and crucified.

This was not a common procedure. A man who was to be crucified was generally not beaten nearly to death. Yet this double punishment was inflicted on both Jesus and the man in the Shroud. In fact, some believe that the man in the Shroud eventually died from the scourging while he hung on a cross.[12]

4. One of the most unusual similarities between the two men is in the head wounds. Since the Romans were, to some extent, emperor worshipers, it is plain that they crowned Jesus with thorns to mock His claims to be the Messianic ruler or King of the Jews. But would this treatment be given to the average criminal who was to be crucified? Probably not. Yet the man in the Shroud had injuries a crown of thorns would create all over his scalp.

5. Another similarity is that both men were nailed to crosses instead of being tied to them. This is not as irregular as some of the other points, for Yohanan, the first-century crucifixion victim whose bones were discovered in 1967, was also nailed to his cross. But tying was an option.

6. The Gospel of John agrees with the Yohanan archaeo-

logical find that normal Roman crucifixion procedure involved breaking the victim's legs to hasten death. But since He was already dead, this was not done to Jesus. The man buried in the Shroud did not have broken legs.

7. Besides the crown of thorns, the piercing of Jesus' side by a Roman spear is the most intriguing parallel. Since legs were regularly broken to hasten death, lancing the victim's side would be a superfluous procedure. But while neither of the two men had broken legs, both were wounded in the chest by a spear. Furthermore, it was reported that blood and water flowed from Jesus' chest wound as are visible from the wound in the man on the Shroud. The soldiers could have done nothing when they detected that the victims were dead, or they could have struck different areas of their bodies. The fact Jesus and the man in the Shroud were similarly wounded raises the likelihood that the two men are one and the same. Moreover, the flow of blood and water would not have occurred apart from the chest wound. John's description of Jesus' death coincides with the Shroud image in that a post-death wound was inflicted, the chest area was affected, and blood and water oozed from the wound.

8. Jesus and the man in the Shroud were both given fine, individual burials in linen, not the common burials generally given to crucifixion victims.

9. Jesus was buried hastily because of the oncoming Sabbath. Therefore, the women returned with spices on Sunday morning in order to finish the burial process. There are also signs that the man in the Shroud was buried hastily (see Chapter 7). What are the chances that two men would be crucified, receive individual burials in fine linen shrouds, and still have to be buried hastily?

10. Last, the New Testament testifies that Jesus' body did not experience corruption (Acts 2:22–32), but that He was resurrected instead. No decomposition stains are present on the Shroud. Since many of the burial garments in existence have even visible decomposition stains on

them, the absence of stains on the Shroud is enigmatic, especially in light of the New Testament testimony concerning Jesus' resurrection (see Chapter 9).

These ten similar crucifixion anomalies between Jesus and the man buried in the Shroud are strong arguments for the identification of the two men. And yet a serious objection must be answered. Couldn't a person actually have been crucified to replicate Jesus' crucifixion? Could not some sadistic person kill another by patterning his death after Jesus', thus reproducing irregularities?

At first glance this is an excellent alternative argument because it claims to account for the rather exact agreements between the Gospels and the Shroud. But while attempting to explain one portion of the Shroud puzzle, it falls prey to numerous other problems. Presumably, the whole project was to make the victim look like Jesus as His death is portrayed in both the New Testament and ecclesiastical tradition. But this is precisely where this thesis is most vulnerable.

For instance, this scenario fails to explain the presence of the wrist wounds on the man in the Shroud. This failure is especially poignant in light of New Testament passages explaining that Jesus showed His disciples His pierced hands, feet, and side as further evidence of His identity (Luke 24:39; John 20:25, 27). Throughout the history of the church, the punctures in Jesus' hands have been pictured in the palms (or lower hands). Art historian Philip McNair claims that in his entire experience with hundreds of examples of medieval art, the nail wounds are always located in the palms of Jesus.[13]

Likewise, the man in the Shroud apparently had his head *covered* by the thorns (or other sharp objects), as opposed to the traditional wreathlet around the forehead. It is also possible that the man in the Shroud was nude. Should this be the case, it would also require an explanation, since this would similarly be contrary to traditional historical depictions of the crucified and buried Jesus.

If, as this alternative thesis supposes, the accounts of Jesus' crucifixion are the model for the Shroud, then these three difficult problems must be overcome. The wrist wounds would be especially noteworthy since the "artisans" would seemingly be forced to follow tradition in order to be believed (even if they thought otherwise or knew of a contrary example in Christian art).

In other words, the Gospels and church tradition would have to be followed for the cloth to be accepted as the burial garment of Jesus. But such is simply not the case in at least these three areas. On the other hand, if it was *not* the point to copy Jesus' passion, then why would there be such the close agreement, especially at each of the anomalies we have noted? This alternative thesis encounters a major dilemma at this juncture.

Other problems abound for this strange forgery thesis. Medical studies have questioned the likelihood of blood and water flowing from typical chest wounds, but these fluids are present on the Shroud as they were with Jesus.

Another serious concern for this view is the cause of the image. This theory would probably require some sort of contact process or perhaps even some type of vaporograph, possibilities that have already been disproven (see Chapter 8). And against the response that the cause of the image is an equal problem for any view, since it is unknown, we would point out a crucial difference. In a case favoring the Shroud as the actual burial garment of Jesus, we would perhaps need to try to identify the cause of the image (see Chapter 9). But the replica thesis involving the crucifixion of another person seems to require a type of image formation that has *already* been disproven. Science may not know *how* the image was created, but it is amazingly adept at discovering that objects have been faked. And since the latter is all that is required, the fact that the Shroud image has not been duplicated is a tremendous blow to this forgery thesis.

Other problems for the replica thesis include the lack of bodily decomposition on the Shroud, the detailed knowledge of Jewish burial customs, the possible presence of first-century coins over the eyes, and, in particular, the advanced medical specifications needed, probably beyond what was known (see Chapter 7).

Although this thesis is possibly the best of the skeptical alternatives, it clearly entails major problems. In fact, the very need to suggest it points out how similar the death of the man buried in the Shroud is to Jesus' crucifixion, especially in the anomalies.

One last consideration makes these similarities even more striking. We only considered the points these two deaths have in common. What is almost equally amazing is that there are no contradictions between the two. It would seem likely that, if they were different men, there would be some obvious disagreements—such as the man in the Shroud having broken legs or no spear wound. But that such is not the case is simply incredible since the thesis that someone copied Jesus' crucifixion is apparently untenable.

Once again, it is not our purpose in this chapter to restate the probabilities we set forth in *Verdict.* But the facts lead us to believe that the Shroud of Turin is still very possibly the actual burial garment of Jesus. Our view could be disproven in light of future data; carbon-14 dating, for instance, still poses a critical, though not unanswerable, challenge. Nevertheless, the evidence *at present* favors this possibility.

It is intriguing that one highly skeptical reviewer, who *disallows* miracles and wrote critically of our book, still stated: "Stevenson and Habermas (p. 128) even calculate the odds as 1 in 83 million that the man on the shroud is not Jesus Christ (and they consider this a very conservative estimate). I agree with them on all of this. If the shroud is authentic, the image is that of Jesus."[14]

The opinion that the Shroud is some sort of painting has been thoroughly investigated and rejected by the vast majority of published researchers. A thesis that the Shroud was painted by some particular method has, indeed, a difficult road to a proof. Even to accept the carbon dating results is not to prove that the Shroud is a painting. This would be an unjustified leap over relevant data, for various theses are certainly possible. Other theories postulating a medieval origin for the Shroud are likewise opposed by substantial research. Contrary to some popular opinions, many views, not just those specifically opposing the 1988 dating attempts, must respond to the relevant scientific and historical data.

SCHOLARLY OPINIONS

Before the results of the 1988 carbon dating were released, a number of scholars investigating the Shroud reached the conclusion that this cloth was probably the actual burial garment of Jesus. It is very difficult to know how many of these and others would still hold the same opinions today. Perhaps some still hold these views, rejecting the 1988 carbon dating for any of several reasons. Others are now perhaps undecided about their former views, and it is certainly possible that some have rejected their previous positions. Nevertheless, their views are part of the history of this subject, and the purpose of this volume is to survey the state of the question since 1981.

Though the question of any possible identification of the man in the Shroud with Jesus is largely historical, many people are understandably interested in the opinions of some of the researchers. In spite of the often-pronounced skepticism on this issue, some offered their personal views.

Robert Wilcox, himself the author of a well-known 1977 book on the Shroud,[15] published a series of four long articles on the subject in 1982. Although little publicized, this series was a valuable report on the 1978 scientific investigation.[16] Wilcox's first article reported his interviews with twenty-six of the scientists in the October 1978 investigation. Of those interviewed, thirteen indicated their belief that the Shroud was the actual burial garment of Jesus, while most of the remaining thirteen did not answer this query. This was a startling revelation in light of what had been a relative hush on this subject.[17]

Some scientists not only stated their belief that Jesus was the man buried in the Shroud, but indicated that they were also impressed by a line of argument which noted the points of similarity between Jesus and the man in the Shroud. Physicist John Jackson proclaimed, "This was no ordinary execution," noting that what happened to the man in the Shroud was consistent with the Gospel accounts of Jesus' crucifixion. One of the scientists willing to give an opinion concerning the identity of the man in the Shroud, Jackson observed that the scourge marks, nail holes, and blood flows on the Shroud are anatomically and medically correct.[18]

Pathologist Robert Bucklin shared Jackson's views most openly. He stated his conviction that "The imprint of the body on the shroud is that of Jesus Christ."[19] This is shown by the exact consistency between the Gospels and the Shroud. In fact, the Shroud adds to our historical knowledge of Jesus and even provides evidence for His resurrection from the dead.

Biophysicist John Heller's recent *Report on the Shroud of Turin* points out that the Shroud is in agreement with the Gospel accounts of Jesus' passion. Could the Shroud be Jesus' burial cloth? Heller answered: "That question is not a trivial one. Nothing in all the findings of the Shroud crowd in three years contained a single datum that contravened the Gospel accounts." Heller followed this statement with a long list of similarities between the two men.[20] Later Heller pointed out that, of the Shroud of Turin Research Project team members, John Jackson, Robert Bucklin, and Barrie Schwortz believed that the Shroud was Jesus' burial garment. Another team member, Donald Lynn, added that the Shroud "matches the Gospels historically," without himself making a commitment concerning identity.[21] By 1984, however, he had come to believe that the Shroud was Jesus'.[22] Cullen Murphy added chemist Robert Dinegar as another team scientist willing to say that he personally believed that the Shroud just might be "the real thing."[23]

According to an article in one popular publication, personal interviews have revealed other scientists who were willing to speak to this issue as well. STURP chief photographer Vernon Miller was quoted as saying, "I have no doubts that this is the Shroud of Christ. I have come to this as objectively and scientifically as I can."[24] Barrie Schwortz, another photographer from Santa Barbara's Brooks Institute of Photography and one of the Jewish members of STURP, said:

> The image on the Shroud matches the account of the crucifixion in the New Testament down to the 'nth degree. Evidence is mounting that the Gospels are quite accurate. This may cause consternation among my family and other Jewish people, but in my own mind, the Shroud is the piece of cloth which wrapped Jesus after he was crucified.[25]

CONCLUSION

In spite of the recent carbon-14 test results, enough facts can be martialed to conclude that the Shroud of Turin is still possibly the actual burial garment of Jesus.[26] Our conclusion about the identity of the man in the Shroud *still* may have to be reevaluated in light of future findings, but the present evidence is sufficient to sustain the possibility that the cloth wrapped Jesus.

That Wilcox's 1982 interviews revealed that half of the scientists contacted (thirteen out of twenty-six) had believed that the Shroud is Jesus' burial garment is, at the very least, enigmatic. It is remarkable that this many of them would publicly give their views when such conclusions are sometimes viewed quite negatively. As Wilcox stated, there are just too many "coincidences" in the agreements between Jesus' crucifixion and that of the man in the Shroud to be explained away easily. These similarities do not fit any other known victim of crucifixion except Jesus.[27]

With regard to this, we must take exception to Heller's conclusion:

> It is certainly true that if a similar number of data had been found in the funerary linen attributed to Alexander the Great, Genghis Khan, or Socrates, *there would be no doubt in anyone's mind that it was, indeed, the shroud of that historical person.* But because of the unique position that Jesus holds, *such evidence is not enough* [emphasis added].[28]

Here Heller admitted that there is much evidence to show that the Shroud is Jesus' burial garment—enough evidence to convince us *without any doubt,* if the identity of a nonreligious person was the question. But since, presumably, too much of religious uniqueness is at stake with Jesus, he would not draw this conclusion.

We disagree. Heller's conclusion reveals an unwarranted separation of faith and facts. Without any dispute from us, Jesus is unique, and the decision to follow Him is immeasurably important. Yet this is *not* to say that facts are not quite as factual in the religious realm. We must guard against such differentiation of these two ways of knowing in religious and nonreligious areas.

Yves Delage addressed this very issue over eighty years ago. Professor of Comparative Anatomy at the Sorbonne in Paris, a member of the prestigious French Academy, and an agnostic, Delage concluded that the Shroud was Jesus' burial cloth. Answering the criticism of his "religious" conclusion, he stated:

> . . . a religious question has been needlessly injected into a problem which in itself is purely scientific. . . . If, instead of Christ, there were a question of some person like a Sargon, an Achilles or one of the Pharaohs, no one would have thought of making any objection. . . . I recognize Christ as a historical personage and I see no reason why anyone should be scandalized that there still exist material traces of his earthly life.[29]

98

Again, although religious stakes are much higher, we must draw our conclusions from the current facts. The data certainly allows at least the tentative conclusion that Jesus was very possibly buried in the Shroud. And if the facts do not *favor* this conclusion or if it is later disproven, then that will have to be faced squarely as well.

To be sure, the 1988 carbon dating results remain a serious objection, and we cannot pretend that they do not exist. However, we have also pointed out numerous reasons for some doubt. And *if* these tests are mistaken or even questionable, the evidence may then still favor the conclusion that the Shroud of Turin is Jesus' burial garment.

7

DEATH BY CRUCIFIXION

The Discoveries and Disputes of Pathology

Since the Shroud of Turin may still very possibly be Jesus' burial garment, it may serve as an added testimony to Jesus' death by crucifixion. But it is *crucial* to understand that even those who reject this possibility can still perhaps gain much medical knowledge about crucifixion from the Shroud. Even if those who accept the carbon dating results believe that the issue is moot and even if they were correct, the Shroud could *still* preserve invaluable information about the effects of crucifixion and hence at least indirect evidence about Jesus' death. If the Shroud is not a fake but the garment of an actual crucifixion victim, it can provide important medical knowledge, whether it is Jesus' burial garment or not.[1]

Studies of the Shroud have always evoked special attention from the medical community, and questions about the nature of crucifixion and the cause of Jesus' death have been at the heart of their discussion. Medical doctors and other specialists have brought their expertise to Shroud study in the twentieth century.[2] In Paris near the turn of the century, biologist Paul Vignon of the Institute Catholique and Yves Delage, professor of anatomy at the Sorbonne, led early endeavors. Pierre Barbet, a surgeon at St. Joseph's Hospital in Paris, has perhaps been the most widely read physician to address the Shroud. His monumental work was largely done in the 1930s.

In the 1950s German radiologist Hermann Moedder of St. Francis Hospital in Cologne experimented with crucifixion technique by suspending volunteer university students by their wrists to measure the medical impact of crucifixion. David Willis, an English physician, tabulated medical studies of the Shroud in the 1960s.

Giovanni Judica-Cordiglia, professor of forensic medicine at the University of Milan, was part of the secret commission organized in 1969 to view the Shroud and make recommendations for further scientific study. Anthony Sava, an American physician, studied the Shroud for many years and was involved in some of the medical studies in the 1970s.

In the last decade the most prominent medical specialist to investigate the Shroud is pathologist Robert Bucklin. In 1978 he served in the Shroud of Turin Research Project.

CURRENT SHROUD PATHOLOGY: AN OVERVIEW

Death by crucifixion is a complicated medical puzzle, especially when it has been preceded by scourging, a crown of thorns, and other mistreatment, as in the case of Jesus. Accordingly, isolating a single cause of death is difficult.[3]

Most medical experts postulate that asphyxiation plays a major role in a crucifixion death—perhaps *the* major role. As the suspension of the body's weight from the wrists places intense pressure on the pectoral and intercostal muscles of the chest, breathing becomes increasingly difficult. Moedder found that all his volunteers—regardless of age, stamina, and physical condition—lost consciousness in a maximum of twelve minutes.[4]

Studies have indicated that trying to relieve the tension in his chest by standing up on the nails driven through his feet, the victim of an actual crucifixion freed his lungs somewhat but suffered great pain. Breaking the ankles or legs caused the victim, now severely weakened, to hang "low" on the cross. Death often followed swiftly.

This rather simplistic description shows how asphyxiation is a major factor in death by crucifixion. But such a terrible death is also complicated by shock and congestive heart failure. In spite of a rather amazing general consensus, details may differ from scholar to scholar.

An additional question of much interest concerns the nature of the spear wound recorded in the Gospel of John (19:31–34) and also found on the Shroud image. The aforementioned medical experts agree that the man in the Shroud was dead when the spear struck his side as is evidenced by both the body in the Shroud clearly being in a state of rigor mortis and by the post-mortem nature of the blood flow from the chest wound. Yet once again details differ on the exact nature of the wound.

Some medical experts follow Barbet, who held that the blood came from the right side of the heart while the water came from the pericardium, a thin sac that surrounds the heart and holds some watery fluid.[5] On the other hand, Sava postulated that the scourging was so severe that it caused chest hemorrhaging. Then the pleural cavity (in particular the membrane sacs that enclose the lungs on each side of the chest) filled with blood from the lower portion of the pleural cavity and lighter-weight fluid from the upper portion. This view thus involves pleural effusion: the "bloody fluid collects between the outer surface of the lung and the inner lining of the chest wall."[6]

Actually, each view contains a degree of truth. The spear probably pierced both Jesus' pleural cavity and His heart, thereby causing blood to flow from both places. The watery fluid could have come from the cavity and the pericardial sac. But Jesus was already dead when this occurred. Moedder, Willis, and Bucklin accept this scenario.[7]

From this rather simplistic summary, we may proceed to consider new research, including the conclusions of another expert, Frederick Zugibe, whose results appeared in 1982.

FURTHER DEBATE

On October 10–11, 1981, in New London, Connecticut, STURP held a semipublic press conference and series of lectures on the scientific research since the October 1978 investigation of the Shroud in Turin, Italy. Representing the medical side of these studies (pathology and forensic pathology) were Joseph Gambescia and Robert Bucklin.

STURP's official press release told the public, among other things, that the Shroud had made contact with a body and that it was "a real human form of a scourged, crucified man."[8] In the later words of John Heller, "It was evident from the physical, mathematical, medical, and chemical evidence that there must have been a crucified man in the shroud. If we followed the principle of Occam's razor, we could draw no other conclusion."[9] These two statements are quite important, especially in terms of our opening assertion that if the Shroud wrapped the body of a crucified man, then we can still perhaps learn much about what happened to Jesus, *even if it was not His garment.*

In some ways this STURP conference was both the end and the beginning of further studies, including medical research. The most rigorous study of a "religious relic" in history was supposedly winding down. At the same time, however, other experts were publicly presenting their conclusions. One of these was Frederick Zugibe in *The Cross and the Shroud.*[10]

In Cullen Murphy's well-publicized *Harper's* article, Zugibe was practically portrayed as the chief disputer of Robert Bucklin's claims.[11] As adjunct associate professor of pathology at Columbia University and chief medical examiner of Rockland County, New York, Zugibe brought an array of medical talents to more than twenty-five years of Shroud studies. He had also participated in the Second International Scientific Conference of Sindonology on October 7–8, 1978, immediately before the STURP testing.[12]

In experimental testing of the crucifixion process, Zugibe suspended volunteers between twenty and thirty-five years of age from an actual cross, strapping gauntlets around their hands and seat belts around their feet. Then he monitored their heart rates with an EKG and kept close tabs on their blood oxygen (with an ear oximeter) and blood pressure.

He noted that with their arms stretched out at an angle of sixty to seventy degrees, their bodies hardly touched the cross. Rather, during their frequent shifting to relieve cramps and other pains, the victims often arched their bodies outward, away from the cross itself. Their most frequent complaint was pain in their limbs. Zugibe observed, however, that none of the volunteers had difficulty breathing. In fact, oxygen level increased. Other observations included moderate rises in blood pressure and heartbeat, pronounced sweating, and muscle twitching.[13]

Zugibe's findings on the absence of breathing difficulties mark a crucial disagreement with the established medical studies of crucifixion. The reason for Zugibe's disagreement may lie with his understanding (or lack thereof) of the angle of Jesus' execution, an area we will explore later. But while Zugibe noted this and several other points of disagreement with the medical consensus, he also held that the Shroud is probably the authentic burial garment of Jesus, that Jesus was definitely dead, and that we have much medical evidence to establish the means of His death.[14] As we focus on the points of his interaction with other medical experts, we will evaluate the strengths and weaknesses of his case.

Pre-Crucifixion Suffering

One aspect of Jesus' passion that is well known but much underplayed is pain. Few realize that Jesus actually experienced two types of capital punishment: the preliminary scourging, crown of thorns, and beating; and crucifixion itself. Of the preliminary abuses, Zugibe wrote:

Jesus was bent over and tied to a low pillar, where He was flogged across the back, chest, and legs with a multifaceted flagrum with bits of metal on the ends. Over and over again the metal tips dug deep into the flesh, ripping small vessels, nerves, muscles and skin. He writhed, rolled, wrenched and His body became distorted with pain, causing Him to fall to the ground, only to be jerked up again. Seizurelike activities occurred, followed by tremors, vomiting, and cold sweats. . . . Unfortunately, the scourging was initiated by the Romans so that the Deuteronomic limit of forty lashes less one was not followed.[15]

There are few disagreements on the scourging and other pre-crucifixion abuses of Jesus. Most researchers have counted between 100 and 120 scourge wounds on the Shroud, perhaps more than the 40 lashes allowed by the Jews (Deut. 25:3; 1 Cor. 11:24). But since there was more than one dumbbell-shaped piece of metal on the Roman flagrum, it is difficult to convert the number of scourge wounds to the number of lashes. Still, we assume that there were more scourge marks on the burnt (and therefore now indiscernible) image of portions of the shoulders and that there may have been lashes that did not break the skin and therefore would probably not be visible at all.

The crown—or more properly, cap—of thorns was apparently placed on the man's head. Some experts agree that the most likely plants for this use were either *Zizphus spina* or *Paliuris spina*, both members of the buckthorn family, with thin, inch-long thorns. The scalp is a sensitive area, especially with regard to the nerves. When the small blood vessels are lacerated, significant bleeding results. In our modern culture, we too often ignore the pain involved in this aspect of the punishment alone.[16]

In addition, on the cross the nails in the wrist area pushed against the median nerve, causing a continual burning pain; the nails in the feet were pressed by the body weight against the plantar nerves, causing similar pain. And perhaps worst of all was the terrible pain in the shoulders, wrists, knees, and feet, the muscle twitching, numbness, and cramping. Bucklin noted that when he once suspended himself on a cross for a short time, "the pain suffered by a suspension of the wrists alone is all but unbearable, with the tensions and strains being directed to the deltoid and pectoral muscles. These muscles promptly ensure a state of spasm."[17] The complications from thirst have been described as the worst agony of all.[18]

We must never lose sight of the suffering that Jesus Christ, who Scripture says was an innocent victim, underwent to pay the penalty for humankind's sin. Regardless of the status of the Shroud's authenticity, His suffering and sin payment were real.

The Positions of the Nails

One point of disagreement between Zugibe and most other researchers is the position of the nails. Zugibe listed three possible positions: the palm of the hand; the wrists; and the lower arm area. But instead of placing the nails in the wrists as virtually all other researchers do, he placed them in the lower palm area, just above the wrists. He suggested finding the spot by touching the little finger with the thumb. He thought that the nail was placed in the lower portion of the resulting gully, the thenar furrow.[19] This places the nail, not in the center of the palm, but only about one inch from the wrist, where it was driven in at an angle, exiting in the back near the wrist, as is indicated on the Shroud. Thus, this disagreement is not as profound as some might think.

Since Zugibe realized that the New Testament word for *hand* can mean anything from the fingers through the lower arm, he gave six reasons for selecting the lower palm. Two, the most subjective, are that the palm is the area most people accept and that stigmata have occurred in the palm, reportedly corresponding to Jesus' wounds. These arguments seem superfluous. While Christian tradition may clarify some issues, it is finally subordinate to the facts. So, too, an argument from stigmata cases is questionable because of the very nature of such manifestations. To resolve the question of where the nails were placed, we must rely on the available data.

Zugibe's other reasons rely more substantially on medical research. He believes that the palm closely corresponds to the location of the wound on the Shroud, which exits on the radial (thumb) side of the hand. By contrast, Destot's space in the wrist, made famous by Barbet's research and favored by many, exits on the ulnar (little finger) side. A nail there would easily hold the human body on a cross without breaking any bones and would explain the apparent lengthening of fingers observed on the Shroud.

This argument presents little difficulty for those who postulated that the nails pierced the wrists, especially since, as Bucklin notes, the position does not need to be Destot's space.[20] The wrist can also sustain the weight of the human body without necessarily breaking bones. And Zugibe's assertion that positioning the nail in the palm explains the lengthening of the fingers makes sense only if it is the only explanation. If the finger length can be explained by other means, there is no need to locate the nail in the lower palm area.

But this is not to say that Zugibe is wrong here. The exact location of the nails is difficult to determine with absolute certainty. Since there is only about one inch difference in front and virtually no difference in back, such a determination may, in fact, be unnecessary.

Another issue is the reason the thumbs are not immediately visible on the Shroud. Barbet's popular answer, supported by experimental results, was that when a nail was driven through Destot's space, it touched the median nerve, causing the thumb to draw inward to the palm. Disagreeing, Zugibe objected that the position of the drawn-in thumbs in front of the index finger "is a relatively natural post-mortem position" frequently observed at the medical examiner's office.[21] At this point, the drawn-in thumbs are difficult to explain, but this is a minor point.

Concerning the nailing of the feet, executioners appear not to have used one prominent method. The skeleton of Yohanan, found in Jerusalem in 1967, shows that he was nailed through both heel bones by a single seven-inch Roman spike. Some researchers have maintained that the feet were crossed, left over right, with two nails holding them together. Others have suggested that after the right foot was nailed, the left was crossed over and a second nail was driven through both feet.[22] The most common theories are that both feet were crossed and affixed with one nail or that the feet were placed side by side with a single nail in each. Noting that the Shroud evidence is ambiguous, Zugibe objected to the one-nail theory because it was more difficult to perform; he favored the view that the feet were placed side by side, with each fixed by a single nail.[23]

Zugibe's arguments on this point are quite weak. The fact that it is easier to nail this way is irrelevant. The question is *how* the executioners did it. That Yohanan's crucifixion apparently dates from the first century A.D. provides some evidence for a one-nail theory. And the Shroud reveals that the left foot slants inward, possibly from rigor mortis fixing it in the position it may have occupied before death—over the right foot. Zugibe's argument that the slant is accounted for by a fold in the cloth[24] is possible but not substantiated. If Gambescia and Bucklin's suggestion is valid, the crossed feet may even have been affixed by two nails, thus answering Zugibe's concern with the "easier" method. At any rate, the skeleton of Yohanan, the location of the wound on the Shroud, and the slant of the left foot all support the crossed-feet view, with most researchers favoring the use of one nail.

Cause of Death

With its theological significance for the Christian gospel, perhaps the single most crucial physical element in the study of the crucifixion is the assurance of Jesus' physical death. Hence, signs of the cause of this death are important.

Bucklin listed the cause of Jesus' death as "Postoral asphyxia related to failure of the cardiovascular system from shock and pain."[25] For Zugibe, the cause was "Cardiac and respiratory arrest due to cardiogenic, traumatic, and hypovolemic shock due to crucifixion."[26] Thus both pathologists included cardiovascular failure, particularly the heart. Bucklin stressed congestive heart failure due to excessive blood in the heart while Zugibe stressed cardiogenic shock, shock of the heart. Bucklin also noted shock and, like Zugibe, identified Jesus' suffering and crucifixion as the root cause of death.

But the importance of asphyxiation in Jesus' death is a matter of serious disagreement. Bucklin followed the majority opinion in his conclusion that asphyxiation was crucial.[27] Zugibe did not find this to be a contributing cause in any of his experiments and called it an *a priori* hypothesis. But Bucklin spent a brief time on a model cross and reported that the deltoid and pectoral muscles "promptly assume a state of spasm, and the victim so suspended is physically unable to make use of his thoracic muscles of respiration,"[28] a statement that has been experimentally confirmed by Moedder, Barbet, and others. Thus Bucklin's conclusion was not *a priori* as Zugibe claimed.

Critiquing Barbet's three major arguments for the asphyxiation theory, Zugibe held first that the bifurcated blood flow on the wrist was post-mortem and thus not due to breathing difficulties, a point we will return to later. Second, he argued that crucifragium (breaking of legs) was a common procedure that did not contribute to asphyxiation. And finally he said that Barbet's evidence from German concentration camps does not apply to first-century crucifixion methods because the camp victims' hands were suspended directly above their heads, which was not the case in Jesus' crucifixion.[29]

In fact, Zugibe appears to have indulged in circular reasoning when he assumed but did not substantiate that sixty to seventy degrees was the arm angle of a first-century crucifixion victim. Although his subjects experienced no breathing difficulties, Zugibe admitted that at different arm angles asphyxiation *will* result.[30] William Meacham and Robert Bucklin had noted that a measurement of the blood flows argues for an arm angle of approximately fifty-five to sixty-five degrees.[31]

Other evidence points to the strength of the asphyxiation theory. The skeleton of Yohanan showed that the nails were driven through the lower arms, between the radius and ulna. One radius was both scratched and worn smooth from constant friction. Although an up-and-down movement to relieve leg pain may explain this, most researchers believe the wear on the bone evidences a frantic effort to breathe.

Second, Yohanan had suffered crucifragium, in keeping with the testimony of John 19:31–35 and other sources. Zugibe, not believing that this practice contributed to asphyxiation, postulated shock as the desired result,[32] an unconvincing explanation since blows to other parts of the body might do the same. That *legs* were the target is evidence for asphyxiation. Crucifragium kept the victim from moving up and down, thereby inducing death.[33]

Third, Meacham judged from the state of rigor mortis that the man in the Shroud suffered asphyxiation:

It has frozen in an attitude of death while hanging by the arms; the rib cage is abnormally expanded, the large pectoral muscles are in an attitude of extreme inspiration (enlarged and drawn up toward the collarbone and arms), the lower abdomen is distended, and the epigastrio hollow is drawn in sharply. The protrusion of the femoral quadriceps and hip muscles is consistent with slow death by hanging, during which the victim must raise his body by exertion of the legs in order to exhale.[34]

Notably, a recent study in the prestigious *Journal of the American Medical Association* (JAMA) has reached a similar conclusion. After studying the relevant literature, the authors noted the primary cause of Jesus' death on the cross as "hypovolemic shock and exhaustion asphyxia." The "major pathophysiologic effect of crucifixion was an interference with normal respirations." Other possible contributory factors included dehydration, congestive heart failure, or cardiac rupture, accenting "acute heart failure." So while death on the cross was "multifactorial," stressing asphyxiation, "Clearly, the weight of historical and medical science indicates that Jesus was dead before the wound to his side was inflicted. . . . Accordingly, interpretations based on the assumption that Jesus did not die on the cross appear to be at odds with modern medical knowledge."[35]

Therefore, although other causes, like shock or orthostatic collapse (in which blood collects in the lower portions of the body) have been presented as primary contributors to crucifixion deaths, the evidence favors asphyxiation. More importantly, however, researchers agree that the man in the Shroud was dead.

The Spear in the Side

Bucklin's view on the chest wound was that the Roman lance entered the dead body between the fifth and sixth ribs, drawing out the post-mortem blood flow.[36] Like Moedder and Willis, he further postulated that the lance pierced the pleural cavity, the pericardium, and the right side of the heart. Most of the water came from pleural effusion (not of Sava's variety) while most of the blood proceeded from the right side of the heart.[37] Heller also holds that the blood flow from the chest was post-mortem.[38]

Generally, agreeing about the location of the wound, Zugibe also places it about six inches from the center of the chest. On the nature of the wound, he entertained several options. Contrary to some medical theories, mostly older ones, he held that Jesus' heart did not rupture for four reasons: Jesus' comparative youth, the rarity of heart attacks

111

in first-century Palestine, the absence of any record of heart attack earlier in His life, and the insufficient time between scourging and crucifixion.

Zugibe then listed eleven hypothetical causes of the flow of blood and water. Of the eleven, some of which differ only in fairly minor details, eight postulate that the lance entered the chest cavity, the pericardium, and the heart. Dismissing Barbet's experiments and theory of the water coming from the pericardium and the blood from the heart on the grounds that the two would be mixed, Zugibe chose two possible theories. One is Sava's, discussed earlier, but Zugibe found it weak because, again, blood and water might be mixed.

The view that Zugibe proposed as better is like that of Willis, Moedder, and Bucklin: the "right atrium of the heart pierced by spear (blood) and pleural effusion from scourging and/or congestive failure."[39] Since the man in the Shroud was dead, his wound yielded a post-mortem flow of blood and water. But even had he been alive, the wound would have killed him. Its very purpose was to make sure he was dead. Zugibe and the others seem generally agreed about the spear wound in the chest.

Signs of Death

Zugibe stated his theory on the wound in the side in virtually the same words as Willis, Moedder, and Bucklin, all of whom agree that the wound was post-mortem. The authors of the JAMA *(Journal of the American Medical Association)* article also conclude, "The spear, thrust between his right ribs, probably perforated not only the right lung but also the pericardium and the heart and thereby ensured his death. . . ."[40]

There are at least three signs on the Shroud that Jesus was dead when He was buried. First, the body of the man in the Shroud is in a state of rigor mortis, in which the muscles stiffen, keeping the body in the position the person occupied just prior to death. Such a state is complete in about twelve hours after death, begins to wear off in twenty-four hours, and disappears in thirty-six to forty hours. Of course, these times are variable and imprecise, and therefore somewhat unreliable. Closely related to rigor mortis is a state called cadaveric spasm, an immediate stiffening, a rather sudden contraction of the muscles that occurs quickly after some violent deaths.

Rigor mortis is observable on the Shroud in several places. The head was bent forward, the feet were somewhat drawn up, and the left leg in particular had moved back toward its position on the cross. Especially visible in the three-dimensional image analysis of the Shroud are the re-tracted thumbs and the "frozen" posture of the chest and abdomen. As was also noted by Bucklin, the entire body was quite rigid and stiff, occupying some of the positions it did on the cross.[41]

The second evidence of death in the man of the Shroud is the post-mortem blood flow, especially from the chest wound. If the heart had been beating after burial, the blood literally would have been shot out onto the cloth. But the blood oozed out instead. Also, a comparatively small quantity of blood flowed, and there was no swelling around the wound. Finally, the blood from the chest, left wrist, and feet separated into clots and serum and was much thicker and of much deeper color than it would have been prior to death.[42]

Zugibe also mentioned a third piece of evidence based on his medical experience. If Jesus had been alive after the spear wound, the soldiers and others at the site would have heard a loud sucking sound caused by breath being inhaled past the chest wound. Zugibe related that when answering a distress call after a man had been stabbed in the chest, he heard the loud inhaling of the unconscious man all the way across the room. He saw this phenomenon as "a direct refutation of the theory that Christ was alive after being taken down from the cross."[43]

Washing the Body

One of the most interesting pathological issues is whether or not the body in the Shroud had been washed. A case could be made for either view.

General Jewish burial customs required that the body be washed (Acts 9:37). In *Verdict,* however, we argued that the body was probably not washed for several reasons. For example, the sixteenth-century *Code of Jewish Law,* in "Laws of Mourning," points out that some bodies were not to be washed, among them the body of a person killed by the government and of one who suffered a violent death. Since both prohibitions applied to Jesus, Jewish law may have forbidden the washing of His body—if this custom was also observed in the first century A.D.[44] The Gospels never state that Jesus' body was washed. Rather, the Gospel of John states that Jesus was buried according to Jewish customs (19:40), which could actually mean that His body was not washed.

The Gospels do assert that Jesus' burial was hurried because bodies could not remain on the cross during the Sabbath (Mark 15:42–43; John 19:31). The women who witnessed Jesus' burial were returning to the tomb on Sunday morning not to greet the risen Jesus but to complete His burial by anointing His body with spices (Mark 16:1–3; Luke 24:1–4). One purpose of spices was to cleanse, so the women may have been prepared to wash His body, especially since the early Jewish tradition known as the Mishnah prohibited such washing on the Sabbath.[45]

An alternate view, however, claims that Joseph of Arimathea was a disciple of Jesus and therefore would have ignored the specific custom and washed the body since, as he saw it, Jesus was not a criminal and should not be treated like one (Matt. 27:57; John 19:38; see also Mark 15:43; Luke 23:41).

Bolstering this idea, some pathologists have recently raised valid questions on the washing of the body. Since

Jesus was alive for much of His time on the cross, His body would literally have been covered with blood. Even small wounds bleed profusely when the heart is beating. So how could the wounds and blood flows on the Shroud be so perfectly outlined? How was the blood kept from smearing during burial? Or if it *was* washed first, did the dead body bleed, even from smaller wounds? And even if all the blood stains occurred after His body was washed, why does some of the blood flow uphill if Jesus was buried on His back?[46]

Some researchers view several of these questions not as evidence that the Shroud is a fake but as indications that Jesus' body was washed before burial.[47] This thesis generally contends that Jesus' body was washed and that the blood on the Shroud is made up of post-mortem flows that came from wrapping and moving His body after the washing. In fact, Zugibe asserted that this is the only possible view in light of the phenomena on the Shroud.[48]

Contrary to popular opinion, dead bodies *do* bleed, especially in cases of violent death. But even after nonviolent, natural deaths, blood usually remains unclotted for about the first eight hours. Much bleeding or oozing can occur, even the next day, when the body is moved about. This is true even of some smaller, fairly superficial wounds, especially if a blood vessel has been cut. Zugibe held that since the body in the Shroud otherwise would have been covered with blood, the clearness of the wounds on the Shroud can only be explained by post-mortem flow after washing.

The post-mortem blood flows can account for just the types of stains present on the Shroud. The blood did not flow "uphill" but, according to Zugibe, probably flowed when the body was being wrapped and carried at various angles to the tomb—after the washing.[49]

As was just shown, there are plausible arguments favoring both the washing and the nonwashing of the body. Either view appears tenable, and fortunately a resolution is not crucial to understanding the nature of Jesus' suffering and death.

115

Marfan's Syndrome

One last issue is Zugibe's contention that Jesus may have had Marfan's syndrome, a condition that Abraham Lincoln also may have had. A person who suffers from Marfan's is usually tall and thin, has a combined arm span greater than his height, is longer from the groin to the soles of the feet than from the groin to the top of the head, and has long fingers and a narrow face. The usual cause of death is a ruptured aorta near the heart. One study showed that the average age of death is thirty-two. According to Zugibe, if Jesus had this disorder, it would have no effect on any theology and would not have been detrimental to Jesus' ministry. And, indeed, Abraham Lincoln's career can be taken as an indicator that Marfan's is not debilitating.

But it can not be known for certain that the man in the Shroud had this condition.[50] Actually, the evidence indicates that this was not the case. The man in the Shroud, at approximately 5 ft. 11 in. and 175 pounds, was neither extremely tall or thin. Zugibe's case is built on the assumption that the average height of a first-century male would have been 5 ft. 4 in., so the man in the Shroud would have been about seven inches above average.[51] However, the average height of adult male skeletons found in a recent excavation of a first-century Jewish grave site was approximately 5 ft. 10 in.,[52] which would make the man in the Shroud of only average height. Meacham observed that Talmudic interpretation also confirms the taller average height.[53] The man in the Shroud was also well built and rather muscular, as if accustomed to physical labor.[54]

The fingers of the man in the Shroud do appear long, but Zugibe has already argued that the nail wounds in the lower palms explain the length.[55] So at least he need not appeal to Marfan's Syndrome to explain this phenomenon. Besides, the elongated fingers may simply be a result of image resolution on the cloth. The claim that the man's face is narrow is also problematical because a face cloth apparent on the Shroud would make the face look slender.[56] Also, the gaps at the sides of the face are from the weave of the cloth, not the man's physical features.

Finally, the claims that the cause of death among those with Marfan's syndrome is often rupture of the aorta and that the average age of death is thirty-two cannot be said to parallel Jesus' death. In Jesus' case, rupture of the aorta cannot be proven; even Zugibe appears to rate it as only a possibility.[57] Even though Jesus was near thirty-two, he did not simply die but was a victim of capital punishment.

There is no persuasive evidence that Jesus had Marfan's syndrome. Zugibe admits that he has only offered "scientific speculation" and that a definitive diagnosis cannot be made from the Shroud. Granted, such a conclusion would not affect theological claims,[58] but, as Bucklin asserts, any claim that the man in the Shroud had Marfan's syndrome is illegitimate. The observed facts do not support Zugibe's thesis.[59]

CONCLUSION

Not all physicians agree on all the details of the exact nature of Jesus' suffering and death.[60] Yet even among those with the strongest disagreements, there is little dispute over Jesus' death by crucifixion. The researchers discussed above largely agree about the pre-crucifixion abuse—beating, scourging, the crown of thorns; the general outline of the type of crucifixion; the fact of Jesus' death—postmortem blood flow, rigor mortis, and other indicators; and most of the elements of burial. The fact of this medical agreement on major issues should not be clouded by disputes over the exact placement of nails, the position of the thumbs, more minute details of the cause of death, and washing. Besides, even on these minor issues, scholarly consensus can be shown.

With the pathologists' views in the background, the central fact of Jesus' crucifixion now commands our attention. In *The Cross and the Shroud,* Frederick Zugibe summarizes that event:

> He was almost totally exhausted and in severe pain. Sweat poured over his entire body, drenching him, and his face assumed a yellowish-ashen color. . . . The burning, exquisite pains from the nails, the lancinating lightning bolts across the face from the irritation by the crown of thorns, the burning wounds from the scourging, the severe pull on the shoulders, the intense cramps in the knees, and the severe thirst together composed a symphony of unrelenting pain. Then he lifted his head up to heaven and cried out in a loud voice, "It is consummated." Jesus was dead.[61]

Whether the Shroud of Turin is or is not the actual burial garment of Jesus, it accurately and movingly portrays Jesus' suffering for each of us. We willingly remind ourselves of that suffering, not for the sake of morbid speculation, but that we might more deeply appreciate Jesus' love and self-sacrifice for us.

8

THE CRUX OF THE CONTROVERSY
The Cause of the Image

We could always be mistaken about the issue of the identification of the man in the Shroud, but we have argued that this cloth could still be the burial garment of Jesus. Regardless, we also have seen that Jesus was dead when He was buried. While medical views differ on some of the details regarding His death, it is agreed that He did not survive crucifixion.

In this chapter we will consider evidence for the cause of the image on the Shroud, especially the testimony since 1981. The cause of the image, the real crux of the controversy, is the issue that has created the most heat. Why? In a sense, everything depends not only on whose image it is, but on the data it reveals.

In *Verdict* we reported scientific treatments of hypotheses that seek to explain the Shroud's image in terms of fakery or natural processes.[1] We included a detailed appendix (reproduced in this book as Appendix C) that lists the objections to such views.[2] Although we will not repeat that discussion here, we will investigate whether scientific statements still verify it.

Before we actually begin our treatment, it must be carefully noted that the views contained in this chapter were expressed *before* the 1988 carbon dating results were released. Therefore these persons *might* not say the same today. Even so, there are at least two reasons for including these data. First, one of the purposes of this volume is to note results from Shroud research since 1981, and the views expressed here are certainly part of the story. Second, in any discussion of the Shroud image, the question of how the image was caused is still important, whatever one concludes on the subject of dating.

So even if the Shroud turns out to be a medieval artifact, it need *not* be simply a human work of art. In fact, many have responded to the recent dating efforts by commenting that the formation process is *still* a major issue. Some now believe that this question has been intensified by the dating process. And if the dating was possibly incorrect, this subject is even more significant.

HYPOTHESES INVOLVING FAKERY

First we will explore the validity of hypotheses suggesting fakery as the cause of the image. Could the image have been created by an application of some sort of foreign material to the linen? A number of scientists have testified that before their investigations they believed the Shroud was a fake. "Give me twenty minutes and I'll have this thing shot full of holes," testified STURP chemist Ray Rogers.[3] Bill Mottern of Sandia Laboratory, another STURP scientist, said, "I went in as a doubting Thomas."[4] Heller reported that, "For numerous reasons, Adler and I had been assuming all along that the Shroud was a forgery."[5] Testimonies like these could be multiplied. Many STURP scientists thought that the Shroud was simply a fake to be exposed by scientific testing.

But in the 1981 meeting at New London, Connecticut, the scientists reported: "No pigments, paints, dyes or stains have been found on the fibrils. X-ray fluorescence and microchemistry on the fibrils preclude the possibility of paint being used as a method for creating the image. Ultraviolet and infrared evaluation confirm these studies."[6]

Ever since then, several STURP scientists have continued to report that forgery could not be the cause of the Shroud's image.[7] Heller notes: "At the end of months of work, we had pretty well eliminated all paints, pigments, dyes, and stains. . . . the images were not the result of any colorant that had been added."[8] Heller points out that fraud can be checked by at least two scientific methods—chemistry and physics. Concerning the first means, he said, "Adler and I had reached the conclusion that the image could not have been made by artistic endeavor."[9] The second method revealed no forgery either: "The conclusion of the physical scientists was that the Shroud could not be the result of eye/brain/hand."[10]

During these studies, a number of published reports appeared which detailed the work of Walter McCrone, a former STURP member. A world-renowned micro-analyst, McCrone announced that he had discovered red ocher (iron oxide and vermilion) and gelatin or collagen tempera on the Shroud, which he believed indicated that the Shroud's image was either painted or at least touched up by this substance.[11] His claim directly opposed the findings and stand of STURP and other reports such as Heller's above. Consequently, one report challenged Heller and Adler to publish their findings in response to McCrone.[12]

So although STURP scientists found no pigments, paints, dyes, or stains on the Shroud,[13] several of them began work on McCrone's specific challenge. Heller and Adler, who did some of the main work, reported that "There was not enough iron oxide or vermilion to account for one painted drop of blood, let alone all the gore on the Shroud."[14] STURP scientists tested and rejected McCrone's claims.

The stage was set for a debate, and one was planned for the 1981 meeting of the Canadian Society of Forensic Sciences. McCrone, Heller, and Adler were invited and hoped that the issue would be resolved. But McCrone did not go, so the confrontation did not occur.[15]

Later McCrone was quoted as saying, "I believe the shroud is a fake, but I cannot prove it."[16] At any rate, STURP objected to his findings.[17] Even one nonteam physicist who appeared sympathetic to McCrone's findings still admitted that "STURP unanimously rejects McCrone's interpretations."[18]

One other well-publicized set of attempts to show how the image may have been faked came from artist Joe Nickell. His chief example involved applying a dry powder mixture of myrrh and aloes to a damp cloth which had been carefully fitted around a bas-relief face. The result is also an image of the face, created by the powder, which, to an untrained eye, resembles the face on the Shroud.[19]

Nickell's methods have been analyzed frequently, especially since his work was first publicized in 1978. He has changed his methods over the years, but his various attempts (as well as similar ones) have all been tested with devastating results to Nickell's claims. The absence of powder on the Shroud and the disproving of any artistic process by both chemical and physical testing wielded death blows to Nickell's theories. Also, Nickell's models failed the 3-D test and were badly distorted when checked by the VP-8 image analyzer, as pointed out by John Jackson. Problems with shading and the fact that Nickell's model is not superficial (despite his claims to the contrary) led to the assessment that it was "unacceptable."[20] Heller likewise listed as a major failure of both bas-reliefs and block prints the fact that they do not reproduce a 3-D image, as the Shroud does. He also pointed out that no such bas-reliefs or artistic method existed in medieval times.[21]

Don Lynn and Jean Lorre of the Jet Propulsion Laboratory discovered that the Shroud's image is nondirectional (has no linear direction). In other words, the image was apparently not caused by any movement of a hand across cloth, which "would not be consistent with hand application"[22]—the crux of Nickell's theories. This poses a big problem, not only for Nickell, but for anyone who suggests that hand artistry caused the image. Many other problems could be mentioned,[23] but as Heller asserted, bas-reliefs were "examined and rejected because they could be ruled out—both theoretically and experimentally."[24] STURP scientists tested many different models and rejected all of them.

Another suggested method of fakery given considerable attention was "acid-painting," a chemical alteration of a linen cloth to produce an image. But STURP's tests with acid also failed to create a viable image. Achieving uniform density like that in the Shroud's image was a problem for this method, as was the presence of capillarity and even the destruction of the cloth itself.[25] For these and other reasons, acid-painting was rejected as a viable cause.[26]

Other fakery hypotheses were concerned with producing contact images, whereby an object with some substance on it is transferred to the linen by contact, apart from any painting methods. One of the more clever attempts involved coating a plaster bust with phosphorescent paint and then dipping the bust into black ink. But this method failed both chemically and physically.[27]

Another attempt at producing a contact image came from draping a cloth over a statue or bas-relief. Although scientists used various designs, their attempts failed to account for the image. In the words of Ron London, "You can scorch cloth. . . . You just can't make it look like what we see [on the Shroud]."[28] Numerous problems, such as the lack of 3-D information, plague these theories involving heated images. Heller noted that these hypotheses are "seriously flawed" with regard to this distance information.[29] Another problem is the inability of heat to cause a resolute image because heat diffuses.[30] STURP also discovered that when the heat was high enough for the contact areas to mark the linen, the contact areas "burned through the cloth,"[31] which again fails to match the characteristics of the Shroud's image.

Consequently, STURP rejected all these theses.[32] In Rogers' words, "The image is too sharp and too uniform for any of the hot statue theories."[33] Heller rejected them on both theoretical and experimental grounds.[34] Even Mueller, skeptical of the Shroud's authenticity, recognized their failure at this point.[35]

For such reasons as these, fakery theories have been ruled out by STURP. The testing revealed no pigments, paints, dyes, or stains on the linen fibrils which could account for the image. As the STURP statement released at New London in 1981 proclaims, "[The image] is not the product of an artist."[36] To quote John Heller again, the Shroud's image "could not have been made by artistic endeavor. . . . The Shroud could not be the result of eye/brain/hand."[37] This conclusion rests on thousands of hours of tests, many of the results of which are not even presented here.[38]

NATURAL HYPOTHESES

Now we will turn to natural hypotheses to see if they can explain the image on the Shroud. None of the options in this category are based on fakery; rather, they point to natural causation.[39] The basic tenet of these models is that perhaps some natural relationship between the cloth and the body buried in it can account for the image. Maybe the image was caused by gases coming from the body or by contact.

In 1902 biologist Paul Vignon hypothesized that the body under the cloth was the source of chemical gases caused by the presence of sweat, ammonia, blood, and burial spices. These gases supposedly diffused upward toward the cloth and account for its image.[40]

Vignon's thesis was fairly popular from its appearance in 1902 until about ten years ago. But further scientific investigations revealed numerous problems with his supposition. Robert Wilcox reviewed several of these problems. Summarizing, he said, "As far as chemicals being able to make such an image, lab tests have shown that chemicals diffuse and 'run' through linen fibers, and thus produce a blurry, and certainly non-3-D image."[41] Chemicals do not travel in straight lines upward, as Vignon's theory requires; rather, they diffuse in the air and lack any clear image, which creates resolution problems. Also, such chemicals cause capillary flow ("run") on the cloth, a phenomenon absent from the Shroud. And, as Wilcox noted, a chemically-induced va-porgraphic image is not three dimensional.

Mueller pointed out two other problems with Vignon's view. Both concern the superficiality and lack of saturation on the Shroud.[42] The Shroud's image is on the surface fibers only, but vaporgraphs permeate cloth. Furthermore, unlike the characteristics present with vapor transfer, the image is not saturated and contains no plateaus. Also, STURP's studies revealed "no evidence of any spices, oils, or any bio-chemicals known to be produced by the body in life or in death."[43] The very chemicals needed to create the image, according to Vignon, were not present on the cloth. For reasons such as these, the vaporgraph theory has fallen from popularity in recent years.[44]

Another natural hypothesis suggests that the Shroud's image was created by the contact between the cloth and the body wrapped in it. Obviously, at least parts of the image, such as the bloodstains, were caused by contact, so the supposition that the whole image could be accounted for by natural contact between the Shroud and the body does not seem farfetched—at least at first. But further research on this hypothesis has revealed that, by itself, contact cannot explain many of the observed phenomena on the Shroud.

One of the major problems for contact theses is that they cannot explain the portions of the image that did not contact the body. As Wilcox pointed out in one of his 1982 articles, areas of the body that apparently did not touch the cloth, such as the ribs, the sides of the nose, the eye recesses, and part of the neck, are still shown on the image. This is a major problem for any direct contact theory.[45]

Another significant problem is that a contact thesis seems to require the image's back side to be more saturated than its front because of the weight of the body when laid to rest in a tomb. Also, pressure from the contact should theoretically cause a different density in the dorsal and frontal images. But the fact is that the back side of the Shroud is neither more saturated nor any more dense than its front side. In short, a contact mechanism requires pressure, but the cause of the Shroud's image is pressure independent.[46]

Still another problem was pointed out by Ray Rogers. Mass spectrometry tests performed at the University of Nebraska revealed that there were no aloes, myrrh, oils, or other substances that could create a contact image on the Shroud.[47] If these or similar substances were not on the cloth, it is very difficult to see how any type of contact image could have resulted. The sensitizing material is just not there.

Mueller noted two additional problems for contact theories. The superficiality of the Shroud's image is a major objection, for even if there were sensitizing chemicals on the cloth, they would not remain superficial but would soak into the fibrils. The Shroud shows no evidence of this ever having occurred. Also, the Shroud's image has no saturation points, as would most likely occur with contact chemicals.[48]

A rather ingenious form of the contact thesis deserves some special attention. Samuel Pellicori of the Santa Barbara Research Center and John German of the Air Force Weapons Lab, both members of STURP, postulated that the Shroud's image might have been caused by direct contact through the transference of bodily chemicals to the cloth, producing the image over a long period of time, with the help of either heat or the linen's natural aging process. This "latent image" theory has some interesting twists, such as the belief that the dampness of the tomb might have caused an originally stiff Shroud to droop over some previously untouched areas. The darker aspects of the image would have been caused by the portions of the cloth that contacted the "higher" points of the body for the longest period of time.[49]

Although this hypothesis makes several improvements on the older versions of the contact thesis, it still suffers from numerous problems, some of which have already been mentioned. The Pellicori-German model is still pressure dependent and, if true, would lead to a darker dorsal image and a lighter frontal one. But the Shroud's pressure independent image does not reveal density differences between the back and front of the image. The absence of sensitizing chemicals on the Shroud is another major obstacle since they are, according to this model, the agents responsible for the image. Moreover, the superficiality and lack of saturation of the Shroud's image are still not accounted for on the Pellicori-German hypothesis.

Perhaps the major problem for the latent hypothesis is still the 3-D nature of the Shroud's image. Heller explained it this way: "The recessed areas of the face could not have been in contact with the cloth, as proved by the VP-8 images and the Shroud-body distance data. Pellicori agreed that that was still a problem for his hypothesis. It was not *a* problem, but rather *the* problem."[50]

Some of the scientists, including Heller, also thought that they had observed capillarity on the samples developed by Pellicori, which is another difference from the Shroud's image.[51] Other problems with this theory could be cited,[52] but we will mention only one more here. If this type of body-on-cloth action is natural, why are there so many burial garments that have no images of the person buried in them? Surely more than one burial cloth with a contact image on it would have been discovered. But so far as we know, the Shroud is unique in this regard. And even if another burial garment with an image caused by natural contact with a dead body were found, the image would still have to display the characteristics of the Shroud's image, which has been shown to be highly unlikely.

Hence, serious flaws in contact theories disallow them, at least at present, as likely explanations for the cause of the Shroud's image. STURP concluded: "It is clear that there has been a direct contact of the Shroud with the body, which explains certain features such as the scourge marks, as well as the blood. However, while this type of contact might explain some of the features of the torso, it is totally incapable of explaining the image of the face with the high resolution which has been amply demonstrated by photography."[53]

For these and other reasons,[54] the contact thesis must be rejected as a viable image-producing mechanism. As Heller remarked, "Any hypothesis based on contact between the Shroud and body chemicals had to be ruled out, because the physics of the images seemed to preclude it."[55]

In conclusion, natural hypotheses have failed to explain the Shroud's image and are untenable at this time. Schafersman even referred to such alternatives as "absurd."[56] Thus, neither fakery nor natural hypotheses are viable. Murphy remarked in 1981 that "it is STURP's conclusion that none of the forgery theories is tenable. Neither are any of the 'natural phenomenon' hypotheses."[57]

THE SCORCH THEORY

At this point, science is unable to explain the Shroud's image completely.[58] On scientific grounds, the cause of the image is an enigma. In the words of the STURP report delivered at New London, "The answer to the question of how the image was produced, or what produced the image, remains now, as in the past, a mystery."[59] As Heller asserted, "100 thousand to 150 thousand scientific man-hours have been spent" studying the Shroud, utilizing the best scientific instruments, and yet the image still remains a "mystery."[60]

In spite of this conclusion, by the early to mid 1980s, numerous scientists had indicated their view that the image was best explained by a scorch theory of some sort. Even Mueller, a critic of the Shroud, pointed out in 1982: "Nationwide, at least, most members still seem to regard the dehydrated-cellulose image as a probable low-temperature scorch, and the image as having been somehow 'projected' across space onto the cloth. This is, of course, the old radiation-scorch hypothesis in thin semantic disguise."[61]

128

Wilcox's 1982 article series, largely based on his interviews with twenty-six scientists from the 1978 investigation, confirmed some of Mueller's suspicions. Noting that possibly the most important single finding of STURP was the oxidized, dehydrated, and conjugated nature of the linen fibrils,[62] Wilcox decided to ask the scientists he interviewed what they believed to be the cause of the image. Only seven ventured a specific answer. Two of them, Pellicori and German, favored the latent-image version of the contact theory[63] even though STURP declared that contact theories are "totally incapable" of explaining crucial portions of the image.[64] The other five scientists who answered Wilcox's query indicated their view that the image was a scorch.[65]

Even though a sample of seven scientists is admittedly very small (about 27 percent of those questioned), it is nonetheless quite significant that those who did answer believed the scorch hypothesis fit the facts better than any other. However, the interesting question here is, how can a dead body under a cloth produce such a scorch on linen? Although no completely scientific answer to this question has been given, some of the scientists who accepted the scorch hypothesis cited data in its favor. We will turn now to consider some evidence for this theory.

Questions about the Scorch Theory

According to Mueller, John Jackson led an influential group of STURP scientists who accepted the scorch theory or a similar view. One major argument they cited was the three-dimensional data.[66]

Roger Gilbert of the Oriel Corporation was one of the scientists who believed that the image was caused by a scorch. He was also involved in one of the tests—visible spectral reflectance—which appeared to indicate this conclusion. The test revealed that the molecular properties of the image were very similar to those of the scorch marks inflicted in the fire of 1532. This provides evidence that characteristics of the fire burns were likely the same as those of the Shroud's image, although those who held the scorch theory generally believed that the scorch was caused by a mild emanation of heat or light at moderate temperatures and not by a burst of intense heat or light. Gilbert, on the other hand, was not prepared to explain how a body might "glow" in order to cause the image.[67]

An important question concerned the fact that testing revealed that the 1532 scorch (fire) marks fluoresced while the image did not, which is evidence against the two types of scorches being caused by a similar action. Answering this result, Gilbert explained, "I think this is due to the physical differences in the two targets, not their inherent natures." The Shroud's image is superficial, for instance, while the 1532 scorch marks extend to the reverse side of the cloth.[68]

Alan Adler was another STURP scientist who reportedly favored the scorch theory. Like Gilbert, he believed this scorch was produced by mild heat intensity, which would account for the oxidation, dehydration, and conjugation of the fibrils observed on the Shroud. But again, the issue was how a body or bodily form, especially a lifeless one, could have been the source of such a scorch.[69]

One question concerning the scorch theory was how heat or light could have caused the high resolution of the image. But Roger Morris, a Los Alamos scientist who also favored the scorch hypothesis, pointed out that heat rays can travel in straight lines, depending on the angle from which they are projected,[70] which is consistent with what scientists have discovered about the Shroud's image.

In Murphy's 1981 interview with Ray Rogers, this chemist also stated his preference for the scorch theory: "A scorch seems a bit more promising. If a scorch is produced at moderate temperatures, the predominant result is creation of conjugated double bonds, which is what we have. . . . I incline toward the idea of a scorch, but I can't think how it was done. At this point you either keep looking for the mechanism or start getting mystical."[71]

130

Digitized computer photo reveals details in the Shroud image that cannot be seen by the unaided eye or by other photographic processes.

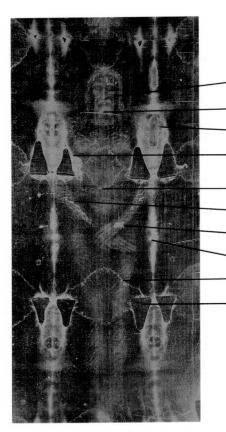

Swollen cheek

Crease in the cloth

Scorch marks from the 1532 fire

Side wound, probably from a Roman lance

Swollen abdomen

Blood flow down arm

Nail wound in wrist

Fold marks in cloth

Water stain

Patches used to repair fire damage

Enhanced photographic negative of the ventral side of the image (above).

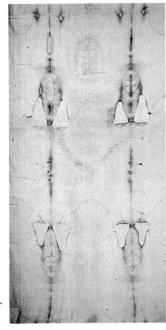

Ventral view of the image in natural color (right).

Holes caused by another fire, date unknown

Blood flow from scalp punctures

Probably a pigtail

Shoulder abrasions, caused by carrying a heavy object

Scourge wounds

Blood from the side wound

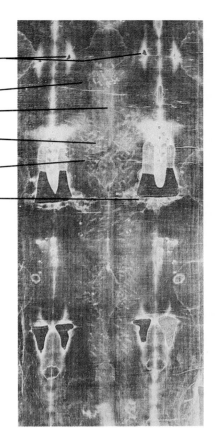

Negative enhancement of the dorsal side of the image (above).

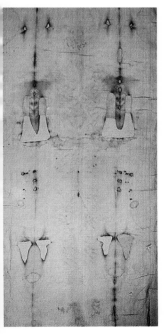

Dorsal view of the image in natural color (left).

Close-up of the face as seen by the naked eye. It shows swollen cheeks and blood flowing from puncture wounds in the scalp.

A photographic process known as isodensity enhances details by highlighting differences in the image. In this photo, the blood on the image is seen as red, clearly showing the severe beating suffered by the man buried in the Shroud.

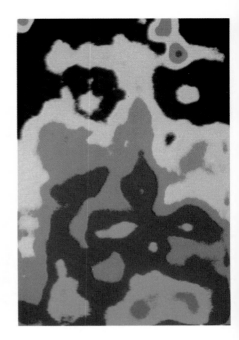

Scientists have confirmed the presence of coins over the eyes of the man imaged on the Shroud. This computer-enhanced picture of the victim's face (right) reveals these coins as circular, cream-colored objects where the eyes should be. Like the lepton pictured below, the coins revealed on the cloth were minted between 29 and 32 A.D., during the reign of Pontius Pilate and toward the end of Jesus' life.

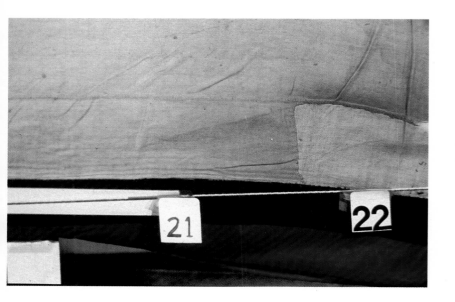

According to textile experts, the herringbone twill weave pattern of the Shroud (above) was rare and costly in the first century. However, traces of cotton found in the cloth's weave strongly suggest that the Shroud was made in the Middle East, not in Europe, since cotton was not grown in Europe but in the Middle East. The discolored yellow portions on the cloth (below left) are of the Shroud image itself, and they appear only on the uppermost layers of the cloth, while the red-colored marks (below right) in the image areas are bloodstains, and they have seeped into the crevices of the fibers.

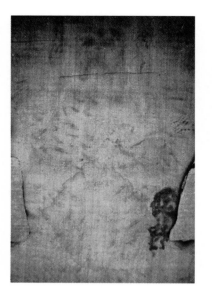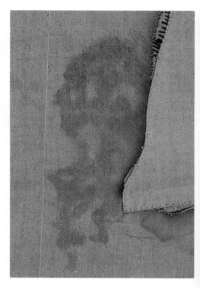

Many characteristics of the Shroud image match the Gospels' descriptions of Jesus' beatings and crucifixion. One of these is the Shroud victim's side wound, which was caused by a sharp object, probably a Roman lance. In these fluorescent photos of this wound, the bloodstains do not fluoresce, but the blood serum does. The light area around the top and sides of the wound is probably a colorless serum that separates from whole blood when it clots. This is yet another indication that the bloodstains are really blood and that the man buried in the Shroud was likely Jesus of Nazareth.

In his book on the Shroud, John Heller also appeared to give the slightest hint that the scorch theory just might possibly be the correct view: "If it turns out that some form of molecular transport we have not been able to fathom is the method whereby the images of the scourged, crucified man were transferred to the linen, we shall have only solved another little micropart of the puzzle."[72]

Kenneth Stevenson, who had served as the scientists' editor and spokesperson until 1981, was also convinced that the Shroud image may have been some kind of scorch. He held that this view was the most viable of the image-formation hypotheses.[73]

Some non-STURP scholars have also defended the scorch theory since the 1978 scientific studies were conducted. Perhaps the scholar who has received the most attention is Giles Carter, professor of chemistry at Eastern Michigan University, who had specialized in X-ray fluorescence analysis for fifteen years. Carter felt the Shroud's image was caused by low-energy X-rays of a secondary nature, which were emitted by the body under the cloth.[74] Carter based his research on STURP photographs supplied by Vernon Miller, chief photographer for the team. After studying them, Carter thought that he could detect the effects of X-rays, taking some hints from what he believed was evidence of knuckles, of some of the backbone, and even of teeth on the Shroud. From this, Carter developed his theory, which proposed that strong X-rays actually proceeded from within the bones and teeth of the dead man and then reacted with dust, dirt, and chemicals on the skin, such as those caused by perspiration. The result was that the elements on the skin fluoresced, thereby producing secondary X-rays and causing the image. In other words, the initial, stronger X-rays were the cause of the secondary, low-energy X-rays. The latter resulted from the fluorescing dirt and other chemicals on the body and then produced the image over the distance between the body and the cloth.

Carter experimented with his method in the laboratory

and had some reasonably good results, even claiming that his model could account for the three-dimensional data on the Shroud. He presented a paper explaining his findings at the September 1982 meeting of the American Chemical Society.[75]

Carter sent copies of his work to Shroud specialists, including several members of STURP. When interviewed, Adler responded that Carter's theory was "great physically, great chemically, but absolutely bizarre biologically. Anyone who was that radioactive would be dead long before he was crucified."[76] In 1983 Carter concluded, "I'm more optimistic because time has gone by and my theory hasn't been disproved."[77]

Another researcher, Jerome Goldblatt, who has been close to Shroud studies in recent years, also espoused a scorch theory, favoring the postulation that a burst of radiant energy from the body projected onto the cloth. On the other hand, he allowed as possibilities the other varieties of the scorch hypothesis: "In the final analysis . . . whether we call the image on the Shroud a scorch, a quasi-photograph, a thermogram, a Kirlian aura, or a hologram is only a matter of semantics."[78]

But the scientific tendency, to the extent to which a scorch was a possible option, was away from high-intensity radiation to the concept of a moderate-temperature scorch (less than 280 °C).[79] Of course, the question regarding how such heat could emanate from a live or dead human body has no purely scientific answer. But the scorch theory did seem to account for more data than any other theory that had been proposed.

CONCLUSION

The scorch thesis was not without problems to be solved if it was to be viable. Yet a scorch could exhibit many of the characteristics present on the Shroud, such as oxidation, dehydration, and conjugation of linen fibrils, superficiality, the absence of saturation or image plateaus, and thermal and water stability and coloration.[80] In other words, a scorch explains such phenomena as the conditions of the image fibrils themselves, the fact that this image is on the surface fibrils only, and that there are no points at which the image soaks into the cloth (except for the blood stains). A scorch can also account for the coloring and the resistance of the image to changes brought about by heat or water.

Hence, just as the scorch theory was probably the most popular thesis before the 1978 scientific investigation,[81] so some form of it appeared to be the most popular option in the eighties, at least until the carbon dating results were revealed. Granted, comparatively few of the scientists answered this critical issue publicly. Instead, many of them labeled the image a mystery.[82] Nonetheless, several scientists professed their views, and most of those espoused some form of scorch thesis. And yet, even for those who postulate a scorch, they may not know its cause. Such a scorch could have a known or unknown origin.

But could the scorch theory still possibly be true? If so, what could account for the emanation of heat or light? That's the question we will address in the next chapter. For those who do not think that carbon dating has eliminated the chance that the Shroud could be the burial garment of Jesus, this may, in fact, be the most important question of all.

9

NEW EVIDENCE FOR JESUS' RESURRECTION?

We have been building a post-carbon-dating case for the possibility that Jesus was the one buried in the Shroud. Medical knowledge has confirmed that Jesus died from the rigors of crucifixion. And concerning the cause of the Shroud's image, there has been no scientific consensus, except that the image is a mystery.

Now we turn to the most controversial subject of the whole debate—Jesus' resurrection. Is there any support for this event from the Shroud of Turin? Could any scientific evidence from the ancient linen cloth add to the strong independent historical evidence for the resurrection of Christ? Now, of course, for those who believe that the results of the carbon dating are authoritative, this question is misplaced. But for those with doubts about the tests, the issue is still important.

SCIENTIFIC OPINION

From 1978 to 1988 the scorch hypothesis appeared to be most popular among scientists who expressed their views on the cause of the image. However, it must be carefully noted that the question of whether the Shroud provides evidence for Jesus' resurrection is *not* dependent on whether the image was caused by a scorch. The Shroud appears to be unique at this point, even if a natural explanation for the image is found.[1] As Wilcox pointed out: "But even if [researchers] come up with some 'natural' process, the failure, so far, to find anything like the shroud amongst the world's body cloths and artifacts leaves them with the further problem of why the process occurred only once in the history of the world, so far as is yet known."[2]

In fact, Wilcox even observed from his 1982 study that the thirteen scientists who indicated their belief that the Shroud was the actual burial garment of Jesus also thought that a natural cause for the image would be consistent with the Christian belief in Jesus' resurrection:

> While all 13 indicated they thought a "natural explanation" (meaning one that can be explained by science) for the cloth's images will eventually be found, they also indicated they believe the shroud's uniqueness (nothing like it has yet been found on earth) will remain, thus keeping it, in their view, consistent with the Christian belief in Jesus' death and resurrection.[3]

John Heller has also commented on the Shroud's uniqueness: "We do know, however, that there are thousands on thousands of pieces of funerary linen going back to millennia before Christ, and another huge number of linens of Coptic Christian burials. On none of these is there any image of any kind."[4]

Therefore, even if a natural hypothesis for the Shroud's image is discovered, it would not discount the image as evidence for Jesus' resurrection. In fact, a natural thesis could even produce evidence for this historical event, since scientific phenomena such as those described later in this chapter still exist.

Some of those who have studied the Shroud have related its revelations to Jesus' resurrection. STURP pathologist Robert Bucklin, who did not support the scorch theory, still believed that the Shroud provided evidence for the Resurrection:

> It was inevitable that the question of the resurrection would come up in relation to the Shroud studies. . . . While the majority of the scientists have been reluctant to take a stand on this matter, a few of us have openly expressed our opinions that there is support for the resurrection in the things we see on the Shroud of Turin.[5]

Elaborating, Bucklin proclaims: "The medical data from the Shroud supports the resurrection. When this medical information is combined with the physical, chemical and historical facts, there is strong evidence for Jesus' resurrection."[6]

Giles Carter's thesis (see Chapter 8) postulates that the body in the Shroud emitted Xrays, which caused surface dirt and chemicals on the body to fluoresce and produce secondary, low-energy Xrays. These, he argued, passed over the distance from the body to the cloth and created the image on the Shroud.

But how did a dead body wrapped in a burial cloth emit strong Xrays? Carter suggested three options. Perhaps the person buried in the Shroud had lived in a cave that had radioactive walls due to the effects of certain materials. Or maybe this person had eaten food that was grown in naturally radioactive soil. Or, according to Carter, "There is a possibility of the unknown, a supernatural cause, if in fact this is the burial shroud of Jesus Christ."[7]

Concerning the likelihood of the last option, Carter held that if the Shroud turned out to date from Jesus' time, this would "provide proof of the resurrection," which would "make some atheists awfully mad."[8]

As was pointed out earlier, Alan Adler's initial response to Carter's thesis was that it was "great physically, [and] great chemically." But in regard to Carter's first two options, Adler concluded they are "absolutely bizarre biologically. Anyone who was that radioactive would be dead long before he was crucified."[9] Now if Carter's thesis was otherwise "great" on both physical and chemical grounds and yet his first two explanations for the image were "bizarre" and physically unexplainable, does this make the supernatural option possible? Several pieces of evidence provide support for this thesis.

Jerome Goldblatt found strong evidence for the Resurrection on the Shroud of Turin. Although not a scientist, Goldblatt is an informed researcher on this subject. He noted that the man buried in the Shroud was in a state of rigor mortis and definitely dead. Yet absolutely no decomposition is observed on the Shroud, indicating that the body apparently left the cloth during the period of rigor mortis, twenty-four to forty-eight hours after death. Neither does the body appear to have been removed by any human agency because the blood stains are not smeared or otherwise marred and no known damage to the image fibrils exists. This entire process is unique. Saying, "Precedents are not only elusive, they are nonexistent," Goldblatt related each of these evidences to the resurrection of Jesus.[10]

Furthermore, a few physicists have recently proposed a testable hypothesis which would attempt to measure a possible neutron flux that could account for the higher C-14 content in the Shroud as well as argue that the resurrection of Jesus would be the supernatural cause of this chemical change in the cloth. We already viewed a somewhat related thesis by German physicist Oswald Scheuermann in Chapter 2. Briefly, he has proposed that a high-voltage, high-energy transfer onto dry cloth can produce an image like that on the Shroud.

Two other noteworthy and similar hypotheses were proposed by Thomas Phillips, a Harvard physicist, and Eberhard Lindner, a German physicist. Phillips has debated his thesis in the British scientific journal *Nature* and elsewhere, explaining how such a neutron flux would be measurable on the Shroud. He argues that such a thesis would account for both the younger date of the cloth and the cause of the image. Without testing this hypothesis further, he concludes that it cannot be ligitimately concluded that the Shroud is a medieval object.[11]

For Lindner, a synoptic theory is needed which accounts for all of the data, not one that accepts just one result over all of the others. He, too, favors a "thermal neutron flux" which altered the C-14 content and caused the image. Complimenting the research of Carter, Scheuermann, and Phillips, Lindner contends that a restricted number of protons disappeared during the resurrection, leaving electrons and neutrons. He favors Carter's thesis that the remaining electrons caused the image of the corpse by a process termed "electron-radiation". Furthermore, like Phillips, Lindner explains how such a cause is definitely testable, with verifiable or falsifiable results.[12]

Wilcox's report that thirteen of the twenty-six STURP members were willing to identify the Shroud as the actual burial garment of Jesus was startling, especially since these thirteen also believed that the Shroud was consistent with Jesus' death and resurrection.[13] Some researchers have even contended that the Shroud is evidence for Jesus' resurrection. What case could be made for this conclusion? Let's see.

THE EVIDENCE

By combining the New Testament record with the scientific, medical, archaeological, and other historical information concerning the Shroud of Turin, an argument can be made. The detailed agreement between the beating and execution of Jesus and that of the man buried in the Shroud, especially in the crucifixion anomalies indicates that the image of the man in the Shroud may still possibly be Jesus.[14] Then the witness of the Gospels to Jesus' bodily resurrection from the dead provides the possible explanation for the scientific evidence pointing to the strange disappearance of Jesus' body from the Shroud. Any other Shroud data could present additional evidence for His resurrection. And we believe, along with numerous other researchers and scientists, that the Shroud does exhibit some additional evidence for this event.[15]

First of all, that the Shroud contains no hint of bodily decomposition indicates a hasty bodily departure. If the body had remained in the cloth, it would have been seriously decomposed after a very few days. The fact that the body was still in rigor mortis indicates that it may have left the cloth before the forty hours or so that the condition generally lasts.

Second, according to Bucklin, the blood stains indicate that the body left the Shroud without disturbing it. Since the cloth was loosely attached to the body from the dried blood, any attempt to remove it probably would have damaged the stains. Yet these blood stains are anatomically correct, even down to their precisely outlined borders. Moreover, we noted earlier that the scientific tests failed to reveal any evidence of damage done to the image fibers, again evidence that no physical separation between the body and the Shroud occurred. Bucklin takes this as further evidence that the body was not unwrapped.[16]

Third, our theory that the Shroud's image was caused by a scorch from a dead body certainly reveals a mystery surrounding the death of the man buried in it and his subsequent departure from it.

But what sorts of theories could account for such a strange disappearance of a dead body? The possible theories are three: (1) naturalistic, which must utilize explanations that proceed solely from the normal operations of nature; (2) supernaturalistic, which require that ultimate explanations derive from a work of God or another agent with powers beyond those of nature; and (3) unknown origin, which either fail or refuse to provide a causal explanation for the phenomena in question. But the current evidence suggests that the naturalistic alternatives are mistaken.

Naturalistic hypotheses that would account for the Shroud must explain at least (a) the absence of decomposition, (b) the fact that the body was apparently not unwrapped when it separated from the cloth, and (c) a very possible light or heat scorch from (d) a dead body in a state of rigor mortis. Theories involving an unwrapped, rewrapped, or stolen body are confounded by (b) and (c). Those claiming that the person in question never died are disproved by (b), (c), and (d). Most other naturalistic theories are refuted by one or more of these phenomena.

Some people might prefer to wait for a yet unknown or future naturalistic hypothesis. And, to be honest, there is some warrant for such attitudes in light of the recent carbon dating, for this is a serious objection. On the other hand, no known alternative thesis can presently explain the image, the results of the dating notwithstanding. In addition, given the significant problems with the 1988 dating procedures, the possibility that the Shroud is authentic is increased, in which case it could still have some relevance to the issue of the Resurrection.

Therefore we conclude that the Shroud does provide some new evidence for Jesus' resurrection. In addition to the absence of viable naturalistic theories, other features of the Shroud support Jesus' resurrection:

- The physics and mechanics of the light/heat image strongly imply the mechanics of bodily separation from the cloth, which is independent of other data.
- Most of the facts about the Shroud image, such as three-dimensionality, superficiality, and nondirectionality, are empirical and repeatable, certainly a new type of evidence for the Resurrection.
- The image may actually be a quasiphotograph of the process of separation, again a new phenomenon.
- That the man was clearly in a state of rigor mortis shows that whatever else occurred, it was not a near-death experience or a resuscitation.

While it is true that none of these conditions *proves* a resurrection, it is also true that they present more than just a strange occurrence. Indications such as a quasi-photographic image caused by heat or light and having the unique empirical and repeatable characteristics of three-dimensionality, superficiality, and nondirectionality, all proceeding from a completely dead body, and that the body apparently exited from the cloth without being unwrapped, produce strong considerations for Jesus' resurrection. Of course, the Shroud's image could have a different cause, and this evidence does not amount to a proof for this event. But there is certainly some evidence here for the cause being Jesus' resurrection. And when it is combined with the Gospel records and other historical evidence, the man imaged in the Shroud is still possibly none other than Jesus. In and of themselves, the Gospels' eyewitness testimony to Jesus' resurrection lends reliable historical support to that event.

But we conclude that the Shroud adds some further empirical evidence.

Consider the analogy of a court case. Even if there is enough evidence to convict a person of a crime, extra evidence could reinforce the conviction. Similarly, the independently reliable Gospels confirm the historicity of Jesus and His resurrection. The Shroud may add some new empirical evidence, strengthening an already strong case.

At any rate, one could either accept this preliminary Shroud apologetic as providing some evidence for the Resurrection, or one could reject it in light of the current data. But when the scientific evidence is combined with the previously and independently validated Gospels, the result may be more than the possible identification of Jesus with the man of the Shroud. The Gospels also record Jesus' resurrection from the dead.[17] The Shroud could add some new, empirical evidence for this event, thereby providing a possible explanation for the scientific mystery that is at least partially generated by the strange disappearance of a dead body from the cloth.[18]

We are not stating that the Shroud supplies any proof for the Resurrection. However, that does not rule out the possibility for there being some evidence on it for the Resurrection. And yet we must be cautious about evidence from the Shroud of Turin. This cloth still might turn out to reveal something different from what we have envisioned, and, of course, Christianity neither rises nor falls on the nature of the Shroud. On the other hand, the Shroud may give some added testimony to that of the early church: "Christ died for our sins according to the Scriptures, and . . . He was buried, and . . . He rose again the third day according to the Scriptures" (1 Cor. 15:3–4).

An important concern needs to be voiced here, however. What if the Shroud turns out, in the end, not to be that of Jesus? What would such a conclusion say about resurrection? Would someone else have been raised? Here it should be remarked that there are at least two differences between the identification of Jesus and that of some unknown victim of crucifixion. First, if it is known for sure that the Shroud is a medieval garment, then an alternative theory of some sort does become a much more likely candidate simply by the fact that its origin has thereby been explained otherwise than was previously thought. If we have been wrong in our previous assessment, then all of our conclusions suffer. Second, the resurrection of an unknown individual would not have the additional and independent backing of either the New Testament or historical data, as Jesus' resurrection does. The evidence would not be sufficient to conclude that a resurrection had occurred to an unknown individual.

A BRIEF APOLOGETIC FOR THE RESURRECTION

At this point, an additional issue needs to be addressed: the relationship between the Shroud and a defense of the Resurrection itself. My [Habermas] recent writings on this subject have stressed the existence of independent historical arguments for the Resurrection which are based on either a reliable New Testament or historically demonstrable facts acceptable even to critical scholars who reject the New Testament's reliability.

In other words, these two independent arguments could either proceed in a rather straightforward manner from the trustworthy New Testament to its testimony concerning the Resurrection or, conversely, we could utilize known and critically accepted historical facts which can be separately confirmed on the basis of the available data. These facts are sufficient to prove the historicity of the Resurrection, even for those who do not believe that the Scriptures are trustworthy. In short, we can reason to the Resurrection either from the overall nature of the New Testament text or from separate facts that are independently demonstrable.

We could pursue the first approach, which begins with the New Testament, by employing evidence regarding authorship, eyewitness testimony, dating, extrabiblical and archaeological sources, as well as manuscript support.

Then we would have to ascertain what these sources report concerning Jesus' resurrection.

On the second approach, facts that are verifiable on separate grounds (beyond the trustworthiness of the New Testament) are utilized to both disprove alternate, naturalistic attempts to dismiss the Resurrection and to provide numerous positive evidences for this event. In particular, these minimal facts (which are accepted by virtually all critical scholars who study this subject) especially affirm the nature of the eyewitness claims to have seen the glorified body of Jesus. And, to repeat, these appearances have not been explained away by naturalistic means.[19]

Some new twists can be added to this second approach. For instance, even the German liberal scholars of the nineteenth century decimated each other's naturalistic and critical theories, revealing many weaknesses in each of their views. Furthermore, these theories are generally rejected wholesale by twentieth-century critics. Hence, numerous nonsupernaturalistic theories of the Resurrection have fallen on bad times—and for many reasons.

But the strongest aspect of the second type of apologetic asserts that a *minimum* number of facts accepted as historical by virtually all scholars who study this subject can provide enough evidence to demonstrate the historicity of Jesus' resurrection. Having accepted these minimal facts, which are established by strict historical and critical methods accepted even by contemporary skeptical scholars, they cannot properly reject the conclusion of the bodily resurrection of Jesus whatever their doubts on other areas of Scripture. Therefore, the Resurrection event is established by the minimal amount of historically validated and accepted facts.[20]

A third approach has already been presented in this chapter. It uses both the independently verified Gospels and the new evidence from the Shroud for the resurrection of Jesus.

It is not the purpose of this chapter to present the pre-

143

vious historical arguments in any detail; the interested reader can pursue them elsewhere. The second argument, in particular, differs from the approach in this chapter in that all of the arguments contained in the former apologetic are built on demonstrated historical facts accepted almost unanimously even by more radical critics who reject the reliability of the New Testament. The present approach, however, uses the trustworthiness of the Gospels and any possible scientific corroboration from the Shroud.

A MIRACLE?

If the image of the Shroud of Turin is a scorch, what significance might it have? Mueller, a critic of the Shroud, surprisingly concludes:

> The celebrated interpretation that the shroud image is a scorch formed by a burst of radiation emitted by the corpse obviously requires nothing less than a miracle. Not only would the source of radiation be unprecedented, but the radiation emanating vertically from every element of the body surface would somehow have . . . properties totally unknown to science.[21]

He makes a similar point in a reference to our earlier work on this subject: "Stevenson and Habermas in their recent book [*Verdict*] regard the radiation-scorch as proved. . . . They fully realize that it clearly implies supernatural intervention."[22]

Beside the fact that we do not believe either the "burst" form of this thesis or that the scorch theory has been proven (but only that a form of it is possible), Mueller has clearly recognized the possibly miraculous nature of the Shroud image, although he does not believe it is a likely option: "The point is that there are really only two possibilities for the origin of the shroud: either it was made by an artist or it is a miraculous reproduction of the image of Jesus Christ."[23]

We have already seen both that scientists have found artistry to be a highly unlikely hypothesis and that some scholars have accepted the scorch theory. However, not all would agree that a scorch would indicate a miracle. In some current philosophical discussions, an argument for a resurrection is not necessarily an argument for a miracle. To determine if a miracle has actually occurred, we need criteria beyond the event itself. Regardless of whether the Shroud is the actual burial garment of Jesus, we do have such criteria for recognizing a miracle in the historical case for Jesus' resurrection.

Reproducing the evidence for this last point would take us far beyond the scope of this chapter. So what we will do here is outline only the conclusions of two sets of arguments for the identification of Jesus' resurrection as a miracle caused by God.[24]

A Philosophical Case

It may be asserted with good reason that we live in a theistic universe. I [Habermas] refer to theism here in a specific way: it entails a universe where God exists and in which He is involved to some extent with man in the process of history. God reveals Himself to human beings in various ways, and they are to respond through prayer and worship. The meaningfulness of history is also shown by moral and other values present in this existence as well as in life after death. In such a universe, we therefore have an important indication of the identity of the power that caused Jesus' resurrection. In other words, the truthfulness of theistic argumentation, including many of the attributes of God and the orderliness of the universe, best identifies the Resurrection as an orderly event brought about by God's power, consistent with His attributes, in order to validate Jesus' truth-claims. Therefore, proceeding from true theistic arguments, God's attributes, and the order and purpose in the universe, the historical resurrection of Jesus should be seen as an orderly theistic event which verifies His theistic message. This evidence agrees with Jesus' theistic worldview much more than with the notion that the Resurrection had some unknown natural cause.

145

A Theological Case

The second argument combines the claims of Jesus with His literal resurrection as further verification for His teachings and worldview. Jesus' claims to be deity, God's chosen messenger, and His agent of personal salvation; Jesus' views on His corroborating miracles; and His having predicted His own resurrection all point to His theistic worldview.[25] The Resurrection was a planned and orderly historical occurrence, and Jesus was in the best position to interpret it. Jesus taught that the Resurrection validated His message and claims.[26] And the only time that a resurrection is known to have happened,[27] it occurred to the only person who made these extraordinary claims concerning Himself and God. The combination of this unique historical event with the unique message of Jesus further verifies His theistic worldview.

In other words, if just anyone had been raised from the dead, the cause might be hard to ascertain. But since it was Jesus who was raised, we must take very seriously His claims to be deity and God's special messenger and agent of personal salvation, as well as His belief that His miracles and bodily resurrection validated His claims. Since these unique claims were coupled with the unique Resurrection event, we judge that Jesus' theistic worldview was validated.

CONCLUSION

We have seen that prior to the 1988 carbon dating, numerous scholars involved in investigations of the Shroud had indicated their belief that it was Jesus' actual burial garment. Furthermore, most of a small sample of scientists who responded to the question favored the scorch theory as the cause of the Shroud image. A number of scientists and scholars have also stated that the Shroud image is either consistent with the resurrection of Jesus or evidence for it.

Next we pointed out some evidence on the Shroud for the Resurrection. The Gospels provide the very possible identification of the man of the Shroud as Jesus and record His

146

literal Resurrection. The Shroud of Turin adds some new, empirical, and repeatable evidence for the Resurrection as the best explanation for such data as the strange bodily disappearance, the absence of decomposition, the lack of unwrapping, and the quasi-photographic image caused by a probable scorch from the dead body. We must look not only to the mere strangeness of these conditions but beyond it to ascertain a cause. The improbability of alternative theses and the suggestive new information reveal some evidence for Jesus' resurrection.

More important and independent of the Shroud, we also presented summarized arguments for both the historicity of the Resurrection and for the miraculous nature of this event as an act of God which provides further verification of Jesus' theistic claims. The Shroud may or may not provide additional evidence for Jesus' resurrection, but the event itself and the claims of Jesus' theistic worldview are validated completely apart from it.

Jesus' call to salvation in the Kingdom of God was His central teaching, as is recognized by virtually all scholars today. His chief message was a challenge concerning a personal decision with one's eternal destiny hanging in the balance.[28] According to Jesus' primary message, all people are sinners by their very nature, the remedy for which is repentance (Luke 13:3, 5) and forgiveness of sins (Luke 24:47). Faith in Jesus and His payment for sin through His death (1 Cor. 15:1–4) allow one to gain entrance into the Kingdom of God and receive eternal life (Mark 1:15; John 3:15–16). The Christian's response to Jesus should be total surrender (Luke 14:25–35).[29]

Since this was Jesus' central message, it is the portion of Jesus' claims and theistic worldview which would most be validated by the Resurrection and other evidences from His life. To ignore this message is to ignore the only entrance to eternal life. Faith is not to be placed in the Shroud but in Jesus, who died for the sins of humankind and was raised by the power of God.

10

QUESTIONS PEOPLE ASK

Since early 1977, when I [Stevenson] was on the faculty of the United States Air Force Academy and became involved with STURP, I've lectured on the Shroud from coast to coast and in Canada and Europe. During that time I've noted that even after a detailed discussion, many questions remain in the minds of the curious, critics, and amateur sindonologists. These questions range from detailed technical issues, normally raised by those with technical backgrounds, to scriptural concerns, normally voiced by scholarly evangelicals or other devout Christians.

Some of the most interesting questions have come from children who have demonstrated an unusual ability to approach the subject of the Shroud without a great deal of emotion. Adults, on the other hand, are often so involved in their own particular points of view that they haven't heard the answer in the lecture.

While neither Habermas nor I is necessarily an expert in all the varied areas, we have spent untold hours of research on their pertinence to the Shroud. Furthermore, having interviewed experts who could resolve the major nagging questions in each area, we feel qualified to address them more than adequately. As only one example of how seriously we took this question of expertise, I have spent hours with two orthodox rabbis to garner an understanding of Jewish death and burial customs. One rabbi was messianic and believed that Jesus was the Messiah while the other was strictly orthodox. I also sent copies of *Verdict* to Jewish archaeological experts and scriptural scholars from as far away as Israel.

From our combined years of Shroud work, Habermas and I have compiled the twenty-nine most frequently asked questions and a few unusual or special interest questions to answer in this chapter.

Q *Doesn't the Shroud conflict with Scripture?*
a) John 20:5–7 mentions linens and at the very least implies there were a minimum of two cloths. Many have suggested that the linens were "strips," however the Shroud is merely one piece of cloth.

b) In 1 Corinthians 11:14, the Apostle Paul declares that long hair is a disgrace to men, yet the man of the Shroud apparently has shoulder-length hair.

c) The prophet Isaiah declared that the Messiah would have "no form or comeliness . . . no beauty that we should desire Him" (Isaiah 53:2). Yet most find the man of the Shroud to be majestic even in death.

d) Another Messianic reference found in Isaiah declares that "his visage was so marred more than any man" (Isaiah 52:14). Why then is the face on the Shroud so distinct?

e) Thomas the doubter is said to have declared that the nails were in the hands (John 20:25–27), yet these marks seem to be in the wrists.

f) Also, John's eyewitness account of the empty tomb on Sunday contains no mention of an image (John 20:1–8).

A All of the other scriptural issues were dealt with heavily in *Verdict*. The answers to these apparent discrepancies are as follows:

First, the Gospels use the following words to describe the Shroud: *Sindon*—burial sheet, winding sheet, shroud; *sudarion*—sweat cloth, face cloth, handkerchief; *othonia*—

149

linens. One way for the synoptic Gospels (Matthew, Mark, and Luke) to be in harmony with John is if a burial method like the one depicted on the Shroud was used. John mentions a cloth that was described as "around his head" and about the face of Lazarus (John 20:7; 11:44). The word is *sudarion,* used in burial to bind the jaw against the effects of rigor mortis. There is evidence on the Shroud that a *sudarion* was used, though the whereabouts of any such cloth has long been unknown. The Shroud is a pure linen garment with some evidence that the head, hands, and feet were bound, most likely with other "linens." The synoptics describe a linen sheet—a single cloth. Most likely, the sheet was more significant to the synoptic writers than other funerary cloths. Since the Jewish burial custom allowed the use of cloths to bind the hands and feet as well as the jaw, the total picture matches Jewish burial customs exactly and explains clearly why the synoptics only mention a *sindon* and John mentions *othonia.*

Second, John's use of *othonia* has led to a widely held belief that Jesus was wrapped like an Egyptian mummy. But such a procedure doesn't conform to what is known of first-century normal Jewish burial ritual. Nor does it match what was previously mentioned in the Word, to wit, that Joseph of Arimathea had purchased a winding sheet and wrapped Jesus in it (Mark 15:46). Even John used the word *edesan,* which is translated *wound* in the KJV but literally means "enfolded." Enfolded would also match the burial custom. Being wrapped with strips of cloth would not. In other words, *othonia* in John should be understood to mean that Jesus' dead body was enveloped from head to feet in one burial cloth, not wrapped like a mummy with numerous strips of cloth.

Third, though the question of long hair seems overly naive, it is frequently asked. Our concept of what Paul meant by "long hair" is usually affected by our own views of what constitutes long hair. While Paul was speaking of effeminate men who wore their hair in styles peculiar to women,

Paul himself would probably have worn shoulder-length hair in keeping with the hairstyle of the other orthodox Jews of his day.[1] As a matter of fact, the traditional style for an orthodox Jewish man of two thousand years ago is much the same for him today: a ponytail of hair and sidelocks—precisely what we see on the Shroud.

Fourth, Scriptures frequently cited in relationship to this question are the "suffering servant" messianic prophecies. In fact, the remainder of Isaiah 53 details much of the passion that would lead to that image that had "no beauty." When all of the passages in the Isaiah messianic chapters are reviewed, we read:

> I gave My back to those who struck Me,
> And My cheeks to those who plucked out the beard;
> I did not hide My face from shame and spitting. (Isaiah 50:6)

Some have interpreted these words to mean that the Messiah was homely, but certainly that is a subjective interpretation at best. Those who feel that the man of the Shroud is too handsome to fulfill this Scripture may never have seen a good color photograph like the cover photo on this book showing the places that show heavy blood flow, severe bruises and abrasions, or missing segments of beard. More importantly, they overlook the obvious attractiveness of a Savior who could win a total stranger's confidence almost immediately. "Come follow Me" seems terribly wanting unless backed by something in the man Himself, not to mention the fact that children were drawn consistently to Him.

Fifth, the Gospels record that Jesus was struck with reeds and fists and that His accusers spat upon Him. The reeds mentioned here were apparently long, slender sticks or rods. As we discussed in Chapter 7, there is clear medical evidence that just such a weapon was used. Isaiah also prophesied that His beard would be plucked. All of these are clearly visible on the image of the crucified man revealed on the Shroud. Those who say this victim was not marred enough to be Jesus should perhaps review the data we gave in Chapter 7.

Sixth, almost all drawings of the Crucifixion depict the nails in the palms of the hands rather than in the wrists. However, the only place that could support the weight of a hanging body is the wrist. The confusion among artists and many Bible exegetes has been most likely caused by the following two passages of Scripture: "They pierced My hands and My feet" (Psalm 22:16), and "Behold My hands and My feet" (Luke 24:39). The Hebrew word for "hands" is *yad* and the Greek word for "hand" is *cheir*. In each case these words do not just refer to the palms, as we might too quickly suppose, but to everything from the fingertips to the armpits. The concept of the nails being in the palms of the hands therefore is based on tradition rather than medical, historical, or scriptural fact. Finally, the only two crucifixion victims' remains that have ever been unearthed and subsequently researched in detail have shown evidence of being nailed through the wrists, not the palms of the hands.

Seventh, the issue of the image was touched on briefly in the first question we addressed, but to clarify it from the scriptural standpoint, we need to understand that the Bible is primarily a Jewish book, written for the most part by Jews to other Jews. With this in mind, it is not hard to imagine that the first-century Jewish believer had just as much difficulty with accepting an image as does any current evangelical Christian. Therefore, it is easy to see why the New Testament writers would not mention an image in relationship to Jesus. After all, the most vitriolic responses have come over this very issue of imagery, and they've come from Christians.

 Couldn't the image be of someone other than Jesus?

152

The identity of the man of the Shroud has always been a major issue. In *Verdict*, our estimate of the probability of it being anyone other than Jesus was very low. The lowest estimate next to ours was 1 in 225 billion.[2]

 Couldn't the Shroud be a satanic deception?

Nearly six pages of *Verdict* deals with satanic deception. If there was an overwhelming response of image worship to the knowledge of the Shroud, this would be a very serious possibility. The fact of the matter is that in my [Stevenson's] experience, those who do respond to the Shroud story respond to the man in the Shroud and not to the Shroud itself. In over a decade of lecturing on the Shroud, I have found no episodes of image worship or idolatry. On the other hand, countless numbers have written to me to proclaim that they have come to a saving knowledge of the Lord Jesus through the story of the Shroud. Perhaps the true issue is whether Satan would allow many to base their faith in the Shroud and then suddenly pull the rug out from under them by having it declared a fake. But from the beginning, religious leaders have usually been the ones to declare the Shroud a fake, while nonbelievers captivated by a sense of spiritual, scientific, or historical curiosity have come to study and stayed to pray. Besides, why would Satan allow for any reason the depiction of the emblem of his ultimate defeat—the death, burial, and resurrection of Jesus Christ?

What are the physical characteristics of the man of the Shroud?

153

The best estimates of the dimensions of the man are approximately 5 ft. 10½ in. and 175 pounds. They are approximate because we must allow a slight margin for error due to the distortion of various forms. The best studies done indicate that a man of those proportions will fit the image with a minimum of problems.[3]

Q *Didn't someone claim to have painted the image on the Shroud?*

A First, the claim of the image being painted is secondhand, has never been substantiated, and was entered into the debate by a hostile source with prejudice. The medieval Bishop d'Arcis, offended by a challenge to his authority, ordered an April 1389 exhibition of the Shroud in Lirey, France, stopped. When his order was successfully challenged, he apparently issued a memorandum to Pope Clement VII, charging that the Shroud's image "had been cunningly painted, the truth being attested by the artist who had painted it. . . ." But we have no evidence that d'Arcis' claims were ever substantiated. In fact, we know the pope was unimpressed since he permitted the exhibition to continue and ordered the bishop, under penalty of excommunication, to keep silent on the subject of the Shroud.[4]

Second, the claim that the Shroud was created by human hands flies in the face of all available scientific evidence.

Third, no one has ever been able to duplicate the image, not in the day of the claim nor since. The only human attempts, even those using sophisticated modern methods, are abysmal by comparison to the image, and early attempts are rudimentary and horribly inaccurate.

The final blow to this claim is that the word used in the d'Arcis memorandum quoted to substantiate it could equally be translated *copied,* not *painted.*[5] There were many copies of the image but no duplicates. Recently a report from France surfaced that claimed to have identified the alleged artist as Ramon Vidal; however, there is still no supporting evidence whatsoever for such a claim.

Finally, Luigi Fossati, sindonologist and professor at the Salesian Institute in Turin, Italy, did a masterful job of putting the d'Arcis memorandum in proper perspective. According to Fossati, "the [d'Arcis] document (memorandum itself) seemed to be only a rough draft never put in final form to be sent to the Pope. Even Chevalier [an eminent French medieval scholar who dismissed the Shroud's authenticity on the basis of this memorandum in the early 1900s] defines it as a pro-memoria. Eschback remarks 'with neither date nor signature, it is a rough draft of such faulty style that one could not attribute it to an episcopal pen.'" Furthermore, Fossati stated, "These documents (including Papal letters and Bulls on the Shroud), absolutely do not prove what Chevalier maintained (that the Shroud was a painting) . . . in fact they contradict each other." Moreover, "The fundamental thought behind the Bull of January 6 [which allegedly condemned the Shroud] was not so much concerned with the authenticity of the Shroud as it was with the mode of exposition. . . . The Bull affirmed, 'the Shroud with the imprint of our Lord Jesus Christ is there preserved with veneration (not allowed for objects made by man).'" Geoffrey II de Charny (who bypassed d'Arcis, bishop of the diocese where Lirey was located, to help his mother get permission from papal authorities to exhibit the Shroud) entrusted the Shroud to the Church "to increase the devotion of the people. Even Bishop Henry de Poiters (who, according to d'Arcis, supposedly uncovered the fraud), "Adds his Laudamus, ratificamus, approbamus (we praise, ratify, and approve)" to the Shroud's exposition. To add insult to injury, Fossati even pointed out that "The proprietor, the canons and the judges themselves . . . always refer to the cloth as . . . (The Holy Shroud of Our Lord Jesus Christ: the most precious object of joy; most holy and venerable Shroud), and they set it above every other relic." Fossati went so far as to note that the de Charny's would have had a minimum of four months and a maximum of one year (between A.D 1354 and 1355) to formulate a plan, search for the cloth, conceive the image, find a painter, and generate the notoriety described in d'Arcis' memorandum as "from the whole world." Not only that but their entire plot would have had to be investigated and uncovered during the same time period. This would have been an incredible feat for anyone.[6]

Many authors have pointed out that Bishop d'Arcis had ample reason to be upset over an exhibition so close to him which would attract so many pilgrims. "It was a cause of annoyance to Bishop d'Arcis," writes Ian Wilson, "that Geoffrey II de Charny had bypassed him and obtained permission for the exposition from Cardinal de Thury, the papal Legate [especially in] a time notorious for abuses related to relics . . ."[7]

However, d'Arcis' memorandum did not stop the exhibition, as one might imagine it would if, indeed, fraud had been demonstrated. As Fossati concludes, "The pope's letter threatened the Bishop with Excommunication if he did not allow exposition of the Linen."[8]

Q *Aren't there many other shrouds?*

A During the Middle Ages there were as many as forty so-called true shrouds, almost all of which can easily be proven to be shoddy copies of the Shroud of Turin. Sometimes the artist even copied the fire and water damage markings. Most, if not all, of these forgeries were destroyed or lost over the intervening years, yet the many paintings of them that still exist discredit any contention for them being the true burial garment of Jesus.

For the most part, the paintings look like primitive and crude renditions of the Shroud image, depicting none of the anatomical accuracy of the image on the Shroud.

 What testing remains to be done?

 The only testing to be done is basically more of the same. Given another opportunity to test the Shroud firsthand as STURP did in 1978, I [Stevenson] am convinced that most of the researchers would opt for using the same nondestructive procedures we used then but for longer time periods. Specifically, there was a need to do more detailed microscopic studies at various levels of magnification; infrared work, which was very promising, was significantly limited by time overruns and would be an excellent choice for further study; more blood analysis could be helpful, as would additional chemical studies, and, of course, an accurate and careful application of carbon-14 dating is a must, at least as long as it satisfies proper scientific protocol and is subject to rigorous peer review. (For additional information regarding testing, see Chapter 3.)

Finally, STURP itself approached Turin for additional testing, and although the proposal was rejected by the authorities, it gives an excellent profile for further study. As of this writing, STURP is still pursuing the matter.

 What was the religious makeup of STURP?

 STURP was composed of people from quite a variety of religious backgrounds. Many were of no particular religious persuasion and claimed to be

157

either atheistic or agnostic. To the best of our knowledge, many others had a faith that they might have been reared in, Catholic or Protestant. Several were Jewish, and one was Mormon. Last, but certainly not least, there were a small number of evangelical Christians who were either "born-again believers" or involved in the Catholic charismatic renewal. In either case these members clearly understood the meaning and importance of the gospel and were determined to remain true to both the scientific facts and their spiritual convictions.

 Were any of the nonbelievers changed after their studies of the Shroud?

 In the years after the STURP project, various articles have appeared in magazines, newspapers, and even the tabloids, all supposedly documenting the stories of STURP members and what the Shroud has meant to each of them. Perhaps the most dramatic statement came from one man who was interviewed by Geraldo Rivera and said, "I began this project with science as my god. I ended it on my knees!"[9] My dear friend Dee German often used to state, "The one thing that could change me from a position of agnosticism to belief in Christ is the Shroud of Turin."[10] Dee accepted Jesus as Savior last year. Jewish members of the team have also been affected dramatically by their involvement. But more will be said about all this in Chapter 11.

 Has the blood on the Shroud been typed yet, and what does it show us?

Sometime after our departure from Turin, it was widely reported that Dr. Baima Bollone had accurately typed the blood on the Shroud as AB.[11] The problem with typing the blood at all is twofold: 1) There is far too little blood material taken from the cloth for most standard methods to be effective, and the amount left on the cloth itself is jealously guarded by the cloth's custodians; 2) the age and condition of the blood matter would also render such typing useless. STURP's blood experts, who had a difficult enough time finding sufficient quantities to demonstrate conclusively that the blood was human, stated at the time of the Bollone announcement that all blood more than three hundred years old will test AB, regardless of what type it originally was. Therefore, even if Dr. Bollone did have enough material to type the blood, the results would be scientifically meaningless.

 What is the Shroud's material like?

 The material on the Shroud is a very heavy well-woven fabric, like burlap in weight, but not as coarse. Some portions of the cloth seem to be drier and closer to eventual decay or dry rot than others, which are still quite supple for the supposed age of the cloth. Areas in closer proximity to the fire damage seem to be in the worst shape.

 Is it true that the human image reveals no navel?

 When this question was first posed to me at a press conference, I nearly doubled over from laughter. Later I learned that to some people the answer is critical because they feel that being born without sin, Christ miraculously would have no navel. Personally I [Stevenson] find that patently foolish. The Scripture de-

159

clared that He would be born of a woman. To be sustained in His mother's womb would require a normal umbilical cord, which would result in a normal navel. At any rate, the photos of that area of the image are not sufficiently detailed to answer this question one way or the other.

 Did anyone consider Kirlian photography as a cause of the image formation process?

 Kirlian photography is the ability to photograph an aura, which may be caused by the release of energy from an object. This aura may be related to moisture coming from that object. Regardless of the aura's cause, however, Kirlian photography has been rejected as a causal factor in the case of the Shroud image. Kirlian still qualifies as a "fuzzy studies" type of field, and its moisture-based type of reaction doesn't seem at all to mesh with the known characteristics of the Shroud. However, others are still investigating this field. (For a detailed discussion, see Chapter 8.)

 Isn't the Shroud image similar to the post-bomb images on walls around Hiroshima and Nagasaki?

 The images caused by radiation effects during a nuclear burst are all unquestionably shadows. They do not contain the clear-cut characteristics of a photographic negative. Therefore, there is no real similarity between them and the image on the Shroud. This question was originally raised because of the so-called flash-photolysis theory of image formation, which has been discounted as an explanation for the Shroud's image.[12]

If the image really occurred at the moment of Jesus' resurrection, will we ever know what about the Resurrection caused it?

Assuming that the Shroud image was created at the moment of resurrection does not in any way rule out the search for an image-formation process. While it is true that we do not have a scientific explanation for the Resurrection recorded in the Bible, some of the descriptions of what occurred did seem to suggest a process that might have matched the known Shroud characteristics. On the other hand, a naturalistic explanation of the image would also not rule out the evidence of resurrection that is present yet not dependent on the image itself. (See Chapters 8, 11.)

How is the Shroud displayed now?

For the moment, the Shroud has been returned to its marble reliquary in the chapel at St. John's in Turin. It cannot be seen, for it is locked behind several layers of protection, including a red silk bag, a silver box, iron and wooden chests, and the glass and bars of the chapel's altar.

Will the Shroud be brought out again, or must we wait another fifty years?

No one knows for certain, and the custodians of the cloth show no urgent concern to make decisions about such expositions. In the past they have been motivated by special events such as the king of Italy's wedding, but never by public interest.

Since preservation seems to be the key factor here, can't the Shroud be put on permanent display without any danger of damage to it?

 Technically, the answer is an unqualified yes. The equipment and procedures for such a display have been known and practiced for years. The use of a bulletproof casing with an inert gas and low-level lighting would ensure safe public viewing for ages. Ostensibly the reason given for not doing this is money, although an occasional comment is also made that the scientists either don't agree on method or cannot ensure the Shroud's safety. To my [Stevenson's] knowledge, at least one philanthropist who has pumped thousands of dollars into Turin has offered to pay to house the cloth, but the Shroud's guardians have not responded to his request.

Personal experience has shaped my opinion that many of those most able to effect changes in the status of the cloth move at best at a snail's pace and even then without much apparent influence from those of us on the outside. The Shroud has almost become a personal treasure to a handful of people who seem to all but control its destiny.

 Will the Shroud ever come to America?

 Without some incredible change in the people responsible for its custody, the chances of this occurring are virtually nonexistent. The Shroud has hardly been out of Turin in over four hundred years, not even to Rome. Surely if the Vatican cannot move the Shroud, except in cases of dire emergency, America would be hard put even to try.

Q *If the Shroud covered a human body, why isn't there any distortion in the image?*

A First of all, there is slight distortion in the image on the Shroud. Perhaps the best discussion of this can be found in the excellent article by William Ercoline and associates in *IEEE*.[13] Ercoline discusses the various forms of distortion, including a slight broadening of the hips, elongation of the arms and fingers, and displacement of the hair. He concludes that all the forms of distortion can be attributed to the drape of the cloth in conjunction with a projection-type image-formation process. The reason we don't see the severe distortion that would be found if one wiped one's pigment-stained face with a cloth is the way the image-formation process apparently projected from the body to the cloth. In other words, the Shroud was not formed by a typical contact mechanism, which would have caused such distortion.

Q *How did the Air Force and NASA get involved with the study of a Christian relic?*

A Neither organization was involved. Members of the 1978 research team who were employed by the Air Force and NASA participated in the research on their own time and largely at their own expense. In fact, for at least some of us, our involvement with the project proved to be a deciding factor in our careers. While at the peak of my [Stevenson's] career in the Air Force— faculty professor at the Air Force Academy, just invited to participate in the Ph.D. program which would assure me of tenure, nominated as Outstanding Junior Officer of the Year, and selected as one of the Ten Outstanding Young Men of America—the Air Force suddenly gave me a bizarre "op-

163

portunity" to drop my involvement with STURP so as to improve my career. This choice was rooted in their world-view, which was secular humanism. Several of my superiors verbally described my involvement in STURP as a frivolous waste of time, even though my work with STURP occurred on my own time. So rather than bow to the pressure to leave STURP, I chose to drop my involvement with the Air Force instead.

 Who paid for STURP's research, and how much did it cost?

 The scientists themselves paid for most of this effort. Many of them came to view the Shroud almost as an avocation. Someone canvassed team members years ago and came up with an average expenditure of $10,000–$15,000 per person. Funds were raised by lectures at churches, civic groups, schools, and other public forums. Also, Mr. Harry John of the De Rance Foundation was singularly generous to STURP. He personally funded the trip to Turin in 1977 to propose the research, and he played a major part in funding the expedition itself. Finally, much of the technical equipment was either loaned or donated to STURP by the respective manufacturers. An accurate total accounting would be difficult to calculate at best. Such an estimate would have to include untold voluntary hours as well as donated equipment worth hundreds of thousands of dollars. However, the amount actually spent by STURP from the inception through 1979 was $142,081.61.[14]

 What do you think about the coins on the image's eyes and the box on its forehead?

Among the Shroud's finer nuances, probably more hackles have been raised over these two items than any other nuances. First of all, there is definitely something in both locations, not merely anomalies in the weave pattern of the cloth as some Shroud opponents and even team members have suggested. In the photographs of the Shroud that have been examined for such items, conditions that could change the research outcome all too often were ignored—by those who believed the coins were present and by those who did not. Such conditions as the contrast of the film, the lighting, the sophistication of the camera, and whether the Shroud was loose or stretched taut on a board all have an impact on what is seen or not seen in a standard photograph. Fortunately, we are not limited to standard photographs alone. All of the three-dimensional images that I [Stevenson] have examined give evidence of something round and solid on the eyes as well as something boxy and solid on the forehead. Despite arguments from experts about why coins and/or phylacteries would or wouldn't be present on the body of a crucified Jew of the first century, the fact remains that something is there, and the most logical explanation still suggests that they are coins and a phylactery.[15]

If the Shroud is really two thousand years old, how did it survive without rotting away?

To begin with, in its known history the Shroud has been protected to a fault. Locked away for hundreds of years at a time in various chests, reliquaries, and containers, it has only on rare occasions seen the light of day. In its speculative history, it would appear to have been almost hermetically sealed in a stone wall for nearly five hundred years. There are thousands of ancient

165

linens in various museums throughout the world. Linen is durable; one of the team members had a piece that had been handed down in his family for over three hundred years. Some discussion also occurred over retting linen in saponaria or soap weed. While none was detected on the Shroud itself (the evidence could have been washed or abraded away over the years), this process or one similar to it was most likely done at the time of manufacture. The result would be the extermination of the types of mites most responsible for the weakening of cloth.

 How sure are you that the Shroud can't be faked?

 Though everyone is entitled to his own opinion, I [Stevenson] believe that the possibility of fakery is so small that, once again, I am willing to stake my reputation on it. The best attempts to reproduce a shroud like this one, even using modern techniques and equipment, have failed miserably. Despite the fact that they now understand the chemical makeup of the image, some of the world's top scientists have failed in their efforts to reproduce this cloth. Finally, those who still claim to have duplicated this image can be rebutted; they have not even come close.

 What is the weakest link in the argument for authenticity?

 When *Verdict* was first published, I would have said the lack of an unbroken historical record. However, after Wilson's history has withstood the onslaught of peer review and criticism, I believe that the history is a little less shaky. As a Christian, the weakest link is the very sketchy references in the Bible, and as an engineer, the lack of a clearly definable formation process. Beyond those three concerns, the total Shroud picture has tremendous evidence for authenticity (see Chapters 2—5).

On the other hand, Habermas is not bothered by the lack of either biblical references or a known image-formation mechanism. For him, the chief issue remains the question of the Shroud's past, including the results of the 1988 C-14 tests.

 Do you really believe the image was produced at the moment of resurrection, and if so, why?

On the question of the Resurrection and the Shroud, there seems to be no neutral ground, except for those who still believe that the image is a mystery. Generally speaking, people either believe or don't believe in the Shroud's authenticity. I [Stevenson] still believe that the single most logical explanation for the Shroud image is the Resurrection.[16]

To my mind, the Resurrection is the only thing that could explain satisfactorily all that we know about the Shroud. If the most logical explanation for the image is some unusual form of "scorch," energy, or "advanced decomposition of the linen"—and if the most logical identity of the man is Jesus of Nazareth—and if the most logical conclusion of science is that this is indeed a burial garment of a crucifixion victim, then the only sensible explanation is the Resurrection.

Of course, anyone can avoid the issue by labeling the image a mystery. But it's more reasonable to investigate the matter seriously in order to make an intelligent and informed decision based on the facts.

167

Q *But why do you still believe the "scorch" theory when there are admittedly problems with it and not all the scientists believe it? Doesn't that imply blind faith?*

A Given the known characteristics of the Shroud, the only reasonable explanation for its image is a "scorch" or an energy-formation process of some type. The problem is that dead bodies do not normally provide the energy necessary to scorch cloth. As STURP concluded, "There is no technologically feasible explanation."[17] Also, normal scorches fluoresce and the Shroud image does not. Nothing in the known laws of this universe can explain how a dead body would do such an unusual thing to a cloth. In addition, as far as we know, this kind of image formation has only happened once in the history of humankind. While some of the scientists might declare that this is simply an as yet unknown phenomenon, to many, if not most, it spells "miracle." Since miracles are outside the domain of scientific study, some immediately shout "Foul" and attempt to discredit such a possibility.

To make matters worse, the most brilliant scientific minds have not been able to reproduce the effect of the image with any methods they've tried to date. (The German-Pellicori and Oswald Scheuermann efforts have been the best attempts, though they still fall short.)

Though much of scientific theory is based on assumptions and limited knowledge, it seems that something of the Shroud's importance requires "proof" in the mind of the average scientist. For example, for years it was assumed that no one would ever fly faster than the speed of sound. Though "experts" constantly warned of the dangers, many brave men with vision died in the attempt. Now we know and understand the sound barrier and its effects; then everyone knew it was there, but no one understood it. For me the Shroud is like that. The most likely explanation may not fit our understanding because of the known laws of physics or chemistry, but the image exists nonetheless. Blind faith is a leap in the dark toward something totally unknown; belief in the "scorch" theory is simply leaning in the most likely direction based on the facts as we know them.

Q *Why would God, who abhors idolatry and knows the natural human tendency to improper worship, leave an image of Jesus behind? Doesn't that violate His own Word, especially the second of the Ten Commandments?*

A As Christians we feel this is perhaps the single most important question to answer. On the surface, interest in the Shroud does seem to be diametrically opposed to the Word of God. Given the sinful nature of humanity, it doesn't seem right that God would violate His own commandment. The major problem with that line of reasoning is that it fails to allow for the sovereignty of God. The Scripture statement that His ways are not our ways and His thoughts not our thoughts should be a warning against our too-swift condemnation. After all, the major criticism of Jesus from the religious leaders of His day was that He violated the Law.

A detailed study of Scripture, however, may offer a more satisfactory answer. Though the Bible is silent concerning the image of the Shroud, there are two Scriptures that deserve consideration here:

1. John 20:5–9:

And he, stooping down and looking in, saw the linen clothes lying there; yet he did not go in. Then Simon Peter came, following him, and went into the tomb; and he saw the linen cloths lying there, and the handkerchief that had been around His head, not lying with the linen cloths, but folded together in a place by itself. Then the other disciple, who came to the tomb first went in also; and he saw and believed. For as yet they did not know the Scripture, that He must rise again from the dead. (KJV)

This verse has led to a myriad of comments on the evidence for the Resurrection. Many scholars believe that the meaning of the Greek is so strong that John must have seen something in the tomb itself that convinced him that Jesus rose from the dead. By and large they have long adhered to the theory that there was some sort of empty mummy casing that could only have been vacated by a miracle. But there is no internal evidence to support that. Furthermore, our studies indicate that Jesus was not mummified, nor was that a Jewish tradition. It is our contention that seeing the image we now see on the Shroud would explain John's sudden acceptance of the Resurrection.

At any rate, the central point of Luke 24:12 is that there was an actual shroud in Jesus' tomb, and it might be the same as the one we have come to know as the Shroud of Turin. So it is hard to say, *before* viewing the relevant data, that God would not allow such an object to exist as a silent witness to Jesus' death, burial, and resurrection. Can we know with certainty that God would not permit this?

2. Isaiah 52:13–15:

Behold, my servant shall deal prudently
he shall be exalted and extolled, and be very high.
As many were astonished at thee;
his visage was so marred more than any man,
and his form more than the sons of men:
So shall he sprinkle many nations;
the kings shall shut their mouths at him:
for that which had not been told them shall they see;
and that which they had not heard shall they consider. (KJV)

Though this reference to the Messiah can have many meanings, a few things should be pointed out. It is obviously a referral to something after the time of Christ, for His passion was seen only by a local monarch and not "kings" or

170

"many nations." Additionally, the Apostle Paul chided King Festus, "The king . . . knows these things; for . . . this thing was not done in a corner" (Acts 26:26), indicating that Jesus' passion was a well-known event. If the marred visage of the Savior was to startle those who had not "heard" or "considered," it had to be later than the time of Paul. Therefore, if Jesus is not coming again to be crucified, how can this Scripture be fulfilled at any future time? If, on the other hand, there is visible evidence that can be seen and discussed, evidence that would startle and yet reveal His "marred" visage and form, evidence that would leave many astonished and yet exalt and extol our Messiah—that evidence would appear to have to be very much like the Shroud of Turin. Although some biblical scholars argue that people will see Jesus' marred form at His Second Coming, it seems plausible that He will *not* return in a form that displays all the brutality of torture and crucifixion He endured. After all, in His resurrected and transformed body, Jesus called on doubting Thomas to verify His resurrection by checking out His pierced hands and feet, not by investigating any other wounds He incurred (John 20:24–27). Perhaps this was because Jesus' other wounds were no longer visible. At any rate, it is at least possible that the Shroud was left behind as a continuous witness to the brutality Jesus suffered for the sins of the world. In this sense, it may be a fulfillment of the prophecy given in Isaiah 52:13–15.

Q *What is your gut feeling about the Shroud?*

 A On the Shroud question, you must finally make a decision for yourself—a decision based on the facts as you see and understand them. My [Stevenson's] gut conviction and scientific conclusion is that the Shroud of Turin is indeed the burial garment of the Lord

Jesus Christ. Furthermore, I'm convinced that it offers corroborating evidence for His resurrection. When friends ask your opinion on people, places, or things that you know or have experienced, they count on your judgment, honesty, and expertise for an accurate response.

When people ask me about the Shroud, I try always to answer from my heart, keeping in mind my responsibility to be fair and evenhanded. I have staked my reputation on how I feel about the Shroud. Someone's eternal destiny might be at stake. How do I know if they are much like doubting Thomas who only lack that one piece of evidence to decide their eternity?

Certainly this is the ultimate question for the study of the Shroud: What is the impact of this cloth on the lives of those who study it? In my experience, this enigmatic cloth has led many to a personal relationship with the living God through faith in Jesus Christ. Is it not interesting that those who are first drawn to the Shroud itself, as they study it further, are invariably led to the One who was probably buried in it?

11

SPEAKING OUT ON THE SHROUD

Since "Christian-bashing" has become somewhat of a national pastime in recent years, it should come as no surprise that Shroud proponents have received their share of hostility. From the very outset of modern sindonology, anyone brave enough to speak out in favor of authenticity has been subject to fierce attack. Yves Delage, a professed agnostic, was booed from the stage where he presented the first scientific defense of the Shroud, though he made it abundantly clear that his findings were based solely on science. Likewise, members of STURP have often been held up to ridicule in the media, not only if they openly advocated authenticity, but also if their scientific data could be interpreted as favorable. The media often challenged the scientific findings on the grounds of the religious orientations of the scientists. In spite of media claims, however, many of the scientists had no particular religious convictions; in fact, out of some forty or more, only six professed a personal faith in Jesus Christ.[1] This small ratio of believers would hardly warrant the often echoed accusation that we were a group of fanatics. In actuality, as the attacks from both the media and their scientific peers escalated and "proof" for the image-formation process became more elusive, some of the researchers retreated behind noncommittal scientific language while others refused to comment about any of their convictions based on the data.

For these reasons, we urge you to read the comments of the scientists with an open mind. The opinions expressed in this chapter do not represent the consensus of a sectarian group but rather the thoughts of various individuals who have touched, studied, and lived with the Shroud in a unique way. Though many of those discussed in the following pages do not necessarily agree with all of our personal opinions regarding the Shroud issues, they each have important perspectives to add to sindonology.

It is my [Stevenson's] personal contention that much of the fuzziness of the Shroud story can be directly attributed to the inability of STURP *(though not their own fault necessarily)* to retain the scientific credibility they well deserved without compromising the facts they alone fully understood. Hampered as they were by a self-imposed agreement of secrecy, I doubt if any scientific team could have managed such a task, especially given the hostile climate of the media attacks on Christianity. Obviously history has proven, given this particular subject matter, that it is practically impossible to separate the Shroud scientific studies from Christianity. Most, if not all, sindonologists readily admit that if this cloth did not cover the dead body of Jesus of Nazareth, it was created by someone very deliberately to give the impression that it did. Given that starting point, it is amazing how many people begin to back-peddle when the evidence refutes a human hand.

The focus of this chapter will be to hear from the scientists themselves, STURP members, and others. You will read personal testimonies concerning the numerous tests run, plus, in their own words, statements concerning what the Shroud means to some of the team members now that their efforts have been subjected to the rigorous scrutiny of their peers. Hopefully, the historical view of events that occurred will also be seen in the best light so that STURP and its members will finally be understood by the general public. Also, our intention is to reflect the variety of opinions that surface over the same basic data.

John D. German

Perhaps one of the most exciting personal stories for me is the story of John D. German. Dee, as he is known to friends, was in the original carpool with myself, Dr. Jackson, and Dr. Jumper, and he considered himself a religious agnostic. "I was the group's resident agnostic, and I was the group's *vocal* resident agnostic. I felt it very important that the world knew that we weren't a bunch of Christians going over there to prove this was the body of Christ. And, indeed we weren't . . . this was good objective science work . . . this wasn't trying to prove anything religiously. . . ." Though his wife Patty had been a believer for years, and as a couple they were intimately involved in the excellent program, Marriage Encounter, Dee remained agnostic. Working with Sam Pellicori, Dee developed a natural explanation for the Shroud's three-dimensional image.

> My own belief is that if you put a fresh brand new linen on a body that laid in a cave, the body gave off moisture. The cave may have been damp. The linen is going to sag over time. So, the highest points were in contact the longest with the linen; [hence there was] more time for the [body's] oil to soak in and do its damage. . . . I proved the 'time of contact' idea by making a mold of my face and putting it into my bathtub and laying linen over it, sealing it with plastic and putting a kitchen humidifier in there. . . . The new piece of linen initially just touched the nose, the forehead, the lips, and the chin. After about twelve hours it had sagged down into the eyewells, down between the lips, down around the nose, and was making contact everywhere but in the narrowest little creases. So that the time-sag theory seems to work. . . . I did that with vegetable oil and still *couldn't make a three-dimensional image.*[2]

So how does he feel about the Shroud now after the scientific studies of 1978 have been hashed and rehashed? In his own words:

> Is it the image of Christ? Is it not? As a scientist you deal in probabilities, and to me all the little things just nibble away at the proba-

175

bilities. In my own mind, the probabilities of the image's identity with Christ is up in the high nineties. You could never prove it. . . . There are a lot of biblical correlations . . . but you could never get away from the argument that the Romans crucified somebody else . . . and because you can't, you could never prove it. All you could do is nibble away at the probabilities and choose to believe or choose not to believe. Based on science, based on faith, whatever . . . again, in my mind, I'm up in the high nineties.[3]

Perhaps most dramatic is the effect the Shroud has had on his life:

It might interest you where I stand on this religiously . . . all of the things that just "fell out of the sky," just happened. . . . To a Christian that wouldn't be surprising, but I was the group's resident agnostic. . . . There were a couple of times I had to remind [them of their] objectivity . . . but over the years I've come to believe in God and a lot more things. . . . I believe that a lot of things were put together at the right time to make this happen. . . . Strong Christians say, "I don't need the Shroud for my faith." . . . Some evangelical Christians get *angry* when I present this: "What are you showing me this for? I don't need this!" They may not. I *did!* There are people like me, who question a lot of things—whose minds get in the way of their hearts, I guess—and need this kind of thing to help them understand. . . . I actually laughed at myself recently when I found myself asking God, "Show me some proof. Show me some evidence." I thought, *Wait a minute. I'm one of probably three or four dozen people in the world that have touched and seen close up the Shroud of Turin, and here I am asking for evidence.* . . . The Shroud has unquestionably played a role in where I am today.[4]

Dee German was once a doubting Thomas who has since put his hands in Jesus' side. Recently German trusted in Christ as his Savior.

Ray Rogers

Another scientist whose life has been forever affected by the Shroud is Dr. Ray Rogers. Rogers, perhaps the single most vocal proponent of the Shroud's possible authenticity prior to Turin, has been quoted and misquoted with statements he probably wishes he had never made. Such phrases as "flash photolysis" (used to describe the "scorch" theory as it was understood at that time), while well received by Shroud fans—including me—and the media alike, produced a tremendous backlash from the scientific community, especially when the process was not reproducible in the lab. During one of the many post-Turin workshop meetings, I distinctly recall discussing the meaning of the data in Rogers' home. A soft-spoken man with incredibly kind blue eyes and a fighter-pilot mustache, Ray was distraught that the data analysis to that point had failed to reveal any "smoking pistol" evidence. He felt that though the evidence had pointed so clearly to a scorch, there was nothing that he could hang his scientific reputation on. He was later quoted saying, "I incline toward the idea of a scorch, but I can't think how it was done. At this point you either keep looking for the mechanism or start getting mystical." I recall, however, that he was also singularly determined to pursue looking for the mechanism. As he put it to Cullen Murphy:

For some reason, the fibrils that make up the image got older faster than the rest of the fabric. . . . I think everyone in STURP concurs that the image is just degraded cellulose, that there's actually nothing "on" the linen. But there's no consensus on just how the cellulose was degraded. . . . There are any number of ways to degrade cellulose, apart from doing nothing and just letting it age. You can bake it or burn it or irradiate it and produce a scorch; or you can add something to it that will soil it or alter it chemically. The problem with chemically induced aging is that we can't find anything on the Shroud to account for it. We've spot tested with reagents looking for likely materials. Mass spectrometry . . . tested for aloes, myrrh, oils, and so on—things that might produce some kind of contact image. Everything came out negative. You'd think we would have found something. I mean aloes, for example, has a bunch of glycosides in it that should stand out like a sore thumb. And these tests are sensitive. We picked up traces of the polythene bag the threads were wrapped in.[5]

In our last meeting together, Rogers felt that much of his work had been terribly misunderstood and consequently used inappropriately, including our discussions in *Verdict*. In spite of those feelings, he has produced some of the most compelling evidence to date for the authenticity of the Shroud. His best efforts included ground work in fields from textiles to chemistry that has increased the interest of other experts. All this came from a man who by his own admission did not want to be involved: "When I first heard about the Shroud project, I didn't want to get involved. I don't like being identified with the lunatic fringe."[6] Now retired from the Los Alamos lab where he worked as a chemist, Rogers could not be reached for comment on how the recent C-14 dating affected his outlook on the Shroud.

Alan Adler

Interestingly enough, STURP had several Jewish members, including Alan Adler, who helped demonstrate the presence of primate, most likely human, blood on the cloth. Alan was asked the somewhat obnoxious question, "What's a nice Jewish fellow doing involved with the Shroud of Turin?" He answered, "Well, everyone's got to be famous for something, though I'd rather be known for my work in porphryns." Or if the questioner is sarcastic, Adler answers, "Funny, I always thought that Jesus was Jewish." After all is said and done, Alan, a chemist, still feels that the most likely theory of image formation involves a high-energy, high voltage process on a relatively dry cloth—a theory most investigated and researched by Oswald Schuermann (see Chapter 2). Alan described it in this fashion:

> If you were able to get a body form at least five to six inches in diameter under a dry cloth and somehow generate from (or on) that body 50KV at 100,000 cycles per second and most likely using at least 10 amps, you would conceivably have a good testing profile to work from. Unfortunately, so far no one has ever done it because it is in reality a much bigger challenge than it appears on the surface.[7]

A latecomer to STURP, he joined after the 1978 trip, helping not only to isolate and identify human blood on the cloth but also to carry out the very detailed chemical analysis. Many have attempted to discredit the chemical analysis for blood, but here's how Alan defended his work: "We have now reported over a dozen separate chemical and/or physical tests consistent with the presence of blood materials," not to mention the fact that all of those results have been subjected to some of the most rigorous and heated peer reviews on record (see Chapter 7). Adler declined to discuss the questions of identity and spiritual significance of the Shroud, other than to state the following: "I study the Shroud because it is an interesting scientific puzzle. What is it? How did it [the image] get there? The data are only understandable as being consistent with a cloth that covered a wounded male body. The fact that it might be Christ's makes it interesting, but not necessarily scientifically demanding. After all, there is no scientific test for Christness."[8]

Barrie Schwortz

Perhaps the most interesting story of a Jewish Shroud researcher is that of Barrie Schwortz. A tireless worker, he personally spent 102 hours photographing the Shroud during the 120 hours of testing. In spite of its excellent photographic and audio documentation, his work received short shrift from some of the team members, who even begrudged his producing a photo essay book as too "crassly commercial." Considering himself the "Jiminy Cricket" of the project, he also was one of our supporters during the attack on *Verdict*. During the trip to Turin in 1978, I spent considerable time discussing with Schwortz the evidence that *Yeshua* (Jesus) was in fact the long-awaited Jewish Messiah and that He was virtually ignored in His day. After many questions, mostly answered from the Hebrew Scriptures (Old Testament), Schwortz told me that he was beginning to get chills just thinking about the possibility. Later during a particularly fast and furious photo session, as we passed each other, Schwortz nudged me and said, "It's happening again. I'm getting chills all over." Even though I learned to distrust almost anything printed in the media at large, I must say that the tabloid articles on Schwortz's "conversion" struck a hopeful chord in me. However, Schwortz has never publicly acknowledged any such conversion. What he has said, as Habermas has already noted, is a belief that the man of the Shroud is Jesus of Nazareth, and that is significant enough in itself.[9]

Bob Bucklin

When Habermas and I were writing *Verdict,* we needed someone to write an afterword—someone whose expertise and scientific accuracy were beyond reproach; someone whose faith would be strong enough to interpret the data for others; someone, in short, able to stand on even ground with other scientists and yet neither fear the scorn of men nor avoid the spiritual issue. We needed Dr. Robert Bucklin. A pathologist, an attorney, and then deputy county coroner for Los Angeles, Bucklin was one of the two men that modeled as well as consulted for the television series *Quincy.* He boldly stated, "A few of us have openly expressed our opinions that there is support for the Resurrection in the things we see on the Shroud."[10]

Bucklin, a devout man, has known the hand of God in his own life in dramatic ways outside of any involvement with STURP. Certainly given his background and expertise, his comments concerning the identity of the man of the Shroud should carry much weight in the scientific community:

Scientifically speaking, one's faith or religious beliefs should play no role in arriving at a conclusion concerning the true nature of the Shroud. On the other hand, it would be a gross injustice to deny to one who believes the biblical account of the passion, death, and resurrection of Jesus Christ that the physical findings on the Shroud of Turin, in correlation with the pertinent historical facts discovered thus far, including those related in the Bible, make a strong

180

argument that the man of the Shroud and Jesus Christ could indeed be one and the same. Obviously, this judgment must in the end be a matter of personal conviction.[11]

From a man who has on many occasions said the evidence would stand up in a court of law, such a statement is indeed significant.

Roger and Marty Gilbert

Before going to Turin, Italy, in 1977, John Jackson did a rough color analysis on the Shroud photographs which seemed at that time to indicate a decided similarity or correlation between the color of the image and the color of the lightest burn-damaged areas of the Shroud. Not surprisingly, everyone waited with baited breath as Doctors Roger and Marty Gilbert (spectography experts and founders of the Oriel Spectographic Corporation outside Danbury, Connecticut), ran their series of spectral analyses on the Shroud image. When the spectrophotometric comparison proved to be nearly identical, we and many others concluded that the most likely image-formation process was some perhaps unknown form of "scorching" mechanism. Because I (Stevenson) was there, I can confirm that it was very easy to get caught up in the excitement of that moment. The most logical question to begin with then in my interview with Roger Gilbert was, Did you then and do you now consider the "scorch" theory to be viable—and why?

Basically, the way I've been describing it . . . it seems similar to a scorch. . . . It's similar to a scorch in spectral reflectance . . . it's similar to a scorch in three-dimensional characteristics . . . in spectral fluorescence it does not seem to be similar to a scorch. If it was a scorch, it would have had to have been scorched by a very high energy source or a very high temperature source and exposed to it for a very short period of time, and that's all we know about it. . . . I think similar to a scorch is as close as I can come to it. . . . I can't call it a scorch exactly. . . . As to the mechanism . . . some sort of high energy process . . . that's as close as I can come to it.[12]

181

Roger originally suspected that the Shroud might have been a fake, but now says, "Of all the tests that I've been involved with and really all that I've read about, I've seen no indication in those tests that the thing is a fake—not even an indication."[13] Though Roger felt that a consistent medieval date from all labs would swing him to believing that the Shroud was a fake, Marty's response was very interesting:

> I want the dating to come out right. That is unscientific, but I say that because I have talked to so many people who I consider are in the wilderness searching, who, if this comes through are going to be pushed a step farther along the way. . . . For those people, I can't tell you the number who come to me and say, "Marty, what's new on the Shroud?" . . . If something came out at least in the ballpark . . . it would lead them a step farther. . . .[14]

Sam Pellicori

During one of the data reduction meetings—occasions when we would analyze, discuss, and collate data for publication—in Colorado Springs, I had an opportunity to discuss with Sam Pellicori, a scientist involved in the realm of scientific, photographic testing, the image-formation process that he and Dee German have continued to investigate. Sam was introduced to the Shroud by Vern Miller, who sought Sam's help in procuring/fabricating special UV filters for the photography testing. Also Sam was involved in the photomicroscopy, visible spectrophotometry and UV fluorescence photography of the Shroud. His theory of image formation, one of only three being seriously considered, is based on contact and testing involved spreading certain oils on his hand and bringing them into contact with a cloth that was then baked in an oven to simulate aging. In spite of all the known problems with contact theories (see Chapter 2), Sam still pursues this approach because:

> The hypothesis for explaining the image formation was tested in the lab and found to reproduce the color, spatial, UV fluorescence

properties and three-dimensionality characteristics that the team found on the Shroud image. The image chemistry was then elucidated during a brainstorming/chemlab session at AFA, with the principal players being Al Adler, Eric, and myself. John Heller was later to claim a disproportionate degree of credit for the chemistry explanation in his book [*Report on the Shroud of Turin*].[15]

(I [Stevenson] was present at that session.) At one point I recall asking Sam why, if he could "bake" such an image, he had such a problem with the so-called "scorch" theory? His response today is:

We understand the image chemistry as a greater degree of degradation (carbonyl chromophore formation) in the body image than is naturally occurring elsewhere on the cloth. It has been demonstrated that this greater degree of (i.e., more rapid) yellowing (or browning) can be promoted by the presence of extremely low concentrations of any number of foreign materials. These discoloring reactions can be made to occur at much less than half the temperature required to scorch cellulose. In fact, they will occur at room temperature given enough time. . . . The chemistry is well established, and the arguments against the scorch hypothesis are quite strong. The high temperature required to scorch cellulose produces a different set of chemical reactions than we observed in the image. Notably, high temperature reactions, whether in abundant oxygen or not, will give products that fluoresce to UV excitation. There have been repeated attempts to ignore the devastating observation that the body *image does not fluoresce!!*[16]

Three-dimensionality and the detail of the image seem to be major hurdles to the German-Pellicori hypothesis. I asked Pellicori how he dealt with those problems, why an image using his hypothesis has been so difficult to reproduce in the lab, and also why there are no other images like the Shroud's in the world? He responded, "We did demonstrate the ability to reproduce three-dimensional images [German does not agree] by the accelerated aging process. [That means baking it in an oven.] The fine detail of the image *is* well reproduced by contact. Reproduction of the face image without distortion has not yet been accomplished."[17]

Asked if he believed this cloth held the body of Jesus of Nazareth, Sam said:

> I believe that the Shroud is a genuine burial cloth in the sense that it was not contrived by an artist or produced by other artificial means. . . . I am bothered by the nonexistence of other burial cloths with images. I wrote a hypothetical scenario for the Dec. 1981 issue of *Sindon* which supposed that this particular burial cloth was retrieved and retained for some reason. Then, over time, the image gradually developed (as a photograph does), and it thus took on a greater significance, and more reason to be treasured and perhaps even revered. The carbon dating will provide another piece of circumstantial evidence that will either support the possibility of the cloth being extant near the time of Jesus, or will remove that possibility.[18]

I then asked if this was a result of all the facts or if Pellicori had any preconceived ideas concerning this cloth. He said, "It seems that faith is blind to reason, meaning that it has a separate reality regardless of the facts. This observation is already evidenced in the 'interpretations' of our research by people holding various prejudiced views."[19]

What is the bottom line of all these points? "I feel that the basic mechanism is the so-called German-Pellicori hypothesis, but with a missing ingredient. The current incompleteness of the hypothesis is not cause to disregard it, especially in the absence of a valid *(i.e., verifiable)* replacement" [emphasis added].[20]

William Meacham

Along the way I had the opportunity to contact several people who wrote on or analyzed the STURP data after peer review was completed. One of the most interesting individuals was Bill Meacham whose *Current Anthropology (CA)* article on the Shroud was comprehensive and yet not at all clouded with the technical jargon of some sindonologists. More importantly, he brings to sindonology the trained eye of the serious archaeologist who can pull the various disciplines together into a composite. Furthermore, Meacham made an excellent case for the importance of bringing historical research to bear on the principle Shroud question: Is the image that of Jesus of Nazareth? ". . . encoded in the image are data of such specificity that the relic can be fixed in time and place, used to generate hypotheses to be tested in the laboratory and in the field, and finally attributed to a single, historical person."[21]

As this book was being prepared, Bill made a visit to New York, and I was able to interview him. I wanted to know whether, since his article, anyone had presented evidence to him that had weakened his strong stance for authenticity. He said, "I'm still at the same point as when I wrote the *CA* article. I haven't mellowed or weakened. I mean the way I see it, the evidence is still very strong."[22] Given his knowledge of C-14 and the strength of the other historical data, my next concern was how he would respond to either mixed dating results or a firm medieval date.

To me the other evidence for the Shroud's authenticity is strong enough to raise questions about any C-14 dating that came out, way off from two thousand years. Say we got a date of 1300–1500. Most people would say, "Well, that's it; it's all over." I would say, "No, it's not." The twenty-first century is going to answer this thing. Or maybe if the church releases some samples, the 1990s will. . . . The technology exists for very refined tests in C-14, but they need bigger samples. . . . These three samples they have now are minuscule little bits. All they can possibly do is give it a kind of a rinse in a very dilute acid and alkaline bath and then date it. . . .[23]

Considering the fact that he was an archaeologist, I asked what significance could be placed on the fact that there are no other burial clothes like this out of the thousands in existence. Meacham replied:

Well actually, it might just be a unique set of circumstances that produced it, such as the cloth being separated from the body in an environment where it would normally decay. . . . As you say, there are in Egypt a lot of burial clothes that have survived from Coptic burials, second and third century A.D.—a relatively dry, desiccating type of environment so the body decomposition is slowed down almost to a snail's pace. It doesn't affect the cloth . . . it hasn't spoiled the cloth . . . but in an environment in, say, Jerusalem . . . where normally the decomposition of the body would be fast, like a few days . . . in those circumstances the cloth is going to decay with it . . . [except in a case where the body is removed] because to my mind, it [the image] originates from before the resurrection.[24]

As with all the researchers, I was also interested in what he thought was the most likely theory of image formation. "As far as image formation is concerned, I think we're still groping in the dark. I mean there are several good methods that produce kind of similar images, but they don't answer *all* the points. . . . it might be worth considering heating a cadaver. . . ."[25]

Finally, I asked if there were any evidences which could move him into a stronger category on the Resurrection issue. Meacham replied:

To my mind, the resurrection is probably something that is so "otherworldly," in the sense that we understand things, that we're speculating—we're in the unknown. . . . If it's authentic, it *is* connected with the resurrection in the sense that the body that was in it came alive again. . . . we don't really know anything about the physical processes that went on. . . . Whatever *could* happen to bring a body back to life that happened in the case of Christ *could* also. . . . Maybe there's some "exuding" of something that caused the image. . . .[26]

PERSONAL WITNESS

In the short space we have in this book, it would be impossible to include all of the significant stories of the Shroud's impact on the life of so many individuals. I've received calls from engineers, attorneys, college students and letters from clergy, homemakers and media personalities, many of whom were not converted to Christianity until they read *Verdict* or heard a lecture on the Shroud. From media personalities like David Hartman to corporate executives, comments like "fascinating . . . inspiring . . . powerful . . . a persuasive argument not only for the Shroud's authenticity, but more importantly for the claims of Christ," continue to convince me of the importance of telling this story.

The Shroud was not meant for dusty shelves or laboratory test tubes only. It was meant for changing lives. As one reader put it, "[your] wonderful book . . . caused me to bring down my Bible, and 'dust it off'. . . . My faith is renewed. . . . *Surely those scientists realize this image was an act of God.* . . . I hope that millions read your book. . . . [it] led me to the ultimate book, the Holy Bible!"[27]

I offer one last note for those who fear idolatry in such "gushy" comments. In over ten years of direct involvement with the Shroud, I have yet to meet a single person who began to worship it. On the other hand, I've met or heard from many who've found Christ as a result of reading *Verdict*.

The members of STURP had in their hands a unique opportunity to witness to the reality of the gospel message. Most of the team's scientists have not taken that step.

Perhaps one of the most significant sindonologists who was willing to speak out was John A. T. Robinson. An Anglican bishop and a noted skeptic who actually set out to use the New Testament to debunk the Shroud, Robinson instead came to believe in Christ because of the Shroud and publicly acknowledged the importance of that fact. ". . . we may have to learn to count ourselves also among those who have 'seen and believed.' But that . . . brings with it . . . rather special responsibility."[28] Until his death, Robinson told the Shroud story and consequently the gospel story. As other sindonologists report on their findings, the gospel will be preached and lives will be changed because the Shroud portrays the gospel in a unique and powerful way. Of course, not everyone will respond positively to the message or to the evidence, but that is no reason to stand silent before those who need to hear both.

Now that you have the pieces of evidence pertinent to the search for the Shroud's authenticity, it is time for you to draw your own conclusions.

12

THE IMAGE THAT WON'T GO AWAY

When D. James Kennedy, one of the finest scholar-pastors, read *Verdict,* he was inspired to write a message and a booklet called *Save the Wrappings.* When Norman Geisler, now the Dean of the Liberty Center for Research and Scholarship at Liberty University in Lynchburg, Virginia, was asked to review the book, he went from certainty of fraud to near certainty of authenticity, calling it the "best evidence in the 20th century for a 1st century miracle."[1] These are just two of the many remarkable responses to the evidence from the Shroud in 1981. In conservative scholars of their caliber, the reversal in position carries additional weight.

Historically, the Shroud image has been the focus of hotly contested battle lines, shared at times by the most bizarre of "bedfellows." For example, it is not unusual to see an evangelical Christian like Josh McDowell align himself with an atheistic opponent of the Shroud like skeptic Marvin Mueller. On the other side of the war zone, you might find Jewish Shroud experts like Barrie Schwortz and Alan Adler in agreement with such Shroud proponents as former agnostic Dee German. Some researchers just as ardently avoid the obvious religious implications of sindonology. More importantly, they actually expect people to regress to *their* purported position of "noncommittal scientific curiosity." Almost no one remains neutral.

What is the public to believe? Is the Shroud of Turin really a burial garment, or is it a pious fraud? Does the scientific research completed thus far give us any reliable conclusions? If in fact it is the Shroud of Jesus Christ, what role does it play in Christianity? What message does it give to the world at large? Where do we go from here? From peer review and discussion, what conclusions can finally be drawn? Is the evidence as strong as we felt it was when we wrote *Verdict,* or should we tone down the enthusiasm that earned us everything from skepticism and outright scorn by opponents to hearty approval? These are the major issues for the conclusion of *The Shroud and the Controversy.*

A HISTORICAL PERSPECTIVE

Perhaps the single most frustrating thing to me [Stevenson] in the entire Shroud saga is the near hysteria that originally greeted *Verdict.* Amazingly, the worst of it came from brothers in Christ, who even went to the extent of leveling false charges at Habermas and me and the book. One critic began an address before IEEE by stating that we claimed "that the Shroud exhibits proof of the resurrection of Jesus," which is patently untrue.[2] Nowhere in *Verdict* nor in public lectures or interviews has either of us made such a wild claim. In fact, we say in the conclusion of *Verdict:*

Throughout this work we have tried not only to present the known facts, but also to be cautious in our evaluation of them. . . .

Even though hypotheses involving fakery and natural explanations have failed to explain the known data, we *did not* therefore assert that the Shroud gives *evidence* for a supernatural occurrence. . . .

Thus the facts point strongly to the two conclusions that the Shroud is an actual archaeological artifact, and that it is Jesus' burial garment.

. . . it is also *probable* that the cause of the image *corresponds* to the historical report that Jesus rose from the dead. . . .

Science can only go part of the way; *it cannot prove* irrefutably that the man of the Shroud is Jesus Christ. . . .

> We must remember that *the Shroud proves nothing* [emphasis not in original].[3]

After line upon line of caveats and disclaimers throughout *Verdict,* to end on such a note is far from "proving" *anything,* much less something as significant as the Resurrection. Nor did our personal opinions on the Resurrection require approval by STURP members. Perhaps the real cause for alarm was that we understood the facts too well and drew from them a probability that some were not willing to accept.

Some of the scientists would say that the "proof" of the Resurrection and the "proof" of the identity of Jesus do not belong in their studies. Their consistent argument is that to answer such questions lies outside the realm of science. For the "nth time" let me state clearly, *We most emphatically agree!* "Proof" of either the Resurrection or of the identity of Jesus cannot come from science alone. However, let us make it clear that while the proof itself may be outside of their bailiwick, evidence is not, hypotheses are not, the connection is not, *and most certainly the issue is not!*

While all of those hostile to the Shroud question have no problem making the connection between Jesus, His resurrection, and the Shroud, and while they even go so far as to use it as an offensive weapon against the scientists, some of the key people providing the most positive evidence for authenticity tend to hide behind the cloak of scientific objectivity. Consider the comments of Professor Gonella given at the Hong Kong Symposium in 1986:

> The operation also showed the difficulties of communicating scientific results and problems to the public and humanistic colleagues. Both the media and scholars of the related humanistic fields seem to make little or no difference between reasoned scientific conclusions by professional scientists and wild hypotheses by amateurs, between measured results and mere opinions. Thus the field is still cluttered by mis-information and thoroughly confuted theories. The media showed an uncanny ability in pushing the wildest news

and overlooking the solid results . . . because too many Shroud enthusiasts (pro and con) choose to address the mass-media instead of
scientific journals. The media interest, fostered by the emotional
attachment in the public, brought about too many misquotations of
those who walk on the narrow path of scientific rigour [sic] and
publication in referenced journals. They were often judged by such
misquotation, and often accused of "religious fanaticism" only because they were studying an object of *obvious religious connection;*
they were therefore compelled to lean over backward in their statements to an extent unheard of in normal research, under the
weight of a *psychological pressure* that constitutes an effective lim-
itation to the freedom of research.[4]

Throughout his report Gonella had made reference to the
"obvious religious connection" and in nearly the same
breath attempted to sever that connection. STURP members were well aware of the nature of the problem they were
attacking in sindonology. We discussed it among ourselves
on more than one occasion, including the overwhelming media interest that would unquestionably follow our work. As
one who primarily handled press relations for STURP from
its inception, I [Stevenson] often stressed the increasing
need to address the general public, but my pleas generally
fell on deaf ears. After three long years of silence and secrecy except for the excellent June 1980 *National Geographic* article and a smattering of others, the leaders of
STURP were content to make the public wait. Unfortunately, men like Nickell and McCrone were quick to provide
answers—answers that *sounded* good but were plagued with
inaccuracies and loopholes.

Also from a personal perspective, I frequently argued
for the inclusion of other disciplines, including Scripture experts, but these were considered "unscientific"
by STURP. Even Father Rinaldi admonished us all, "When
you take up the cause of the Shroud, you take up the
cross."[5]

Now it seems that because we failed to find the "missing
link" of sindonology—the image formation process—there is

an overwhelming desire to remove all connection with Jesus of Nazareth. Let me state emphatically that *if it were not for the gospel of Jesus Christ, the Shroud would be no more than a scientific oddity, a museum piece, a mere curiosity*. Anyone who is honest must concede that point or accede to intellectual dishonesty.

Also, to deny public access to the data because of "media misquotations" or an inability of the public to distinguish between facts and opinions strikes me as a form of intellectual snobbery. Is the problem that we, the public, may not understand the scientific theories? Certainly a reasonably accurate report could be prepared for public consumption without scientific compromise. After all, such has been done many times before—the *National Geographic* and *Current Anthropology* articles on the Shroud are cases in point.[6] One letter expressed this feeling very well: "It does seem to me that ever since the American scientists—seemingly great numbers of them—came on the scene with all their manifold scientific tests (which never seem to provide an answer!) the whole conception of the truth of the Shroud has come to a sort of shuddering stop. It seems to me also that we were much better off before the tests were embarked upon. I do wonder if other people think the same, or is mine an uninformed viewpoint?"[7]

Humorous, perhaps. Uninformed? Decidedly not! Nor can the scientists expect us truly to believe that the media and public pressure is too great when they knew in advance what to expect. More importantly, how long do they expect to limit Shroud knowledge to a privileged few, a sindonology club for members only? Not *all* the scientists acted or responded this way, but personal opinions and conclusions have elicited quite volatile responses, especially from those who feel their work is misunderstood.

SKEPTICAL ANTAGONISM

First, to address the issue of whether or not the concerns of some STURP members were actually justified, let's examine the "mis-information" problem as it really exists. Are science and religion truly at war?

Delage's 1902 comment seems particularly relevant in dealing with such a touchy issue, for he manages to *separate science from religion without separating the Shroud from Jesus:*

> A religious question has been injected into a problem which is in itself purely scientific with the result that feelings have run high, and reason has been led astray. If, instead of Christ, there were a question of some person like a Sargon, an Achilles, or one of the Pharoahs, no one would have thought of making any objection. . . . I have been faithful to the true spirit of science in treating this question, intent only on the truth, not concerned in the least whether it would affect the interests of any religious party. . . . I recognize Christ as a historical personage and I see no reason why anyone should be scandalized that there still exist material traces of his earthly life.[8]

What we actually characteristically face in dealing with most of the Shroud opponents is an oversimplification of the technical qualities of the image, which then allows an easy solution but actually one that does not exist.

As *Chemical and Engineering News* correctly points out, we're now faced with a serious problem: "These differences are difficult to reconcile. Neither side hesitates to question the scientific objectivity of the other."[9] Both proponents and opponents of authenticity justifiably claim scientific expertise, yet both can't be correct. How do we break the tie—if one really exists? Most Shroud opponents seem to have a special ax to grind. For example, Nickell and Schafersman make much ado about Jesus Himself or the narratives concerning the miraculous events of His life being mythical, topics certainly not at issue here or within their expertise.

In *Current Anthropology* Schafersman states, "Meacham's painstaking rendition of this ritual [that the image on the Shroud represents Jesus Christ] is therefore characteristic and only serves to reveal his dogged belief in the authenticity of the Shroud of Turin and of Jesus Christ, a personage best considered by available evidence to be mythical."[10] If that were not strong enough, he clarifies his position in the *Skeptical Inquirer* (a self-appointed watchdog publication of the supernatural): ". . . there are serious doubts that, if he [Jesus] existed, he was crucified; that there are serious doubts that, if he was crucified, he died; and there are serious doubts (to say the least) that, if he died, he was resurrected."[11] Nickell even claims to be writing a book that concludes Jesus was simply a magician, obviously intending to imply that Christ's miracles recorded in the Gospels were simply sleight of hand.[12] Does that mean that Jesus' walk on water was done with mirrors à la David Copperfield?

McCrone and Mueller have another ax to grind. They seem bent on demonstrating STURP to be a clique of religious zealots out to prove a point. According to Mueller, "Shroud investigators have usually been characterized by their pro-authenticity enthusiasm and markedly religious interpretations. About this there can be little disagreement."[13] Certainly many of the members of STURP would not agree with such a harsh blanket statement by Dr. Mueller and would in fact disagree wholeheartedly. Mueller offers a further caustic comment: ". . . it would be surprising to find in these times a fairly large, well-funded, well-organized program of experimentation with predominately theological motivations. . . . Yet, for several years now, such an enterprise has been subjecting a most famous relic, the so-called Shroud of Turin, to an impressive panoply of scientific tests. . . . Concluding that the Shroud is the work of an artist would dash the hope of changing the prevalent scientific world-view. Also the strong religious inclination of nearly *all* of the STURP membership doubtless plays a role here."[14]

To the evangelical Christian, if no one else, warning bells should be sounding at this point. The issue at hand is not Christianity nor the historical existence of Jesus Christ.

The issue is not the particular religious bent of the individual scientists who happened to be among the privileged few selected to study this enigmatic cloth—although that *has* been badly misrepresented in much of the literature opposing the Shroud. Nor is the issue some supposed agenda to change the prevailing scientific view of the "cosmos." The issue is what the scientific evidence does say concerning the possible authenticity of the Shroud.

Oddly enough, the Shroud opponents have actually helped to make our case. Certainly the need to resort to a denigration of the scientists on the basis of their religious preferences shows a decided bias on their part. In addition, if critics feel the need to declare Jesus a myth, are they not actually suggesting that the Shroud evidence indeed matches the Gospel narratives of Christ's passion and death? At least a few of them are willing to admit this in print. For example, Schafersman states, "Stevenson and Habermas even calculate the odds as 1 in 83 million that the man of the shroud is not Jesus Christ . . . a very conservative estimate. *I agree with them on all of this*. If the shroud is authentic, the image is that of Jesus. Otherwise, it's an artist's representation. . . ."[15]

The bottom line then is that either the image is that of Jesus of Nazareth or it was intended by its creator to portray Jesus. Since we've virtually ruled out human artifice, are we crazy or unscholarly or unscientific to suggest the image is likely that of Jesus?

Most of the misinformation available is clearly attributable to hostile sources and can be easily refuted by the facts. Therefore, we're squarely back to the main issue: we know *what* the image is, but not *how* it got there. The known characteristics can't be accounted for by any natural chemistry known so far, nor do they match any known "scorching" mechanism.

In the movies, situations like this are called Mexican standoffs. Neither of the primary research directions concerning the image-formation process has resulted in a lab-reproducible product that matches all of the known characteristics of the Shroud image. The easy out for all involved is to state that the Shroud is a mystery, wipe the sweat from their brows, and head off into the sunset. Habermas and I would readily do this, if only the Shroud existed in a vacuum. But *it does not.*

THE TESTIMONY OF THE NEW TESTAMENT

Let's see where the facts lead. Assuming that the Shroud is in fact a burial garment, assuming that the most likely person to have been wrapped in that burial garment was Jesus of Nazareth, then there is a reliable record to give us additional input—*the Bible.*

When I accepted Christ and began to read the Bible to understand my new relationship with Him, I did not have a frontal lobotomy as some might assume. Nor did I, because I began to believe the claims of the Bible, forfeit or trash all my years of higher education. On the contrary, things that I had never before understood concerning this universe and all of the good and bad connected with it began suddenly to make sense as I found a totally reliable central reference point. Science-versus-Bible debates have long been heated and have led to inflamed emotions. The Shroud story is no different. Some would deny us even the liberty to discuss what the Bible says concerning the resurrection of Jesus but given our still extant laws of freedom of speech/press I will have a go at it.

After spending fifty verses of a letter to the Corinthian church developing the following facts: (1) Jesus Christ did rise from the dead; (2) His resurrection was both the *type* and assurance of our promised resurrection; (3) the resurrection of Jesus demanded a moral change in His followers; and (4) the resurrected body was different from the mortal body, the apostle Paul said concerning the unknown process of resurrection, "Behold I tell you a mystery: We shall not all sleep, but we shall all be changed—in a moment, in the twinkling of an eye, at the last trumpet. For the trumpet will sound, and the dead will be raised incorruptible, and we shall be changed. For this corruptible must put on incorruption, and this mortal must put on immortality" (1 Cor. 15:51–53).

Paul was a formerly hostile antagonist to the gospel whose dramatic resurrection encounter led not only to his own life change, but to his authoring 60 percent of the New Testament and changing millions of lives. The key words in this passage are, in order: 1) mystery: *musterion*—secret, something hidden or not fully manifest, unknown to human reason, known only by revelation from God; 2) sleep: *koima*—to put to sleep, to decease, to be dead; 3) changed: *allasso*—to change, transform, exchange; 4) twinkling of an eye: *rhipe*—a jerk of the eye, an instant; 5) incorruptible: *aphthartos*—not capable of corruption, exempt from wear, waste, or deterioration; 6) immortality: *athanasia*—without death, rendered immortality, glorified body, resurrection body.[16]

In common English, the protégé of the famous Rabbi Gamliel says that we will partake of the same type of resurrection Jesus had and that as a result, our dying mortal bodies will "metamorphosize" in a split second into a body that can never die, a body that according to the Gospel accounts has incredible powers and abilities and yet is touchable and even partakes of food (Jesus was not a ghost).

When I asked chemist Alan Adler if such an event could bridge the gap between what we know of the image and its still elusive formation process, his answer was, "Yes, but if such an event took place in which that much matter was exchanged, you'd still have an incredibly huge crater where the Middle East used to be."[17] However, I'm not sure I agree. As my dear friend Dr. Richard Eby recorded in *Caught Up into Paradise,* when Jesus changed the water into wine, there had to be a tremendous energy release, and yet it was contained in an earthen jug. If Adler's supposition were to hold true across the board, then the changing of water into wine should have also blown Cana off the map. In actuality, Dr. Eby's father wed the knowledge of that incredible energy exchange to design a bushing to serve as an insulator to contain the energy of the Boulder Dam project.[18] Are bodies described in Scripture as earthen jugs? Perhaps there are yet a few "secrets" or "mysteries" that we don't understand concerning these earthen jugs. As Sam Pellicori said concerning his image-formation thesis, "The current incompleteness of the hypothesis is not cause to disregard it, especially in the absence of a valid (i.e., verifiable) replacement."[19]

Certainly if that logic holds for his theory, it will hold for ours. After all, does anyone really know what happens in a resurrection?

One final consideration about the Resurrection connection has been raised by the pathological evidence. If indeed the image was caused by the Resurrection, why does it show a dead body in rigor mortis instead of a wakening body? Certainly this is a difficult question. However, one theory that was never fully developed that is in harmony with this concern was first proposed by Joe Accetta. He was a member of STURP during the 1978 research effort. While in Turin with the team, he produced some fascinating infrared photography that showed the image, not as a negative, but as a positive. At the time, some of us believed that Accetta had supplied a critical key to the image-formation process. Unfortunately, however, his work was given short-shrift by others on the team.

Recognizing that Scripture states that Joseph of Arimathea bought a large quantity of aloes, which are known to be photosensitive, to use in Jesus' burial, Accetta derived an equation for image formation based on the known properties of radiant light. He felt that if the light source came from outside the cloth, the weave pattern would act as a sort of focusing mechanism, giving us the excellent resolution and the three-dimensional effect on the cloth. As with many other turns in sindonology, Accetta may have provided a key to further research into image formation and its connection to the Resurrection regardless of what his personal beliefs may be.

Throughout Scripture there are references to the "glory of God" as being an incredible light—from Moses who had to cover his face with a veil against the strength of the light to Jesus, who was transfigured on the Mount of Olives to show the disciples His "glory." If in fact the resurrection of Christ is involved, perhaps what truly happened is that the "glory of God" enveloped the body of Jesus as He lay in the tomb. The Hebrew and Greek words involved in these specific passages are exactly what we initially thought concerning the image-formation properties of the Shroud: "glory": *kabod/doxa*—glory, brilliance, reflecting brightness, giving off beams of light; "shine," "shone": *qaran/lampo*—shoot out rays of light, radiance as the sun; "transfigured": *metamorphoo*—metamorphosed, a change denoted by brilliance.[20] Certainly if it was a process such as this, it would have to display a corpse and yet would still imply the resurrection process was occurring.

On the other hand, on a purely logical basis, if a completely natural process caused the Shroud image, why are there *no* others known in the entire world—especially since the Egyptians left us so many burial linens? Numerous sindonologists who believe in a natural process are troubled by this fact. And if the response is that because it was Jesus' cloth and the disciples *chose* to retain it, why would they go against the biblical injunctions which were so built into them that it required several books of the New Testament for God to change their hearts? After all, a Jewish believer would have destroyed any burial garment, much less one with an image on it, because of the Mosaic injunctions against uncleanliness and idolatry (Lev. 22:4; Num. 9:6–10; Deut. 5:8–9). It is interesting to note that even after Jesus' earthly ministry, the early church still struggled with a legalistic understanding of such scriptural commands. Peter and numerous other Jewish believers had to be convinced that associating with Gentiles and eating foods previously considered unclean were now kosher (Acts 10:9—11:18). At one point, Paul even had to rebuke Peter publicly over the issue of eating with a Gentile, which was thought to be an unclean practice (Gal. 2:11–21).

Admittedly we are dealing with evidence from outside the realm of modern science, but the source has been demonstrated to be extremely reliable, especially in the singularly most related scientific field of Shroud study—archaeology! The biblical accounts concerning the cities of Sodom and Gomorrah, Jericho, Ur, Ninevah, and Babylon have all been confirmed by the archaeologist's shovel.

Perhaps Paul waxed prophetic when he warned Timothy to avoid "the profane and idle babbles and contradictions of what is fasely called knowledge" (1 Tim. 6:20). Furthermore, if scientists are to be considered more objective auditors of the facts, then we have too soon forgotten the scientific frauds of the Piltdown man, Neanderthal man, Hesperopithecus haroldcookii (Western ape-man), Pithecanthropus erectus, and even australopithicines, *all* of which were touted as the "missing link" necessary to support the theory of evolution and which have been determined (by truly objective researchers) to be respectively: a man-made fraud, a man with rickets, an extinct pig, a large gibbon, apes. Moreover, most of these frauds were admitted to in the end by the very perpetrators themselves.[21] Perhaps those "scientists" (I do not include *all* scientists in that category but merely those who have gone to any length against the evidence to *"prove"* their pet theories) should consider the statements of two of the leading spokesmen for evolutionary theory, Aldous and Sir Julian Huxley. By their own admission, these two men denied the existence of a Creator for self-serving reasons. Aldous Huxley, leading atheist and evolutionist said:

I had motives for not wanting the world to have meaning; consequently assumed that it had none, and was able without any difficulty to find satisfying reasons for this assumption. . . . For myself, as, no doubt, for most of my contemporaries, the philosophy of meaninglessness was an instrument of liberation. The liberation we desired was simultaneously liberation from a certain political and economic system [capitalism] and liberation from a certain system of morality. We objected to the morality because it interfered with our sexual freedom.[22]

More recently, Sir Julian Huxley, a famous evolutionary biologist, admitted on a television talk show, "We all jumped at the *Origin* [Darwin's *Origin of the Species*] because the idea of God interfered with our sexual mores."[23] Perhaps some of Paul's comments in his letter to the Romans are appropriate here:

For the wrath of God is revealed from heaven against all ungodliness and unrighteousness of men, who suppress the truth in unrighteousness, because what may be known of God is manifest in them, for God has shown it to them. For since the creation of the world His invisible attributes are clearly seen, being understood by the things that are made, even His eternal power and Godhead, so that they are without excuse, because, although they knew God, they did not glorify Him as God, nor were thankful, but became futile in their thoughts, and their foolish hearts were darkened. Professing to be wise, they became fools (Rom. 1:18–22).

Though obviously evolution is not *the* issue in this particular work, I believe it is more than germane *to the issue*. Historically, the leading scientific theorists of their day were men whose belief in the Bible did not in any way hamper their objectivity nor their scientific excellence. A partial list of them would include: bacteriology, Louis Pasteur; calculus and dynamics, Sir Isaac Newton; anatomy, Georges Cuvier; surgery, Joseph Lister; chemistry and gas dynamics, Robert Boyle; electromagnetics and field theory, Michael Faraday; genetics, George Mendel; galactic astronomy, Sir William Herschel; computer science, Charles Babbage; dimensional analysis and model analysis, Lord Rayleigh; energetics, Lord Kelvin; entomology, Henri Fabre; electrodynamics, James Maxwell; geology and ichthy-ology, Louis Agassiz; fluid mechanics, George Stokes; hydrostatics, Blaise Pascale.[24] The list could go on. On the other hand, when two leading theorists of modern evolution-ary thought, Dr. Stephen Jay Gould and Dr. Nils Eldredge admit that the "trade secret" of paleontologists has been that *transitional forms do not exist* and then leap to a totally bizarre theory of punctuated equilibria, which requires the first bird to hatch from a lizard's egg, could we not suggest intellectual bias of the worst order? Bias is especially possi-ble since both men are by their own admission atheists as well as Marxists.[25]

If the Shroud could indeed be demonstrated to be authen-tic (just for sake of argument! *I in no way mean to imply that the case has been made*), would it not also require a consid-ered decision on the part of all concerned? After all if Jesus did indeed rise from the dead and there were evidence to that effect, then we must consider the claims of Christ. Some of the researchers call any religious conclusions about the Shroud "blind faith" but fail to acknowledge that belief in *any* unproven theory requires faith. For whatever reason, many sindonologists want nothing to do with the possibility that the image–formation process involves Jesus' resurrec-tion. Some, like McCrone, Mueller, Nickell, and Schafers-man, have even "altered" the facts to suit their own interpretations of the existent data. McCrone, in his text-book on microscopy, even suggests that data be altered to achieve the desired result.[26] Others seem reluctant to voice the possibility that the image is of Christ for fear of what people may think of them.

Certainly we cannot prove that this cloth held Jesus Christ's body. Nor indeed can we prove that the image was a direct result of His resurrection from the dead. But there is almost no basis for the incredible histrionics that follow comments such as the following: "To assume it's a painting would be a greater miracle than the resurrection."[27] When Jewish chemist Alan Adler makes such a statement, he does so without emotion exactly because to his studied eye, that is the fact. And yet the scoffing that follows such a statement from many quarters is deafening.

When Habermas and I have made the statement that the image-formation process was probably some form of "scorch" that most likely occurred at the moment of resurrection, it was simply our best shot at describing the facts as they were then known and understood. As late as 1986, Luigi Gonella, who serves as a scientific advisor in Shroud testing to the Archbishop of Turin, put it this way:

> The "3-D characteristic" brought forward the hypothesis of a radiation burst among the image-formation mechanisms to be investigated. This hypothesis, vastly misunderstood, elicited much attention from the media and has often been dubbed "miracolistic," though it was nothing of the kind. Rather it is the obvious reaction of a physicist faced with the structural features of the Shroud image: the agent acting at a distance with decreasing intensity is, *almost by definition, radiation.* The limitation of the cloth darkening to the outermost surface pointed to a non-penetrating, non-diffusing agent, like radiant energy; the absence of plateaus pointed to an effect limited by the exposure time (hence a "burst") and not by saturation of the receiving material; whatever the mechanism might be, it must be such to yield effects as if it were a burst of collimated radiant energy.[28]

The only thing that has changed since this statement was made is that it has been demonstrated that any known or heretofore postulated form of "scorching" mechanism will not match all the known Shroud image characteristics. The image does not fluoresce, burn through, damage the fibrils, or blur as all known methods of scorching do. We readily admit all of these facts and still stand by our original judgment because it still best fits the known facts. The Shroud does *not* exist in a vacuum. On the contrary, if the medical and scientific evidence confirms the biblical record in every other detail, we conclude that the only remaining detail is also accurate: Jesus Christ rose from the dead and the image on this cloth is in some as-yet-unknown way connected with that event. Whether it was the effect of body chemicals over a period of time, an effect that has escaped our duplication attempts, or some high-energy, high voltage transformation for which we lack both name and knowledge, that historical episode—the resurrection of Jesus Christ—is the single most feasible explanation for the image on the Shroud.

The scientists of STURP even conclude the following concerning the image-formation process:

> The cause, then, of the yellowing is chemically altered cellulose consisting of structures formed by dehydration, oxidation, and conjugation products of the linen itself. . . . This conclusion is supported by laboratory simulations using controlled accelerated aging processes that produce the same spectral reflectance curves as the body-only image areas and the background areas on the Shroud. . . . It is important to note that this chemistry is similar to the chemistry that causes the yellowing of linen with age. The fact that we can see the body image tells us that the body image is due to a more advanced [cloth] decomposition process than the normal aging rate of the background linen itself. For this reason, we will from this point on refer to the chemistry of the body-only image as *advanced* [cloth] *decomposition*.[29]

The STURP scientists go on to state:

> The Shroud's mapping relationship, however, poses the strongest objection to a contact mechanism. Contact mechanisms have not been able to produce a convincing cloth-body distance relationship. In fact, taken alone, this mapping function seems to suggest some kind of "projection" mechanism, because there seems to be image present even where it does not appear to have been possible that the cloth was in contact with the body. We are left to identify what kind of "projection" mechanism, and this we have been unable to do. Simple molecular diffusion and "radiation" models, for example, fail to account for the apparent resolution of the image as we understand it. . . . We really do not have a satisfactory, simple explanation for how the body image got on the cloth. We think this

205

fact is underscored by the fact that to our knowledge no other image on any cloth—grave cloth or art form—like the body image on the Shroud is known to exist today. If another example were to exist, our task of identifying the origin of the body image would be much simplified.[30]

Immediately following that remark, the members of STURP began a discussion of whether or not the Shroud might be Jesus'.

To put all of the above in common English, they concluded that the Shroud image is caused by an unknown form of "advanced decomposition" of the cloth, which *seemed* to "project" from body to cloth—a process which has thus far eluded all attempts at duplication. The image is unlike any art form and also has no natural counterpart. Again recall that the lab-induced "advanced decomposition" was accomplished by "baking" linen in an oven. I [Stevenson] clearly recall asking Sam Pellicori if we could induce "shroud-like" characteristics by baking the linen, and what was so hard to accept about an unknown process that might have occurred in a split second of time two thousand years ago in Jesus' garden tomb? Sam had no answer.

Nor is it necessary for science to have an answer. Human beings are not limited to science for answers. Would you choose a spouse because his/her genes are scientifically perfect or because of your love for that person? If you answered "love," could you give a scientific definition for love and demonstrate how to reproduce it in the laboratory? Surely we know many of the chemical reactions involved in the human body when love is in action, but can we reproduce it in a pill or in the lab? Not at all. Why then do human scientists cringe when Christians talk about the Resurrection? One of the most notable intellectual scholars and skeptics of his day, the late John A. T. Robinson wrote, "The quest for the Shroud can lead only to the quest for Christ."[31] Considering that his initial intent was to disprove the Shroud, this statement is highly significant—especially in view of the fact that he professed faith in Christ before his death.

A SCIENTIST'S CONVICTION

I [Stevenson] believe the case for the authenticity of the Shroud of Turin would hold up in any court in the land. Furthermore, I believe the case for the Resurrection can be made beyond a "reasonable doubt." More importantly, it is my firm conviction that the Shroud does have a role to play in Christianity. Indeed, though I by no means consider these things to be *"proven,"* if what *I believe* about the Shroud is accurate, then its purpose is as follows:

After all is said and done, the Gospel of Jesus Christ neither rises nor falls because of the Shroud of Turin. Certainly if more evidence were found to buttress a medieval date, the case for authenticity would be much more questionable. On the other hand, even if a first-century date were scientifically confirmed, the Shroud is not now, nor indeed should it be, an article of faith.

What the Shroud does best is provide an extremely accurate window back in time to the passion of Jesus Christ. As medical doctors from Barbet to Bucklin have discovered, the Shroud allows a virtual autopsy of Calvary. Historians and biblical scholars alike have marveled at the accuracy and level of detail on the cloth of that brutal death. Perhaps the Shroud even allows the modern-day doubter to put his or her finger in His hands and side. Most impressive is the life-changing impact that an open, objective study of the facts can cause. Over and over during the past eight years since *Verdict* was published, people have told me that the straightforward presentation of the facts was responsible for a new direction in life. These people did not become rabid, fanatical, or somehow lose touch with reality. They merely chose to believe in Jesus. The Shroud was only a catalyst to their conversions.

DECIDE FOR YOURSELF

My question to all who read these words is, What will *you* decide about the Shroud? You have heard the evidence pro and con. The final decision for or against authenticity rests squarely with you.

Beyond the issue of the cloth itself, What have you learned about the man who may have been wrapped in the cloth two thousand years ago? The One who in love predicted His own death, burial, and resurrection. It has been well-stated that the Shroud is "God's love letter in linen to all mankind."[32] What better evidence could God offer of His love to a technical generation than something that has stumped some of the best technical minds of their day, while at the same time revealing a depth of love few could even imagine?

For the scientist in you, we close with the words of one of your own:

It seems as if physics and chemistry [would have] provided better explanations of the formation of the image nowadays . . . and yet, the genuine arrangement of simultaneous and successive causal steps that formed this expressive and informative image cannot be attributed to a series of coincidences. Neither was it possible for human beings to produce such an image. . . . Consequently, one cannot help reaching the following conclusion:

"A Dead Man Rose from the Dead and Left Behind His Image as an Evidence for Posterity."[33]

APPENDIX A

Summary of the Cases for and against a Medieval Date

I. Medieval Date of Origin

  A. Evidence for:

    1. Three highly credible C-14 labs using the same methodology have arrived at the same date of A.D. 1260–1390, for which they claim 95 percent accuracy.

    2. At least some members of the scientific community have apparently been willing to accept this dating without question or peer review.

    3. The D'Arcis memorandum claims that an unnamed artist painted the Shroud for unspecified reasons with unspecified techniques.

    4. The Shroud has no known unbroken historical chain before the 1300's.

  B. Evidence against:

    1. The C-14 dating may have been inaccurate due to contamination of the cloth that was missed during pretreatment. Such contamination caused these *same* labs to be off by as much as 1,500 years in an earlier testing of an Egyptian burial linen.

    2. The sample site from the Shroud that was used is suspect. At the very least, it is immediately

adjacent to severely fire damaged portions of the cloth. And some scientists have argued that the piece selected was actually different from the original material—namely, either a patch or an edge strip. Also, a report made of the sampling indicated that random "anomalous" threads were merely snipped from the sample, not unwoven. Moreover, the strip is an addition of unknown age, and the patches were added after the 1532 fire.

3. Only one method of C-14 dating was used while the protocols strongly encouraged a minimum of two. Additionally, only one method of pretreatment was used.

4. Only one sample site was selected from the Shroud. The protocols suggested several to avoid anomalies.

5. Inherent errors and variation in the C-14 methodology would argue strongly for close peer review of all results.

6. The method selected has been used little in the dating of cloth. In fact, one lab using this method had extremely poor results on dating linen of *known* origin.

7. The results were compromised because the tests were not truly blind, as the protocols had required. The labs in question knew which samples were from the Shroud and which were from the dummy. Additionally, they knew the date of the dummy cloth. Indeed, based on the evidence, at least one Shroud scholar, Werner Bulst, has suggested the possibility that some of the labs' scientists conspired to violate documented procedures that had been established for properly removing test samples from the Shroud.[1]

8. C-14 experts from around the world have been mounting a protest over these and other issues. One protester, William Meacham, has experience using C-14 on more than seventy-five field samples.

9. The 1532 fire unquestionably set up an isotope exchange between the Shroud's silver casing, the case's lining, and the Shroud itself, which would of necessity alter the date. This is most significant in view of the proximity of the sample to a severely fire-damaged area of the cloth.

10. A 1982 secret dating performed at the University of California nuclear accelerator facility on a single thread from the Shroud reportedly disclosed two divergent dates from each end of the thread. One end dated to A.D. 200 while the other dated to A.D. 1000. Not only do these dates present significant differences from the 1988 testing, but the older end of the thread dates from about the time of Jesus Christ when the plus-minus factor for C-14 is considered.

11. Another possible option is that the medieval date is correct, but it does not suggest what many think it does. Several physicists have contended that both the higher C-14 content, which would yield a medieval date, and the Shroud image may be explained by a "neutron flux" in the cloth caused by Jesus' resurrection. They argue that this hypothesis is testable and accords with the bulk of Shroud data.

12. There is evidence that the D'Arcis memorandum may have been improperly translated and improperly motivated.[2]

13. All other scientific evidence points to authenticity.

II. A Pre-Medieval Origin—Evidence for:

A. Historical references to a shroud-like cloth begin in Edessa in the second century A.D. Multiple references, including mention of full-length and facial images, continue from that period and become pronounced from the eighth to the twelfth centuries.

B. A miraculous image of Christ from Edessa becomes known, revered, and copied, and its likeness to the Shroud of Turin is unmistakable. The image becomes famous worldwide.

C. The Emperor of Constantinople sends an army to Edessa, captures the Shroud, and returns it to his city. From 944–1204, the Shroud of Christ is mentioned on lists of relics in Constantinople.

D. Artistic likenesses between the first and second centuries are sporadic but do display similarities to the Shroud.

E. From the fifth century onward, artistic renditions of Christ are so similar to the Shroud that they virtually match when overlaid on the Shroud. Even coins from that era show clear evidence of the Shroud's influence.

F. The Shroud violates artistic traditions by depicting nails in the wrists, not in the hands; the crown as a cap, not as a wreath; and a long pigtail of hair, which is decidedly Jewish style in the first century. This argues strongly against a human artistic effort.

G. The textile evidence includes the following: (1) The cloth weave analysis reveals that the cloth is consistent with an early Middle East origin; (2) the cloth material includes threads from a type of cotton specific to the Middle East; (3) the three-to-one

212

twill weave with a "Z" twist is found within 200+ years of the time of Christ.

H. Pollens and mites are found on the Shroud, which mitigate strongly against a medieval European origin. Pollens specific to Palestine, Turkey, and Constantinople are found. The pollen trail matches the Edessan history proposed for the Shroud's missing years. And the mites are specific to Middle East burial garments. The Shroud's known history precludes any movement outside of Europe.

I. Medical and pathological evidence on the Shroud predates scientific knowledge in those areas. Crucifixion by nails was done during a very limited historical time frame, and it was outlawed at least twelve centuries before the Shroud's documented existence. No known medieval artistic renditions ever depicted Christ nude, but the Shroud does. The pathological evidence of postmortem bleeding, rigor mortis, death by asphyxiation, and chest-wall trauma all pre-date medical knowledge of them. Also, the phylactery and crown evidenced in the Shroud image are unusual to crucifixion and/or specific to Jews.

J. Scientific analysis confirms the existence of first-century coins covering the eyes on the Shroud image. The letter shapes on these coins, including a peculiar misspelling in their inscription, match Roman coins which are known to have been minted during the reign of Pontius Pilate—the ruler who permitted Jesus' crucifixion. Computer enhancement and analysis also show that these Shroud coins have twenty-four coincidences of dimension, location, selection, order, and angle which fit only a coin issued by Pontius Pilate between 29 and 32 A.D.

APPENDIX B

Comparison of Image-Formation Theories with Image Characteristics

THEORIES CHARACTERISTICS	*Paint, Dye, or Powder	*Direct Contact	*Vapor	*Direct Contact and Vapor	Unknown Energy Source	German-Pellicori Direct Contact + Unknown Variable
Superficial	No	No	No	No	Yes	Possible
Detailed	No	No	No	Possible	Possible	No
Thermally Stable	No	Possible	No	Possible	Yes	Yes
Pigment	No	Possible	Yes	Yes	Yes	Yes
3-D	No	No	No	No	Yes	Possible**
Negative	Yes	Possible	Possible	Possible	Yes	Yes
Directionless	Possible	Possible	Yes	Yes	Yes	Yes
Chemically Stable	Possible	Possible	No	No	Yes	Possible
Water Stable	Possible	Possible	No	No	Yes	Yes
UV Image Fluorescence	—	—	—	—	No	No

*Discounted by scientists.
**Researchers disagree.
Note: Known forms of heat/light scorch dismissed.

APPENDIX C

Summary Critiques of Alternative Image-Formation Hypotheses

After much research on the Shroud of Turin, we have concluded that the most probable theory is that the image on the cloth was formed by some kind of scorching process. However, other hypotheses have been suggested to explain how the image was formed, and many of them have appeared in the popular press. For documentation and further explanation, see Chapter 8 and *Verdict,* pp. 191–197.

I. **Fraud Hypotheses: These Theories Maintain that the Shroud Was Created by One of Several Forms of Fakery.**

    A. General theories of fraud which indicate that the image was created by the application of paint, dye, powder, or other foreign substance to the Shroud

        1. Microchemical analyses revealed no pigments, stains, powders, dyes, or painting media on the Shroud. Several such tests were performed, including photoreflectance and ultraviolet fluorescence, all agreeing that no fakery is involved. In particular, X-ray fluorescence was considered the major test for detecting such fraud, and it revealed no foreign substance in the image area which could account for the image itself.

2. Fraud is refuted by the Shroud's 3-D characteristics.

3. Fakery is disproven by the superficial nature of the image.

4. There are no plateaus or saturation points on the Shroud image, as would be expected with applications of pigment, dye, etc.

5. The nondirectionality of the image rules out brush strokes or other directional application of a foreign substance.

6. No capillary flow appears on the Shroud, which further rules out any liquid movement on the cloth.

7. The 1532 fire would have caused chemical changes in organic pigments, but no such changes are visible on the Shroud.

8. The water applied to the Shroud after the 1532 fire would also have caused chemical changes in many pigments, but none can be observed on the Shroud image.

9. The nontraditional body image (pierced wrists, a cap of thorns, and possibly nude body) also militates against fraud.

B. Walter McCrone: Iron oxide was used to touch up or to create the Shroud image

1. McCrone must account for refutations IA:1–9 above, which invalidate his hypothesis.

2. The scientists specifically checked McCrone's thesis with highly sensitive microchemical tests and found that Fe_2O_3 does not account for the Shroud image.

3. Submicron-size Fe_2O_3 has been available only within the last two hundred years, making its use in medieval times highly problematical.

216

4. McCrone's observations have not been verified by independent testing.

C. Joe Nickell: Various ideas that ink or powder application produced the Shroud image (see Bibliography)

1. Refutations IA:1–9 above invalidate Nickell's thesis.

2. Nickell's photographs were specifically tested and failed the three-dimensional VP-8 analysis, thus indicating high probability that his methods did not create the true 3-D image on the Shroud.

3. Such a method would probably involve image saturation, which would invalidate it.

4. Nickell's experiment did not recreate the resolution of the Shroud image.

5. Nickell's "squeeze" method apparently is not historically verified as a known technique used before the nineteenth century.

D. "Acid-painting": Addition of an acid or other chemical to cloth to produce an image

1. Refutations IA:1–9 above also invalidate this thesis.

2. Experiments revealed that acid painting is not superficial. That is, the chemical does not remain only on the surface of the material.

3. Testing also revealed that densities from such techniques differ from densities in the Shroud image.

4. Acid-painting involves an additional consideration in that if the acid is not neutralized, it will destroy the cloth.

II. **Vaporgraph Theories: These Theories Assert That the Shroud Image Was Created by the Diffusion of Gases Upward onto the Burial Cloth from Such Sources as Sweat, Ammonia, Blood, and Burial Spices.**

A. Vaporgraphs cannot account for the 3-D nature of the Shroud image.

B. The superficial Shroud image refutes vaporgraphic theories because such gases permeate the cloth and are not superficial.

C. There are no plateaus or saturation in the image, as would happen with vapor stains.

D. Vaporgraphs don't yield a clear image like that on the Shroud. Since vapor does not travel upward in straight or parallel lines, but diffuses in the air, vapor images are comparatively unclear.

E. No gaseous diffusion or capillary flow can be observed on the Shroud's image fibrils. These should be present in a vaporgraph.

F. Vaporgraphic images do not preserve the shading found in the Shroud image.

G. More ammonia is needed to create a vaporgraph than would probably be available on a dead body.

H. No foreign material is found on the Shroud image from such chemical reactions.

I. Few of these chemicals from or on the body are thermally stable, as is the Shroud image.

J. Many of these chemicals are active in water, but the Shroud image is stable in water.

K. Vaporgraphic theories cannot account for the transfer of the images of hair or coins.

III. Contact Theories: These Hypotheses Assert That the Shroud Image Is from Either Natural Contact with a Body or Contact Due to Fakery.

A. General objections to all contact theories, natural or fake:

1. Contact images would not be 3-D, thereby eliminating them as viable hypotheses.

2. The superficial nature of the image is also a major critique of contact theories.

3. The absence of plateaus or saturation in the Shroud image also militates against contact.

4. A contact image would rely on pressure. The fact that the Shroud reveals virtually the same density on the frontal and dorsal images indicates a pressure-independent image formation.

5. That there are no chemicals on the Shroud is an important indicator that mitigates against any chemical transfer by contact.

6. The shading in the Shroud image probably eliminates contact.

7. The 1532 fire militates against the Shroud being formed by contact with natural organic materials.

8. Many chemicals are water active, but the Shroud image is not.

9. Resolution is still very difficult to explain by contact.

10. The question of whether contact theories can properly explain the transfer of the hair or the coins should also be considered.

B. Direct contact-latent image hypothesis: Attributes the Shroud image to natural contact with a body, transferring chemicals and causing the image over a period of time

1. This hypothesis is still shown to be untenable by refutations IIIA:1–10 above, which disprove it, as some specific examples will show.

2. The latent image form of direct contact still cannot account for the 3-D image. For instance, not all areas of the body (the face, for example) were contacted by the cloth, yet even these areas are found on the Shroud image. To use our example, there are no face "drop outs" in the Shroud image. Therefore, this contact theory cannot adequately explain the image.

3. Superficiality is still a major problem for this method as well since the Shroud image does not generally follow dips in the threads.

4. The Shroud image lacks saturation points or plateaus, which severely limits the time dependence of this model.

5. Whereas the Shroud image is pressure independent, this contact hypothesis would be pressure dependent, as with the weight of the body on the dorsal image and the cloth on the frontal image being responsible for the image. This is a very serious obstacle for this model.

6. There are no traces on the Shroud of sensitizing chemicals from any such contact procedures.

7. It would seem that this hypothesis also cannot explain the transfer of the hair in the Shroud image.

8. Some question the experimental method used to represent accelerated aging.

9. If such a reaction can normally occur between

a dead body and a burial cloth, why don't more burial garments also have such an image? Many grave clothes exist, but the Shroud image is unique. No others are known to have a body image at all.

C. The "hot statue" and "hot flat-plate" theories: A statue or flat-plate image of a man was heated and a cloth laid across it, producing a contact or near-contact scorch

1. Many of the objections (IIIA:1–10) above still apply to these theories and thereby render them untenable.

2. The 1532 fire is very helpful here in that it did produce a contact scorch in a variety of densities. However, ultraviolet fluorescence photographs showed that these scorched areas do fluoresce while the body image does not, thereby revealing that they are different. There is also a color difference between the two types of fibrils.

3. Experiments have shown that hot statue or hot flat-plate images are not superficial, thus invalidating these methods.

4. A hot statue or hot flat-plate is distorted. The Shroud image distinctly lacks distortion.

5. Experiments revealed that such a hot statue or hot flat-plate scorch would not produce the shading found on the Shroud.

6. A hot statue or hot flat-plate forgery would be very difficult to create without burning the cloth beyond recognition of any image.

7. The resolution of the Shroud image is another difficult issue for a hot statue or hot flat-plate.

APPENDIX D

Biblical Questions Addressed

A major question in the study of the Shroud of Turin is the correspondence between the Shroud image and the New Testament accounts of Jesus' burial. This appendix summarizes answers to some of these questions. (The topic is covered in detail in Chapter 10 and in *Verdict*, pp. 201–203.)

A. Did first-century Jews bury the dead by wrapping a Shroud lengthwise around the body?

1. In a Qumran community cemetery, at least one person was found buried lying in the same position as the man in the Shroud, with elbows extended.

2. The *Code of Jewish Law*, "Laws of Mourning," states that a man executed by the government was to be buried in a single sheet.

3. No New Testament text describes a wrapping like that of a mummy. To the contrary, Lazarus came out of the tomb under his own power, although impaired (see question *B* below). Such is not in harmony with Egyptian wrapping but is compatible with the Shroud.

4. Even with 1–3, it could still be held that the burial depicted in the Shroud was only temporary because of the oncoming Sabbath. The

222

women were returning on Sunday to finish the
burial (Luke 23:54—24:1; Mark 16:1–3).

B. The Gospels speak of more than one strip of linen
being used (Luke 24:12; John 19:40; 20:5–7), while
the Shroud is only a single piece.

    1. The man buried in the Shroud was apparently
also wrapped in strips around the head (see
question *C* below), wrists, and feet, which
agrees exactly with the description in John
11:44. These were in addition to the main sheet
known as the Shroud. So more than one piece
of linen was used.

    2. Luke (or early Christian tradition) used the
singular and the plural interchangeably to describe the cloth(s) (cf. 23:53 with 24:12). Mark
15:46 and Matthew 27:59 also use the singular,
apparently referring to one major sheet, as in
the Shroud. The use of the plural thus apparently refers to additional strips.

C. Was a napkin placed over the face of Jesus, or was it
folded up and placed around His head?

    1. John 20:5–7 describes the napkin as being
folded up and fitting around Jesus' head. John
11:44 also asserts that a napkin was tied
around Lazarus' face. This position supports
the view that the small cloth was folded up and
tied around the head.

    2. The Mishnah (Shabbath 23:5) instruct Jews to
tie up the chin before burying a body.

    3. The "Laws of Mourning" also instructs Jews to
bind up the chin of the dead person.

    4. Evidence indicates that the man buried in the
Shroud also has such a napkin wrapped
around his head.

D. Jewish burial practice included washing the body. Were there any exceptions?

   1. The "Laws of Mourning" explains that persons killed by the government or those who died a violent death are not to be washed. Thus Jewish customs actually may have prohibited the washing of Jesus' body.

   2. Even without this previous point, it could still be held that Jesus' body was not washed because of His hurried burial. The women were returning with spices to anoint the body (Luke 24:1–4; Mark 16:1–3), and one purpose of spices was to cleanse. The Mishnah effectively prohibited washing bodies on the Sabbath (Shabbath 23:5).

   3. The Gospels never assert that Jesus' dead body was washed.

   4. But we have argued that is also possible that the body of the man in the Shroud was washed.

E. What can you say about the spices used in burying Jesus?

   Since neither the Gospels nor the Shroud give any specifics on how the spices were placed or even what form of spices were used, there is no contradiction. They may have been packed along each side of Jesus' body. However, since there is no evidence of any spices on the Shroud, this matter remains unsolved.

F. Wasn't Jesus nailed to the cross through His palms instead of His wrists?

   1. Even apart from the Shroud, evangelical scholars have long believed that Jesus was nailed through the wrists. Nails in the palms

of the hands would tear out under the weight of the body.

2. The Greek word *hand* includes the wrist, meaning that either area could be indicated.

G. Conclusion

Not only are there no contradictions between the Shroud and the Gospel accounts of Jesus' burial, but Scripture and early Jewish tradition even support the type of burial depicted in the Shroud. At any rate, the Shroud cannot be dismissed on the grounds that it is inconsistent with Scripture.

NOTES

Foreword

**Chapter 1   The Cloth and the Controversy: Where
We Are Today**

1. Associated Press reports, 28 Sept. 1988.
2. Associated Press reports, 13 Oct. 1988.
3. Kenneth E. Stevenson and Gary R. Habermas, *Verdict on the Shroud: Evidence for the Death and Resurrection of Jesus* (Ann Arbor, PA: Servant Books, 1981; Wayne, PA: Dell, 1982). This book will be referred to as *Verdict* in the text and the rest of the notes.
4. Although this section of Chapter 1 was written well before any rumors circulated about the C-14 dating, the release of the results did not affect our willingness to reconsider some former positions.
5. David Graf, review of *Verdict, First Edition,* 1 (Oct. 1981): 46–47.
6. See, for instance, *Verdict,* 6–7, 179–86.
7. Gary Habermas, letter to the editor, *Biblical Archaeology Review,* 10 (July–Aug. 1984): 24–25.
8. *Verdict,* Chapter 9.
9. Ibid., 121.
10. For example, what was earlier identified as a pigtail (*Verdict,* 35–36, photo 9) is dismissed by some researchers today as a peculiarity of the photographs.
11. Steven Schafersman, "Comment," *Current Anthropology,* 24 (June 1983): 301.
12. John Cole, ibid., 296.

13. Gordon Stein, review of *Verdict, The American Rationalist* (Jan.–Feb. 1982): 76–78.

14. William Meacham, "The Authentication of the Turin Shroud: An Issue in Archaeological Epistemology," *Current Anthropology,* 24 (June 1983): 306.

15. Kenneth Stevenson, ed., *Proceedings of the 1977 United States Conference of Research on the Shroud of Turin,* 23–24 March 1977, Albuquerque, NM (Bronx, NY: Holy Shroud Guild, 1977).

16. Gary R. Habermas, *The Resurrection of Jesus: A Rational Inquiry* (Ann Arbor, MI: University Microfilms, 1976); *The Resurrection of Jesus: An Apologetic* (Lanham, MD: University Press of America, 1984); *The Verdict of History: Conclusive Evidence for the Life of Jesus* (Nashville: Thomas Nelson, 1984); with Antony Flew, *Did Jesus Rise from the Dead? The Resurrection Debate,* ed. Terry Miethe (San Francisco: Harper and Row, 1987).

17. Meacham, "Authentication," 289, 307.

18. *Verdict,* 6–7, 179–86.

19. Brigid Elson, review of *Verdict, Queen's Quarterly,* 90:2 (1983): 570.

Chapter 2   Science, Skepticism, and the Shroud

1. Pamela Zurer, "Archaeological Chemistry," *Chemical & Engineering News* (21 Feb. 1983): 34.

2. Ibid.

3. Ibid.

4. Meacham, "Authentication," 298.

5. Natalie Angier, "Unraveling the Shroud of Turin," *Discover* (Oct. 1982): 60.

6. Post-Testing Meeting, Santa Barbara, California, 24–25 Mar. 1979.

7. Marvin M. Mueller, "The Shroud of Turin: A Critical Appraisal," *The Skeptical Inquirer,* 6 (Spring 1982): 29.

8. Ibid., 28.

9. Meacham, "Authentication," 298.

10. Angier, "Unraveling," 60.

11. L. A. Schwalbe and R. N. Rogers, "Physics and Chemistry of the Shroud of Turin: A Summary of the 1978 Investigation" (Amsterdam: Elsevier Scientific Publishing Co., n.d.), 60.

12. Walter McCrone, letter to John Jackson, *STURP Newsletter* (June 1980).

13. Meacham, "Authentication," 298.
14. Post-Testing Meeting, Santa Barbara, California, 24–25 Mar. 1979.
15. Walter McCrone, "Chemical Microscopy," *American Laboratory* (Dec. 1986), 24.
16. Ibid., 25.
17. Joseph Lambert, ed., "Of the Various Stains and Images on the Shroud of Turin," *American Chemical Society* #205, 467.
18. Ibid., 468.
19. Schwalbe and Rogers, "Physics and Chemistry," 60.
20. Meacham, "Authentication," 308.
21. John P. Jackson and William R. Ercoline, "The Three-Dimensional Characteristics of the Shroud Image," *IEEE 11982 Proceedings of the International Conference on Cybernetics and Society,* #0360–8913/82/0000–0559 (Oct. 1982): 573.
22. Meacham, "Authentication," 308.
23. Ibid., 299.
24. Jackson and Ercoline, "Three-Dimensional Characteristics," 575.
25. Robert A. Wild, S.J., "The Shroud of Turin: Probably the Work of a 14th-Century Artist or Forger," *Biblical Archaeology Review,* 10:2 (Mar./Apr. 1984): 46.
26. Schwalbe and Rogers, "Physics and Chemistry," 28.
27. Lambert, ed., "Of the Various Stains and Images," 470.
28. W. R. Ercoline, R. C. Downs, Jr., and John P. Jackson, "Examination of the Turin Shroud for Image Distortions," *IEEE 1982 Proceedings of the International Conference on Cybernetics and Society,* #0360–8913/82/0000–0576 (Oct. 1982): 579.
29. Alan Whanger and Mary Whanger, "Findings on the Shroud of Turin" (Raleigh Durham, NC: Mar. 1986).
30. Mary Whanger, interview with Ken Stevenson, July 1988.
31. Kenneth Weaver, *National Geographic* staff member, speaking in Data Reduction Meeting, Los Alamos, NM.
32. Robert Haralick, *Analysis of Digital Images of the Shroud of Turin* (Blacksburg, VA: Spatial Data Analysis Laboratory, Virginia Polytechnic Institute and State University, 1983): 2.
33. Alan Whanger and Mary Whanger, "Polarized Image Overlay Technique: A New Image Comparison Method and Its Applications," *Applied Optics,* 24 (Mar. 1985): 771.
34. Max Frei, "Nine Years of Palynological Studies on the Shroud," *Shroud Spectrum International,* 1 (June 1982): 7.

35. Meacham, "Authentication," 307.
36. William Meacham, interview with Ken Stevenson in Tarrytown, NY, 15 July 1988.
37. Schwalbe and Rogers, "Physics and Chemistry," 45, *ACA,* 1982.
38. Eric J. Jumper, et al., "A Comprehensive Examination of Various Stains and Images on the Shroud of Turin," *ACS Advances in Chemistry, No. 205, Archaeological Chemistry III,* ed. Joseph B. Lambert (1984): 456.
39. Ibid., 467.
40. Ibid.
41. Ibid.
42. Alan Adler, interview with Ken Stevenson, July 15 1988.
43. Adler quoted in Zurer, "Archaeological Chemistry," 35.
44. Oswald Scheuermann, "Shroud of Turin—Image Formation: New Biblical Basis" (8501 Behringersdorf, Nürnberg, West Germany, June 1986): 67.
45. Adler, interview, July 15, 1988.
46. Scheuermann, "Shroud" (West Germany: June 1986): A1, 5, 7.
47. Ray Rogers quoted in Walter C. McCrone, "How the Shroud Was Created," *The Microscope,* 30:3 (1982): 234.

Chapter 3   Carbon 14: Is the Shroud a Medieval Object?

1. According to the gas-counter method of dating, C-14 measurements are made on the gas products of a material's ionization and carbonization. This method of dating is viewed by scientists as able to give more accurate results because residual gas can be redated, allowing for multiple testing on only one sample.
2. Bill McClellan, "Secrets of the Shroud," *St. Louis Dispatch,* 15 May 1988, C1, 16.
3. Adler, interview, 15 July 1988.
4. William Meacham, in a paper delivered at the March 1986 Hong Kong Symposium on the Turin Shroud.
5. "Wrapped in Mystery," *Los Angeles Times,* 29 May 1988, 1.
6. Ibid., italics added.
7. Bill McClellan, "Secrets of the Shroud," *St. Louis Dispatch,* 15 May 1988, C1, 16.
8. Meacham, 1986 Hong Kong Symposium.
9. Ibid.
10. *McGraw-Hill Encyclopedia of Science and Technology,* 6th ed., s.v. "radiocarbon dating," italics added.

11. Ibid., 125.
12. Ibid., 126, italics added.
13. Ibid., 123.
14. Ibid., 128, italics added.
15. Michael Tite, "An Inter Comparison of Some AMS and Small Gas Counter Laboratories," *Radiocarbon,* 28 (1986): 575.
16. Ibid., 576.
17. Ibid.
18. Willy Wolfi, *Nuclear Instruments and Methods in Physics Research,* B29, 1987, 1–13.
19. Harry Gove, Univ. of Rochester, letter to Sir David Wilson, 27 Jan. 1988, British Museum.
20. William Meacham, "Comments on the British Museum's Involvement in Carbon Dating the Turin Shroud," Hong Kong, Nov. 1988, 2.
21. News release, "Turin Shroud Dated to A.D. 200–1000 in Secret Testing: Results Inconsistent with Recent Dates," 14 October 1988.
22. It should be remembered that the difference between these tests is not three samples (1988) versus one sample (1982). The 1988 tests were conducted on only a single sample, as we mentioned earlier. So the two testings are definitely at odds.
23. Wolfi, *Nuclear Instruments,* 1–13, italics added.
24. Meacham, interview, 15 July 1988.

Chapter 4   Other Tests for Age: Their Reliability and Their Results

1. Gilbert Raes, "Rapport d'Analise," *La S. Sindone* supplement to *Rivista diocesana torinese,* Turin Commission on the Holy Shroud, January 1976, 83.
2. Max Frei, as quoted by Ian Wilson, *Shroud of Turin* (New York: Doubleday, 1978): 63.
3. Werner Bulst, "The Pollen Grains on the Shroud of Turin," *Shroud Spectrum,* 10 (1984).
4. Ibid.
5. Post-Testing Meeting, Santa Barbara, California, 24–25 Mar. 1979.
6. Eric Jumper, Kenneth Stevenson, Jr., and John Jackson, "Images of Coins on a Burial Cloth?" *The Numismatist,* July 1978, 1356.
7. Josh McDowell and Don Stewart, *Answers to Tough Questions*

Skeptics Ask About the Christian Faith (San Bernardino, CA: Here's Life, 1980), 168.

8. Haralick, *Analysis,* p. 34.
9. Eleazor Erbach, interview with Ken Stevenson, Denver, Colorado, April 1978.
10. Meacham, interview, 15 July 1988.
11. Noel Currer-Briggs, *The Shroud and the Grail* (London: Weidenfeld & Nicholson, 1987), 241. Reviewed in *British Society for the Turin Shroud Newsletter,* May 1987, 13.
12. John Tyrer, "Looking at the Turin Shroud as a Textile," *Shroud Spectrum,* 6 (1983): 38.
13. Ibid., 43.
14. Luigi Fossati, S.J., "Was the So-Called Acheropita of Edessa the Italy Shroud?" *Shroud Spectrum,* 3 (June 1982): 23.
15. Rex Morgan, *The Holy Shroud and the Earliest Paintings of Christ* (Manly, Australia: Runciman Press, 1986), 121–22, italics added.
16. Rex Morgan, telephone conversation with Ken Stevenson, Oct. 1988.
17. Morgan, *Holy Shroud,* 121–22, italics added.
18. Currer-Briggs, *The Holy Grail and the Shroud of Christ* (Middlesex: ARA Publications, 1984), 156.
19. Ian Wilson, *The Mysterious Shroud* (Garden City, NY: Doubleday and Co., 1986), 82. For a complete discussion of Bishop d'Arcis and his forgery claims, see *Verdict,* 100–104.

Chapter 5   The Witness of History

1. Robert L. Wise, *The Scrolls of Edessa* (Wheaton, IL: Victor Books, 1987), 9.
2. Ian Wilson, *The Shroud of Turin: The Burial Cloth of Jesus Christ* (Garden City, NY: Doubleday, 1978).
3. Heinrich Pfeiffer, S.J., "The Shroud of Turin and the Face of Christ in Paleochristian, Byzantine and Western Medieval Art, Part I," *Shroud Spectrum,* 9 (Dec. 1983): 9.
4. One of the best discussions of this "speculation" is found in Josh McDowell's *Evidence That Demands a Verdict* (Campus Crusade for Christ, 1979) pp. 228–31. The first conclusion the scholars reach is that something about the grave clothes themselves convinced John that Jesus had risen from the dead. We agree. However, some if not most of them incorrectly surmise that it was an

231

empty mummy wrap, "like a discarded chrysalis" (p. 230, McDowell).

5. See, for example, William Stuart McBirnie, *The Search for the Twelve Apostles* (Wheaton, IL: Tyndale House, 1973), 204.
6. Ibid., 195–97.
7. Wilson, *The Mysterious Shroud.*
8. Ibid., Chapter 7.
9. Wilson, *The Shroud of Turin,* 127.
10. Ibid., 95, 241.
11. Ibid., 99.
12. Wilson, *The Mysterious Shroud,* 112–14, 120.
13. Wilson, *The Shroud of Turin,* 135, italics added.
14. Ibid., 135, italics added.
15. Ibid., 136, italics added.
16. Ibid., 136, italics added.
17. Ibid., 145.
18. Nicholas Mesarites quoted, ibid., 144.

Chapter 6 The Burial Cloth of Jesus?
1. See *Verdict,* especially Chapters 8 and 9 for details in the movement from the reliability of the Scriptures to the question of the identity of the man buried in the Shroud.
2. Giulio Ricci, "Historical, Medical and Physical Study of the Holy Shroud," *Proceedings,* ed. Stevenson, 60.
3. Dr. David Willis concluded that the marks on the back of the head were "caused by independent puncture wounds of the scalp." Quoted in Wilson, *The Shroud of Turin,* 23; cf., 36–37.
4. Questions about the relationship between the burial of Jesus and that of the man in the Shroud are common. For a summary treatment, see Chapter 10 and Appendix D; for a fuller treatment, see *Verdict,* Chapter 4 and Appendix C.
5. Francis Filas shared this conclusion in a television interview, "Inquiry into the Shroud of Turin," CBN University, 4 April 1980.
6. Vincent J. Donovan, "The Shroud and the Laws of Probability," *The Catholic Digest* (Apr. 1980): 51–52.
7. Ibid., 51.
8. Ibid.
9. See *Verdict,* Chapter 9.
10. Donovan postulated 1 chance in 500 for both men having been

crucified, which, as he noted, is quite conservative. But he also noted a 1 in 2 probability that both are males. Thus, by his estimate, chances are 1 in 1,000 that the Shroud wrapped a crucified man. The problem here is that once it is agreed that the Shroud is the burial garment of a crucified person, it probably *would* be a male because males were more commonly crucified. While probability of its being a male would be slightly increased, it should not be doubled. See Donovan, "The Shroud," 50.

11. For statements by Stewart and Coon, see Robert K. Wilcox, *Shroud* (New York: Macmillan, 1977), 130–31, 136.

12. For instance, see Anthony Sava, MD, "The Holy Shroud on Trial," in *Proceedings,* ed. Stevenson, 50–57.

13. Philip McNair, "The Shroud and History: Fantasy, Fake or Fact?" *Face to Face with the Turin Shroud,* ed. Peter Jennings (Oxford: Mowbray, 1978), 35.

14. Steven D. Schafersman, "Science, the Public, and the Shroud of Turin," *The Skeptical Inquirer,* 1 (Spring 1982): 41.

15. Robert K. Wilcox, *Shroud* (New York: Macmillan, 1977).

16. Wilcox's series, entitled "The Shroud: What Does Science Say About the Ancient Cloth of Turin?" appeared in four consecutive issues of *The Voice,* beginning with "Shroud: Real or Fake?", 26 Feb. 1982, 12.

17. Wilcox, "Shroud: Real or Fake?", 12.

18. For Jackson's statement, see Cullen Murphy, "Shreds of Evidence," *Harper's* (Nov. 1981): 61.

19. Robert Bucklin, cited by Richard Lewis, "Pathologist at Calvary: Examination of Turin Shroud Provides Crucifixion Details," *American Medical News* (13 Apr. 1979): 21.

20. John H. Heller, *Report on the Shroud of Turin* (Boston: Houghton Mifflin, 1983), 217.

21. Ibid., 219–20.

22. Donald Lynn, personal communication with Ken Stevenson, 1984.

23. Murphy, "Shreds," 47.

24. "The Shroud: It's Even Changed the Lives of Scientists Studying It," *Globe,* 22 Sept. 1981, 26.

25. Ibid.

26. Concerning problems with dating, see also Charles Foley, "Carbon Dating and the Holy Shroud," *Shroud Spectrum,* 1:1:25–27. See also Meacham, "Authentication," 289.

27. Robert Wilcox, "Fake or Not, Shroud Leaves Mark on Scientists," *The Voice*, 19 Mar. 1982, 12.
28. Heller, *Report*, 219.
29. For this statement in context, see Wilson, *Shroud*, 20.

Chapter 7   Death by Crucifixion: The Discoveries and Disputes of Pathology

1. Heller, *Report*, 17.
2. For background information, see *Verdict*, Chapter 5.
3. For summaries, including sources, see Wilson, *The Shroud of Turin*, Chapter 3; Wilcox, *Shroud*, 23–25, 72–73; *Verdict*, Chapter 10.
4. Wilcox, *Shroud*, 161; cf. 23–25.
5. Pierre Barbet, *A Doctor at Calvary* (New York: Doubleday, 1953).
6. Sava, *Proceedings*, ed. Stevenson, 50–57.
7. Wilson, *The Shroud of Turin*, 29; Wilcox, *Shroud*, 72–73.
8. The Shroud of Turin Research Project (STURP) press release was marked "Text" and dated 8 October 1981. Future references will be noted as STURP, "Text."
9. Heller, *Report*, 210.
10. Frederick T. Zugibe, *The Cross and the Shroud* (New York: Angelus Books, 1982).
11. For this confrontation, see Murphy, "Shreds," 56–57.
12. Zugibe, *Cross*, 138–40, 199.
13. For an account of the experimental design and the results, see ibid., 96–115.
14. For Zugibe's evaluation of the Shroud, see ibid., 138.
15. Ibid., 195–96.
16. See Robert Bucklin, "The Legal and Medical Aspects of the Trial and Death of Christ," *Medicine, Science and the Law* (Jan. 1970): 25; Bucklin, cited by Lewis, "Pathologist at Calvary," 21; Zugibe, *Cross*, 24–35.
17. Bucklin, cited by Lewis, "Pathologist at Calvary," 21.
18. Zugibe, *Cross*, 77, 85–88, 105–9, 117–18, 195–99.
19. For Zugibe's research on the location of the nails in the hand, see *Cross*, 56–79, 87.
20. Robert Bucklin, interview with Gary Habermas, 15 March 1984.
21. Zugibe, *Cross*, 159–60.
22. Joseph Gambescia and Robert Bucklin, "Pathology and Forensic

Pathology," STURP Conference, New London, CT, 10 October 1981.

23. Zugibe, *Cross*, 79–88.
24. Ibid., 80, 85.
25. Bucklin, cited by Lewis, "Pathologist at Calvary," 21. Gambescia agrees with Bucklin's assessment. See Reginald W. Rhein, Jr., "The Shroud of Turin: Medical Examiners Disagree," *Medical World News* (22 Dec. 1980): 47.
26. Zugibe, *Cross*, 136; cf. 132–37.
27. Zugibe recognizes this fact in *Cross*, 89–90.
28. See Bucklin, "Legal and Medical Aspects," 24; "The Shroud of Turin: A Pathologist's Viewpoint," *Legal Medicine* (Philadelphia: W. B. Saunders, 1982), 37, 39. Cf. "Medical Aspects of the Crucifixion of Christ," *Linacre Quarterly* (Feb. 1958): 1–9; rpt. *Sindon*, 7 (1961): 6.
29. Zugibe, *Cross*, 89–95.
30. Ibid., 68–70, 94–95, 105.
31. Meacham, "Authentication," 285; Robert Bucklin, in the film *Silent Witness*.
32. Zugibe, *Cross*, 92.
33. See *Verdict*, 116–17. Cf. Nicu Hass, "Anthropological Observations on the Skeletal Remains from Giv'at ha-Mivtar," *Israeli Exploration Journal*, 20 (1970): 38–59.
34. Meacham, "Authentication," 285.
35. William D. Edwards, Wesley J. Gabel, and Floyd E. Hosmer, "On the Physical Death of Jesus Christ," *Journal of the American Medical Association*, 255 (21 Mar. 1986): 1455, 1461, 1463.
36. Bucklin, "Medical Aspects," 8.
37. Bucklin, "Shroud," 25–26; interview with Gary Habermas, 5 and 30 May 1981.
38. Heller, *Report*, 217.
39. Zugibe, *Cross*, 118–31, 162, 171.
40. Edwards, Gabel, and Hosmer, "On the Physical Death," 1463. For Bucklin's proposed combination of the views of Barbet and Sava on this point, see "Medical Aspects," 25–26; "Shroud," 38–39; interview with Habermas 30 Apr. and 5 May 1981; Zugibe, *Cross*, 127, 130.
41. On the issue of rigor mortis, see Zugibe, *Cross*, 148–50, 152; Meacham, "Authentication," 285; John P. Jackson, Eric Jumper, and

R. William Mottern, "The Three-Dimensional Image," *Proceedings,* ed. Stevenson, 92: Bucklin, "Legal and Medical Aspects," 22, 24; Bucklin, "Shroud," 36.

42. Cf. Zugibe, *Cross,* 165, with the more detailed reports in Bucklin, "Legal and Medical Aspects," 25; "Shroud," 25; Heller, *Report,* 217; Meacham, "Authentication," 286.

43. Zugibe, *Cross,* 165.

44. *Verdict,* Chapter 4 and pages 202–3. It is true that the *Code of Law* is much later than the New Testament, but its prescriptions frequently reflect earlier tradition. For an excellent article on this subject, see Bonnie LaVoie, et al., "In Accordance with Jewish Burial Custom, the Body of Jesus Was Not Washed," *Shroud Spectrum,* 1 (June 1982): 8–17. The authors provide much evidence from the Old Testament through the sixteenth century that Jewish custom in Jesus' time would be in agreement with the *Code of Jewish Law,* meaning that Jesus' body would not have been washed before His burial.

45. Shabbath 23:5.

46. For questions such as these, see Robert A. Wild, "Shroud of Turin," *Biblical Archaeological Review* (Mar.–Apr. 1984): 40; Frank C. Tribbe, *Portrait of Jesus? The Illustrated Story of the Shroud of Turin* (New York: Stein and Day, 1983), 90–93; Zugibe, *Cross,* 91, 151–52.

47. See Tribbe, ibid., and Zugibe, ibid. Wild prefers the view that the Shroud is a forgery but admits he does not know what kind (ibid., 30, 45). Numerous other problems in his article are answered in this present book, especially in Chapter 8. Cf. Gary Habermas, "To the Editor," *Biblical Archaeological Review* (July–Aug. 1984): 24–25.

48. Zugibe, ibid., 151–52.

49. Ibid., 91, 125, 150–52, 157, 159–63.

50. Ibid., 192.

51. Ibid., 42.

52. Haas, "Anthropological Observations," 38–59.

53. Meacham, "Authentication," 291.

54. Cf. Wilson, *The Shroud of Turin,* 21.

55. Zugibe, *Cross,* 65–66, 160.

56. See *Verdict,* 49–51, 202.

57. Zugibe, *Cross,* 125–27, 189.

58. Ibid., 192, 189.
59. Robert Bucklin, interview with Gary Habermas, 15 March 1984.
60. Some have used the testimony of Michael Baden, deputy chief medical examiner of New York, Queens County, against the "traditional" views of pathologists who have investigated the Shroud. Baden was quoted as disputing most of their pathological conclusions. Bucklin points out, however, that Baden's testimony is somewhat muted by such factors as his making no personal examination of the Shroud and not spending much time studying it. Baden himself admits, "In no way do I hold myself out as an expert on the shroud. . . ." Bucklin, a friend of Baden, asserted that if he [Bucklin] and others "could sit down with him for a few hours, we could get him to change his mind." See Rhein, "The Shroud of Turin," especially 40, 49–50, for this discussion. Meacham is a bit more direct:

> Baden . . . is a lone sniper laying siege to a fortified city. Regardless of his prestige, his opinions appear off the cuff. He has not seen the Shroud, nor does he appear to be familiar with the vast medical literature or to have been in contact with other scholars; he has not published on the subject; he is said to be "something of an iconoclast" [quoting Bucklin in Rhein, 50]; his opinions were given on the basis of magazine photographs. . . . This is not to say that Baden may not have something useful to contribute to Shroud studies, but the fact that skeptics quote him at this stage demonstrates their desperation in the medical arena. ("Authentication," 307–8).

61. Zugibe, *Cross,* 199.

Chapter 8   The Crux of the Controversy: The Cause of the Image

1. See *Verdict,* Chapters 5 and 6.
2. Ibid., 191–97.
3. Ray Rogers, cited by Murphy, "Shreds," 44.
4. R. William Mottern, cited by Murphy, "Shreds," 47.
5. Heller, *Report,* 201.
6. STURP, "Text," 1.
7. See Murphy, "Shreds," 47, 61–62, including comments by Jackson and Jumper. For the same view from Zugibe, see *Cross,* 192.
8. Heller, *Report,* 198.
9. Ibid., 207.

10. Ibid., 209.
11. For one report on McCrone's work, see Angier, "Unraveling," 54–60. For a technical discussion by McCrone, see *The Microscope,* 28 (Mar.–Apr.): 105–15.
12. See Schafersman, "Science, the Public, and the Shroud," 49.
13. STURP, "Text," 1; Murphy, "Shreds," 56.
14. Heller, *Report,* 194.
15. Ibid., 205, 213.
16. McCrone, cited by Murphy, "Shreds," 54–55.
17. Murphy, ibid., 55; Meacham, "Authentication," 289, 308. See also Jackson, Jumper, and Ercoline, "Three-Dimensional Characteristics," 566–69.
18. Mueller, "Shroud," 29. For a further critique, see *Verdict,* 191–92.
19. Joe Nickell, "The Turin Shroud: Fake? Fact? Photograph?", *Popular Photography* (Nov. 1979): 99, 147. Nickell has published other works on the Shroud, including articles in *The Humanist,* Jan. and June 1978, and a book, *Inquest on the Shroud of Turin* (Buffalo: Prometheus Books, 1983).
20. Jackson, cited by Murphy, "Shreds," 58, 60–61; Jackson, Jumper, and Ercoline, "Three-Dimensional Characteristics," 573.
21. Heller, *Report,* 208.
22. Don Lynn and Jean Lorre, cited by Murphy, "Shreds," 55.
23. Zugibe, *Cross,* 180.
24. Heller, *Report,* 203. Cf. *Verdict,* 191–93.
25. Heller, ibid.; Murphy, "Shreds," 55.
26. STURP, "Text," 2. Cf. *Verdict,* 193.
27. Heller, *Report,* 207–8, 211.
28. Ron London, cited by Murphy, "Shreds," 56.
29. Heller, *Report,* 203, 208, 211.
30. Ibid., 203.
31. Ibid., 211.
32. STURP, "Text," 2.
33. Rogers, cited by Murphy, "Shreds," 65.
34. Heller, *Report,* Chapter 14.
35. Mueller, "Shroud," 27.
36. STURP, "Text," 1–2. Cf. Jackson, Jumper, and Ercoline, "Three-Dimensional Characteristics," 559, 569, 575.
37. Heller, *Report,* 207–9.
38. See *Verdict,* 191–93.

39. One might, for instance, speak of heated statues and bas-reliefs in this category, but we have already discussed these options.
40. Paul Vignon, *The Shroud of Christ* (New Hyde Park, NY: University Books, 1970).
41. Wilcox, "What Caused Shroud Images?" *The Voice,* 12 Mar. 1982, 10. Cf. Jackson, Jumper, and Ercoline, "Three-Dimensional Characteristics," 569.
42. Mueller, "Shroud," 27.
43. STURP, "Text," 1.
44. For other problems with this view, see *Verdict,* 193–94.
45. Wilcox, "Half of Shroud Scientists Say Image Is Authentic," *The Voice,* 5 Mar. 1982, 12.
46. Cf. Heller, *Report,* 209.
47. Rogers, cited by Murphy, "Shreds," 65.
48. Mueller, "Shroud," 27.
49. Schwalbe and Rogers, "Physics and Chemistry," 35–36, 43–45.
50. Heller, *Report,* 210.
51. Ibid., 209.
52. *Verdict,* 195–96.
53. STURP, "Text," 1.
54. See *Verdict,* 194–95.
55. Heller, *Report,* 201.
56. Schafersman, "Science, the Public, and the Shroud," 42.
57. Murphy, "Shreds," 47. See the conclusions of Jackson, Jumper, and Ercoline, "Three-Dimensional Characteristics," 559, 575.
58. STURP, "Text," 1; Murphy, "Shreds," 47.
59. STURP, ibid., 2
60. Heller, *Report,* 218–20.
61. Mueller, "Shroud," 28.
62. Wilcox, "Half," 12.
63. Wilcox, "What Caused Shroud Images?", 11.
64. STURP, "Text," 1.
65. Wilcox, "Shroud: Real or Fake?", 14, 11.
66. Mueller, "Shroud," 23.
67. Cf. Wilcox, "What Caused Shroud Images?", 10–11; Murphy, "Shreds," 65.
68. Wilcox, ibid.
69. Wilcox, "Shroud: Real or Fake?", 13–14.
70. Wilcox, "Scientists," 11.

71. Rogers, cited by Murphy, "Shreds," 65.
72. Heller, *Report*, 220; interview with Gary Habermas, 19 May 1980.
73. See *Verdict*, Chapter 6.
74. Zurer, "Archaeological Chemistry," 35.
75. Giles Carter, quoted by Emma Jackson, "Prof Thinks X-Rays Caused Shroud Image," *Christian Herald*, Feb. 1983, A1, 5. For a technical discussion, see Giles F. Carter, "Formation of the Image on the Shroud of Turin by X-rays: A New Hypothesis," *Archaeological Chemistry*, 3 (1984): 425–46.
76. Zurer, "Archaeological Chemistry," 35.
77. Emma Jackson, "Prof Thinks," A5.
78. Jerome Goldblatt, "The Shroud," *National Review* (16 Apr. 1982): 419.
79. Schwalbe and Rogers, "Physics and Chemistry," 30–33.
80. Ibid.
81. For instance, see suggestions by Ray Rogers, "Chemical Considerations Concerning the Shroud of Turin," *Proceedings*, ed. Stevenson, 188; Wilson, *The Shroud of Turin*, 207–12; Wilcox, *Shroud*, 171–73.
82. STURP, "Text," 2.

Chapter 9   New Evidence for Jesus' Resurrection?

1. Of the three categories of image explanations—artificial (fakery), natural, and unknown-source scorch theories—the artificial hypotheses are most problematical in terms of the facts. They remain possible explanations but are not likely. Still, if the Shroud is medieval in origin, it of course *cannot* offer any evidence for Jesus' resurrection.
2. Wilcox, "Half," 13.
3. Wilcox, "Shroud: Real or Fake?", 12.
4. Heller, *Report*, 220.
5. Bucklin, "Afterword," *Verdict*, 190.
6. Bucklin, interview with Gary Habermas, 30 April 1981. See also *Verdict*, 155–57.
7. Emma Jackson, "Prof Thinks," A5.
8. Ibid.
9. Zurer, "Archaeological Chemistry," 35.
10. Goldblatt, "Shroud," 418–19. See also *Verdict*, 155–57.
11. Thomas Phillips, *Nature*, 337 (1989): 594, and *The British Society*

for the Turin Shroud Newsletter, May 1989. The latter is also reproduced in Joseph Marino's newsletter, "Sources for Information and Materials on the Shroud of Turin," July 1989.

12. Eberhard Lindner's lecture was presented at the International Scientific Symposium on the Shroud, which was held in Paris, France, 7–8 September 1989. This lecture was reproduced in Joseph Marino's newsletter, ibid., September 1989.

13. Wilcox, "Shroud: Real or Fake?", 12–14.

14. See *Verdict,* Chapters 1–9 and p. 158 for a summary of this argument. If a person was simply crucified to copy Jesus' death, then one must still explain the Shroud phenomena listed in Chapter 8 of this present volume.

15. For this argument in greater detail, see Gary R. Habermas, "The Shroud of Turin: A Rejoinder to Basinger and Basinger," *Journal of the Evangelical Theological Society,* 25 (June 1982): 219–27.

16. Bucklin, interview with Habermas, 30 April 1981.

17. See Habermas, "Shroud," 220–22, for further support of the reliability of the Gospels.

18. For further detail and a similarly worded argument, see ibid., 224–25.

19. For an abbreviated form of this argument, see Habermas, "Shroud," 225–26. More details are provided in Habermas, *The Verdict of History* and *The Resurrection of Jesus.*

20. See especially Habermas, *The Verdict of History.*

21. Mueller, "Shroud," 17.

22. Ibid., 29.

23. Schafersman, "Science, the Public, and the Shroud," 43.

24. For a brief treatment, see *Verdict,* 163–73. For the actual argument, see Habermas, *The Resurrection of Jesus,* Chapters 2–3. The next two paragraphs in the text of this book are a fairly close rendering of material in *Verdict,* 168–70.

25. For examples of such claims by Jesus, see Matt. 11:27; 19:28–29; Mark 2:1–12, 17; 8:34–38; 9:31; 10:33–34, 45; 14:61–63; Luke 24:46–47; John 10:30; 14:6; cf. 5:18.

26. For Jesus' view of the corroborating nature of both His resurrection and His miracles in general, see Matt. 11:1–6; 12:22–28, 38–40; John 5:36–37; 10:36–38.

27. We are, of course, differentiating here between Jesus' resurrection in a glorified body and a miraculous return to one's mortal body, as in the case of Lazarus. For an investigation of the charge

that other religious figures were actually raised from the dead, see Gary Habermas, "Resurrection Claims in Non-Christian Religions," *Religious Studies,* forthcoming.
28. Habermas, *The Resurrection of Jesus,* Chapters 4–5.
29. See also *Verdict,* 171–72.

Chapter 10 Questions People Ask
 1. *Verdict,* 35–36.
 2. *Verdict,* Chapter 9. An area of statistical study not yet applied to the connection between Jesus and the Shroud concerns the fulfillment of Messianic prophecies. In his book *Science Speaks* (Peter W. Stoner and Robert C. Newman [Chicago: Moody Press, 1958]), Peter Stoner calculates the probability that anyone other than Jesus of Nazareth could have fulfilled eight major prophecies on the Messiah's death, burial, and resurrection. Stoner's conclusion is 1×10^{17}. Amazingly enough, the man depicted in the Shroud displays the fulfillment of the same eight prophecies Stoner used in his calculations. Further evidence that the Shroud is Jesus'?
 3. Ercoline, Downs, and Jackson, "Examination," 576–79.
 4. See *Verdict,* 100–104.
 5. *Verdict,* 102–4.
 6. Luigi Fossati, "The Lirey Controversy," *Shroud Spectrum,* 6 (Sept. 1983): 26–27.
 7. Wilson, *The Shroud of Turin,* p. 68.
 8. Fossati, "The Lirey Controversy," p. 27.
 9. John Heller, *20/20,* ABC, 16 April 1981.
10. Dee German, interview with Ken Stevenson, Oct. 1976, following lecture at Air Force Academy.
11. Pier Baima Bollone, "Identification of the Group of the Traces of Human Blood on the Shroud," *Shroud Spectrum,* 6 (Mar. 1983): 5.
12. *Verdict,* Chapter 5.
13. Ercoline, Downs, and Jackson, "Examination," 576–79.
14. Shroud of Turin Research Project (STURP), "Financial Statement," 1979.
15. Whanger and Whanger, "Polarized Image"; Haralick, *Analysis.*
16. *Verdict,* 143–59.
17. Schwalbe and Rogers, "Physics and Chemistry of the Shroud of Turin," *Analytica Chimica Acta* 135 (1982): 3–49.

Chapter 11 Speaking Out on the Shroud

1. Heller states the following about the religious affiliations of the 1978 STURP team: "there were six agnostics, two Mormons, three Jews, four Catholics, and all the rest Protestants—Methodists, Lutherans, Congregationalists, Baptists, Presbyterians, Episcopalians, and Dutch Reform" (Heller, *Report,* 88).
2. John D. German, lecture, Albuquerque, New Mexico, May 1988, italics added.
3. Ibid.
4. Ibid., italics added.
5. Ray Rogers, quoted by Murphy, "Shreds of Evidence," 65.
6. Ibid.
7. Allen Adler, interview with Ken Stevenson, 15 July 1988.
8. Ibid.
9. Barrie Schwortz, telephone conversation with Ken Stevenson, 27 Sept. 1988.
10. Bucklin, "Afterword," *Verdict,* 190.
11. See, for example, Robert Bucklin, "Comments," *Current Anthropology,* 24:3 (1984): 295.
12. Roger Gilbert and Marty Gilbert, interview with Ken Stevenson, Danbury, CT, 27 Sept. 1988.
13. Ibid.
14. Ibid.
15. Sam Pellicori, letter to Ken Stevenson, 5 Oct. 1988.
16. Ibid.
17. Ibid.
18. Ibid.
19. Ibid.
20. Ibid.
21. Meacham, interview with Ken Stevenson, Tarrytown, NY, 15 July 1988.
22. Ibid.
23. Ibid.
24. Ibid.
25. Ibid.
26. Ibid.
27. Name withheld, letter to Ken Stevenson, 1982.
28. John A. T. Robinson, "The Shroud of Turin and the Grave Clothes of the Gospels," in *Proceedings,* ed. Stevenson, 23–30.

Chapter 12   The Image That Won't Go Away

1. Norman Geisler, *Songtime* radio interview, Oct. 1981. Since the announcement of the 1988 C-14 results, Geisler has taken a more skeptical stand on the Shroud's authenticity.
2. Eric Jumper, "An Overview of the Testing Performed by STURP with a Summary of Results," *IEEE* (Oct. 1982): 535.
3. *Verdict,* 176, 177, 179, 186.
4. Luigi Gonella, "Scientific Investigation of the Shroud of Turin: Problems, Results, and Methodological Lessons," paper delivered at the 1986 Hong Kong Symposium, 39.
5. Peter Rinaldi, S.J., STURP meeting, 1978.
6. See the "Select Bibliography" for these and other sources.
7. Letter to the editor, in *The General Report and Proceedings of the British Society for the Turin Shroud* (Autumn 1979—Summer 1981):13.
8. Yves Delage, quoted by Wilson, *The Shroud of Turin,* 20.
9. Schafersman, *Chemical and Engineering News,* 21 Feb. 1983, 302.
10. Schafersman, "Comments," *Current Anthropology,* 24:3 (June 1983): 302.
11. Ibid.
12. Joseph Nickell, personal letter to Ken Stevenson, 1977, in reference to *The Shroud of Turin—Unmasked.*
13. Mueller, "Comments," *Current Anthropology,* 24:3 (June 1983): 299.
14. Mueller, "Shroud of Turin: A Critical Appraisal," *Skeptical Inquirer,* B, 1982: 16.
15. Schafersman, "Science, the Public, and the Shroud," *Skeptical Inquirer,* B, 1982:41, italics added.
16. Spiros Zodhiates, "Lexicon," *The Hebrew-Greek Key Study Bible* (Grand Rapids, MI: Baker Book House, 1984), 1659.
17. Alan Adler, interview with Ken Stevenson, 15 July 1988.
18. Richard E. Eby, *Caught Up into Paradise* (Old Tappan, NJ: Revell, 1978), 99.
19. Sam Pellicori, letter to Ken Stevenson, 5 Oct. 1988.
20. Zodhiates, "Lexicon," 1684, 1600, 44, 1711.
21. D. James Kennedy in pamphlet "Evolution's Bloopers and Blunders," 11.
22. Aldous Huxley, ibid.
23. Sir Julian Huxley, ibid.

24. Kennedy, "Creationism: Science or Religion?" 9–10.
25. Ibid, 12.
26. See Walter McCrone, *Methods in Chemical Microscopy* (pub info. coming from Ken), + p. #.
27. Alan Adler, "Archaeological Chemistry," *Chemical and Engineering News,* 35.
28. Gonella, "Scientific Investigation," 31.
29. STURP, *Analytica Chemica Acta.*
30. Ibid.
31. Robinson, quoted in Peter Rinaldi, "Some Reflection on the Shroud," presented at the *Hong Kong Symposium on the Shroud,* 3–9 March 1986, 18.
32. Kim Dreisbach, "Behold the Man" TV documentary, Good Friday 1985, produced by Ken Stevenson.
33. Oswald Scheuermann, "Shroud" (West Germany, June 1986).

Appendix A
1. Werner Bulst, *Shroud News* 54 (August 1989): 4–17.
2. See Luigi Fossati, "The Lirey Controversy," *Shroud Spectrum* 8 (September 1983): 24–34.

SCRIPTURE INDEX

SUBJECT INDEX

248

SUBJECT INDEX